WHAT ENGLISH LANGUAGE TEACHERS NEED TO KNOW VOLUME I, 2ND EDITION

Designed for pre-service teachers and teachers new to the field of ELT, *What English Teachers Need to Know Volumes I, II*, and *III* are companion textbooks organized around the key question, *What do teachers need to know and be able to do in order for their students to learn English?*

In the Second Edition of *Volume I*, Murray and Christison return to this essential question and call attention to emerging trends and challenges affecting the contemporary classroom. Addressing new skills and strategies that EFL teachers require to meet the needs of their shifting student populations who are impacted by changing demographics, digital environments, and globalization, this book, which is grounded in current research, offers a strong emphasis on practical applications for classroom teaching.

This updated and expanded Second Edition features:

- a new chapter on technology in TESOL
- new and updated classroom examples throughout
- discussions of how teachers can prepare for contemporary challenges, such as population mobility and globalization.

The comprehensive texts work for teachers across different contexts—where English is the dominant language, an official language, or a foreign language; for different levels—elementary/primary, secondary, university, or adult education; and for different learning purposes—general English, workplace English, English for academic purposes, or English for specific purposes.

Denise E. Murray is Professor Emeritus at Macquarie University, Australia, and Professor Emeritus at San José State University, USA.

MaryAnn Christison is Professor in the Department of Linguistics at the University of Utah, USA.

ESL & Applied Linguistics Professional Series
Eli Hinkel, Series Editor

For more information about this series, please visit: **www.routledge.com/ESL--Applied-Linguistics-Professional-Series/book-series/LEAESLALP**

WHAT ENGLISH LANGUAGE TEACHERS NEED TO KNOW VOLUME I

Understanding Learning

2nd edition

*Denise E. Murray and
MaryAnn Christison*

Routledge
Taylor & Francis Group

NEW YORK AND LONDON

Second edition published 2019
by Routledge
52 Vanderbilt Avenue, New York, NY 10017

and by Routledge
2 Park Square, Milton Park, Abingdon, Oxon, OX14 4RN

Routledge is an imprint of the Taylor & Francis Group, an informa business

First edition published by Routledge 2011

Library of Congress Cataloging-in-Publication Data
Names: Murray, Denise E., author. | Christison, MaryAnn, author.
Title: What English language teachers need to know / by Denise E. Murray
    and MaryAnn Christison.
Description: 2nd edition. | New York : Routledge, 2019. | Series: ESL
    & applied linguistics professional series | Includes bibliographical
    references and index.
Identifiers: LCCN 2018041671 (print) | LCCN 2018052290 (ebook) |
    ISBN 9781351139847 (ebook) | ISBN 9780815351962 |
    ISBN 9780815351962q(vol. 1 : hardback) | ISBN 9780815351979q
    (vol. 1 : paperback) | ISBN 9781351139847q(vol. 1 : ebook)
Subjects: LCSH: Second language acquisition—Study and teaching. |
    Language and languages—Study and teaching. | English language—
    Study and teaching—Foreign speakers.
Classification: LCC P118.2 (ebook) | LCC P118.2 .M89 2019 (print) |
    DDC 428/.0071—dc23
LC record available at https://lccn.loc.gov/2018041671

ISBN: 978-0-8153-5196-2 (hbk)
ISBN: 978-0-8153-5197-9 (pbk)
ISBN: 978-1-351-13984-7 (ebk)

Typeset in Perpetua
by Swales & Willis Ltd, Exeter, Devon, UK

CONTENTS

CONTENTS

FIGURES

TABLES

PREFACE

English language teaching worldwide has become a multi-billion-dollar enterprise, one that the majority of nations in the world are embarking on to lesser or greater extents. For many countries, English is seen as a commodity through which they will become more competitive in the global marketplace. While English may have national and personal advancement potential, it is also pervasive in the global media. Youth culture in particular is influenced by English-dominant media and marketing. As a result, English is being consumed and transformed transnationally.

The settings where English is taught vary from countries where English is the official and dominant language, such as the United States or Australia, to those where it is an official language, usually as a result of past colonialism, such as in India or the Philippines, to those where it is taught in schools as a subject of study, such as in Japan or the Czech Republic. In the first set of countries, when English is taught to immigrants or to international students, the language is often called *English as a second language (ESL)*, and its teaching *TESL*. In the second set of countries, where it is taught to citizens and increasingly to international students, it is usually referred to also as *ESL*. In the third set of countries, the language is often referred to as *English as a foreign language (EFL)*, and its teaching as *TEFL*. Because *ESL* and *EFL* carry ideological baggage, there is much discussion in the field about the use of more appropriate terminology. Some English language teaching professionals prefer to use *(T)ESOL—(teaching) English to speakers of other languages*—because it acknowledges that the learners may have more than one previous language, and the term can be used to include both ESL and EFL contexts. Others prefer *(T)EAL—(teaching) English as an additional language* for the same reason, whereas *ESL* implies there is only English, plus one other. Other terms in use include *English as an international language (EIL)* and *English language teaching (ELT)*. Whatever the terminology used, distinctions across the different contexts of English language teaching are increasingly becoming blurred as people move around the globe and acquire their English in a variety of different settings, being taught by teachers from a variety of different linguistic backgrounds.

In the volumes in this series, we will use the terms *ESL* and *EFL* because they are still the most widely used terms, while recognizing the inherent reification of English in their use. When referring to teaching, we will use *ELT* to avoid confusion between the field TESOL and the professional association called TESOL International.

Similarly, the terminology used to define the users of English has been contested. The most commonly used terms have been *native speaker* (*NS*), in contrast to *nonnative speaker* (*NNS*). Both terms assume ideological positions, especially because the NS has been traditionally valued as the norm and the model for language learning, not only in those countries where English is the dominant language, but also in many EFL settings. Yet, the majority of English language users and teachers do not have English as their mother tongue or dominant language. In some ESL contexts, such as the United States, immigrant learners are referred to as English language learners (ELLs), even though all English speakers, no matter their immigration status, are English language learners— we both are still learning English! Leung, Harris, and Rampton (1997) have, therefore, proposed refining what it means to know and use a language with three terms: (1) language expertise (linguistic and cultural knowledge), (2) language affiliation (identification and attachment), and (3) language inheritance (connectedness and continuity). What is important, then, about a learner's (or teacher's) language is their linguistic repertoire in relation to each of these criteria, not whether they are NSs. Because there is no general acceptance of alternate terms, we shall continue to use *NS* and *NNS*, while noting that they establish a dichotomy that is neither valid nor descriptive.

Much of the literature also refers to people learning English in formal settings as students and sometimes as learners. We have chosen to use the term *learner*, except when it leads to infelicitous expressions, such as *learners learning*. For us, the term *student* implies some passivity, while *learner* implies agency. For us, learners are vital collaborators in the educational enterprise.

Who Is This Book For?

We are writing this book for pre-service teachers and teachers new to the field of ELT. Whether you are teaching in an English dominant country, a country where English is one of the official languages, or a country where English is taught as a foreign language, the information in this book is relevant to your context. We have also designed it for whatever level you may be teaching—elementary (primary) school, secondary school, college or university, or adult education. The series also includes the information teachers need to teach general English, workplace English, English for academic purposes (EAP), or English for specific purposes (ESP). We realize that creating a book that works for many different contexts is a big ask, but we have used examples from the diversity of ELT settings. Of course, we cannot include examples from every country or grade level, but we have tried to be inclusive and ensure that, whatever your current or future teaching situation, you will find the material relevant to your learners and situation. At the same time, we have been as specific as possible, rather than relying on generic characteristics of the field.

Our own experiences have covered a vast array of different age groups, contexts, and content areas—between us, we have taught in English-dominant countries, EFL contexts in every continent, young people, adults, university students, general English, English for business, English for the workplace, English for science and technology, and EAP.

What Is This Book About?

In order to teach in these different contexts, teachers need understandings about the nature of language and language learning. With those understandings, they need to be able to facilitate student learning. Because student learning is the goal, we have oriented the volumes in this series to the notion of learning, by asking the question *What do teachers need to know and be able to do in order for their students to learn English?*

Therefore, the first book provides the background information teachers need to know and develop to be able to use it in their classrooms. Teachers need to know about (or know how to find out) the characteristics of the context in which they work. These characteristics include the nature of their learners, the features of their institutions, the policies and expectations of their state/province/region/nation, and the broader world in which their learners will engage. They need to know how English works and how it is learned. To become proficient in English, learners need to be able not only to create correct sentences in the classroom and read and write texts for different purposes, but they also need to engage in conversations with other English speakers. To accomplish these tasks, teachers need to know how learning takes place both within the learner and through social interaction. Teachers need to understand their role in the larger professional sphere of English language education so that they can continue to grow as teachers and expand the profession through their own participation in its various enterprises. Finally, teachers also need to engage in their local communities to be informed of their needs and to inform their communities about the nature of English language learning.

While we have provided separate sections on each of these important themes, the challenge of successful teaching is to know how to blend an understanding of learners, language, and language learning with knowledge of their content goals and how to achieve those goals, which is the subject of Volume II.

The material in this volume is based on current research in the field and in other disciplines that we believe can inform English language teaching. These fields of interest include psychology, neuroscience, pedagogy, sociology, anthropology, cultural studies, and linguistics. The focus throughout the entire volume is on *outcomes*—that is, student learning. The material in Volume I is can be presented to teachers in different configurations, depending on the length of the course and the topics on which the course might focus. You may decide to use all of the chapters for your course—for example, if you are using this book in a semester-long course (16 weeks). For shorter courses, you might decide to use different parts of the book or a subset of the chapters. We have found the volume useful for both long and short courses.

Each chapter in this volume includes a variety of activities for the reader, such as activities that provide you with a chance to reflect on the information based on your own experiences, to read further on a topic, or to conduct small scale investigations into teaching and learning. We hope that you will have as much enjoyment engaging with the materials as we have had writing them.

Reference

Leung, C., Harris, R., & Rampton, B. (1997). The idealised native speaker, reified ethnicities, and classroom realities. *TESOL Quarterly, 31*, 543–560.

ACKNOWLEDGEMENTS

We are grateful to our many students and colleagues over our careers, whose wisdom and experiences have enhanced our own understandings of the field. We are especially grateful to Karen Adler for her enthusiastic support for the volumes in the series and for encouraging us to move forward with second editions. A very generous thank you also goes to Eli Hinkel for her willingness to read and respond to, yet again, another manuscript from us. And we are, as always, tremendously grateful to our families, especially Bill Murray, Adrian Palmer, and Cameron Christison, who have supported our work, even when it has meant less time together and sometimes distracted dinnertime conversations! You continue to inspire us to be creative and professional.

Part I

IDENTITY AND CONTEXT

In Part I, we offer five chapters that explore the contexts for language learning and teaching. In order to develop the most appropriate language programs to facilitate learning, educators need to know about the characteristics of their learners and the aspects of their environments that affect student learning. We therefore begin with a chapter that examines what the research tells about learner identity and its impact on learning. The next two chapters explore broadly the three major contexts for English language teaching: (1) countries where English is the dominant language (e.g., New Zealand), (2) countries where English is one of several functional languages (e.g., Singapore), and (3) countries where English is taught in schools as a foreign language (e.g., Spain). The fourth chapter discusses the relationships between language, culture, language learning, and the roles that teachers and learners adopt in the language classroom. The final chapter in this section provides research methods and classroom activities that teachers can use to investigate their own contexts of teaching.

We begin with an exploration of the context because the learner and the learning environment are essential starting points for understanding language teaching and learning. Learning is more than the accumulation of knowledge and skills. Learning is a sociocultural engagement that transforms the learner. Further, language learning, whether it is a first or second language, is a process of socialization through which individuals in a society construct and reproduce dominant beliefs, values, behaviors, and role assignments. This socialization is also a site of struggle among competing beliefs, values, behaviors, and role assignments. In the classroom, therefore, the socialization in the home language and culture can come up against those of the new language being learned (English).

1

LEARNER IDENTITIES

VIGNETTE

In an interview about the settlement of young refugees from Africa in Australia, a Sudanese leader (Paul) talked about why he wanted to become a youth leader in his community. This young man was one of the "Lost Boys of Sudan":

There is a lot of culture shock. The children go into a middle culture; they are not Australian, and they are not African. You know what they are? They are in the middle. They are confused. I have seen them. They need a coach to tell them how life is. Most young people want to adapt to American culture, and first we are not in America; and second youth are the bright future of our community. We need them to have a better understanding of how life should be. If I become a youth worker, I'll know more about how I should deal with teenagers. Teenagers have problems—some of them are drug-addicted, some are into guns, and they need good care. Some young people came with a single parent. If a youth worker has been trained fully, and he has an organization that can work with them, you need to engage them so that they can have a good life. I have seen the needs of young African people here and thought, "Why should I not do this?" They have a lot of culture shock. They have a lot of new systems to understand. They want to get into new things that they do not belong to, like if you talk about the way they react in the school, the way they behave, it is different to the way white children behave. Before people came here, they have a high expectation: "I go there, I am free, free to do everything." But freedom is different. Some people took it the wrong way rather than the right way.[1]

Task: Reflect

1   How does Paul position himself in relation to the Sudanese community in Australia and the wider Australian community?
2   Why do you think some of these Sudanese young people want to be "American"?
3   Why do you think some of these Sudanese young people have the "wrong idea" about freedom in Australia?
4   What types of educational programs would help these young people who are in a "middle culture"?

Introduction

The young Sudanese man in the vignette above talks about his own identity—that of someone who identifies with his own Sudanese community in Australia. He also talks about the identity conflict experienced by other young people who want to assimilate and become Australian but who misinterpret some of the cultural values they see among their Australian-born peers. In fact, their identifying with these peers and copying some of their behaviors leads to conflicts with their parents, with school officials, and sometimes with the police. In this chapter, you will read about the various experiences that affect how language learners shape their identities.

While the development of identity among language users and learners has long been studied, earlier approaches saw the effects of context on language and language learning as essentially static and residing in the individual. For example, early work on dialect speakers by Ryan and Giles (1982) found that the patterns of language of the dominant group in a society are the model for social advancement, whereas varieties used by minority groups are considered less prestigious and result in their users being less successful. In a similar vein, work on attitudes and motivation by Gardner and Lambert (1972) identified two dichotomous types of motivation: integrative and instrumental. The former refers to learning a language in order to become a member of that community, that is, to identify with that language and its community. Instrumental motivation, on the other hand, refers to the need to learn a language for another purpose, such as study, with no desire to identify with the community. Schumann's (1978) acculturation model of language acquisition also took this position. However, his model hypothesized that the distance in values between two cultures affected language acquisition, such that learners coming from a culture close to that of the language they were trying to learn would be more successful in acquiring that language. What all these approaches have in common is the belief that the choice is *either/or*: people either choose to assimilate to a group or nation, or they choose to keep their variety or language in order to identify with their native group. However, such views ignore the multiple group memberships that individuals have, such as gender, race, language, language variety, social institutions. Furthermore, research on language and learning that focuses on the social and interactive nature of both has shown that identity is dynamic, formed, and transformed through language and learning (Cadman & O'Regan, 2006; Mohan, Leung, & Davison, 2001; Norton, 2013).

Task: Reflect

Think of your own identity. List all the communities to which you belong. How do you position yourself differently in each of these communities? What different language do you use to express your identity? Do you express solidarity with the values of all these communities? Which values, beliefs, and behaviors do you ascribe to and which do you resist? Why?

What Is Identity?

What, then, do we mean by identity? It is generally agreed that identity is the view that individuals have of themselves and of their place(s) in the world in the past, now, and in the future. Teachers as well as learners hold views of themselves. However, in this chapter we will only discuss learner identities; teacher identities will be discussed in Chapter 2. We have called this chapter *learner identities* because learners' places in the world are multiple, changing, sometimes conflicting, and influenced by the power relations in individual interactions and in society more widely. This influence may result in the desire to assimilate, adapt, or reject. As individuals construct their identities, they position themselves through their language (and non-verbal behavior); that is, they use language to let others know who they are and what their sociocultural allegiances are. At the same time, identities, both welcome and unwelcome, are imposed on individuals. Changing identities has been posited to explain why some learners may communicate effectively in some language situations, yet apparently fail in others. Both the power relations between the people interacting and the wider structural inequalities can lead to such differences (see, for example, Norton, 2000, 2013). Norton developed the notion of investment in the target language to explain the dynamic relationship between the learner and the social worlds in which they interact. When learners invest in acquiring a new language, they expect some return on their investment, whether it be education, jobs, friendship, or other advantages. How and what variety of English they invest in depends on what future identities they imagine for themselves. So, for example, learners may stay silent or appear less proficient, not because they are not motivated, but because they are resisting the identity being imposed on them. Learner investment, therefore, affects which of the "imagined communities" (Norton, 1995) they choose to participate in. One such community is the language classroom, where learners may not invest in the language practices of the classroom because they perceive them as inequitable, of not acknowledging their own lived experiences. Inherent in discussions of identity, then, is the concept of agency, that is, that people shape their identities as a result of what is important to them; they are not merely victims on whom identities are imposed. Furthermore, these identities are shaped through interactions.

One of the difficulties for language learners and those who teach them and interact with them is how to interpret learners' language in any specific instance. We may not know whether they make their linguistic choices deliberately, or because they do not have the linguistic tools to express the position they wish to take. For example, a learner in class may choose not to use a modal to mitigate a request, using *Open the window* in preference to *Could you open the window?* in order to express displeasure with a classmate who has been deliberately baiting her by opening the window near her desk on very cold days. However, the cause may be an imperfect acquisition of modal questions.

Learners' past and present experiences can influence how they understand their relationship to the society and culture of the language they are learning and, therefore, how they utilize, resist, or even create opportunities to use the language. In TESOL, then, it is crucial to investigate and analyze the experiences and social structures that influence learner identity, their acquisition of English, and so the enterprise of English language education. These past and present experiences include nationality, race, and ethnicity; gender; family role; and bi- or multilingualism. These experiences are inevitably intertwined; however, for clarity of discussion, we will discuss each of these facets of learners' lives separately.

Nationality, Race, and Ethnicity

Often, nationality is the silent identifier in much of the literature, especially in ESL situations, where race and ethnicity are more often cited as sites of struggle. Race and ethnicity are both sociological constructs, with little objective, physical evidence for their assignment.

Nationality, also a sociological construct, is as well a political construct with the physical evidence of assignment of citizenship by birth or naturalization. All three terms are highly contested. Rarely are nationality, race, and ethnicity singular in one setting. A particular ethnic group may include people of different races and vice versa. We have, therefore, discussed the three concepts as separate sections within a larger whole.

Nationality. Defining oneself within one's larger social context is fundamental to human life and one such social context is one's national identification. However, nationality is often not examined in the work on learner identity because it is assumed that race and ethnicity subsume nationality. A further reason why nationality is often ignored is because it is considered to have little role in the construction of identity in an era of intense globalization. For English language learners around the world, different national identifications are available, depending on whether learners are learning within their own country, are immigrants or refugees to a new country, or are sojourning in a second country for study or work purposes.

People who move to another nation must (re)define themselves in terms of their new national context. However, research shows that cultural identity is essential for self-identity (Fantino & Colak, 2001; McKay & Wong, 1996). A move from one's country of origin results in abandonment of previous relationships, along with loss of daily contact with interactions that are characterized by the cultural values, beliefs, and behaviors that define one's identity. Therefore, loss of one's country can be a dehumanizing experience. However, many immigrants experience a conflict between the cultural identity of their home country and that of their new country of residence. This conflict can result in trying to deny their heritage and assimilate, or in rejecting identification with their new country. Thus, many immigrants refer to themselves by the nationality of their country of origin (Nieto, 1992).

In addition, for most immigrants and refugees their identity as immigrant or refugee is externally imposed. Further, the attributes of these identifiers are imposed by the dominant group. Even their identification based on nationality may be an external construct. For example, refugees from Sudan may be identified in an English-speaking receiving country as Sudanese, when they themselves identify by ethnicity, such as Dinka, Nuer, Nuba, or Achole. Often, refugees reject identification with the nation-state where they were born, because in fact their identity as a minority in that country and the resulting persecution is what led to their becoming refugees. Such is the case for many Assyrians from Iran or Hazaras from Afghanistan.

For those learning English in their country of origin, nationality is important for their self-identity and their perceptions (or the perceptions of their nation) as to what they may be losing (or not) in acquiring English. We recall a telling incident from the early 1970s. One of us (Denise) was teaching in Australia at the time when China was just opening to the West and was looking to develop English language programs. Several Chinese officials, in the gray Mao suits, visited our program to get ideas and stated emphatically, "We want English; we do not want culture." In countries that were former British colonies, English has played different roles. It has been used as the national language in order to prevent the dominance of any one indigenous linguistic group. In other countries a local language has become the national language to reinforce a singular nationality, such as in Bangladesh, which adopted Bangla as the national language, maintaining English as a language of the privileged (Imam, 2005). Thus, many poor, rural children in Bangladesh may have no investment in learning English because they do not perceive that it will provide them with any advantages.

In other settings, national boundaries may be the result of war or imposed by former colonial powers. Thus, within the boundaries are people who identify with their ethnicity, rather than their nation. For example, on a visit to China, one of us (Denise) met a student from a university near the Korean border. The medium of instruction at her university was Korean. She herself identified as Korean, not Chinese. In Spain, many Basques and Catalans do not identify themselves as Spaniards. For our purposes here, it is sufficient to note that nationality and the extent to which learners' identity is tied to their national beliefs, values, and even myths, is as relevant in EFL as in ESL situations.

However, with English being consumed transnationally, the sociolinguistic environment is liquid (Schneider, 2014), with people from all linguistic traditions interacting via English. These interactions have been identified as *English as a lingua franca*, or ELF. Young people (and other adults) may choose to identify with the consumerism promoted by global media through choices of clothing, music, and even behaviors. Or they may choose to identify through English as part of the informal virtual global world created through social media (Murray, 2018). In fact, many virtual communities are forming, evolving, and dissolving through online interaction. People have agency, and, therefore, some appropriate or resist identification with any one vision, especially because they have access to a variety of alternative views.

Race. While race is a highly contested concept, with no scientific basis, the attributes assigned to race are often socially salient. Immigrants are often assigned particular identities based on their perceived race. So, for example, McKay and Wong (1996) found that immigrant Chinese young adolescents were being ascribed values of the "model minority," that is, as being conscientious, academically inclined, and uncomplaining. In contrast, their Latin American peers were being ascribed values of "illegals," that is, as being academic failures and lazy.

Some learners resist the assigned racial identity while others deliberately choose one they identify with. For example, Ibrahim (1999), in his study of French-speaking refugee African youths in Canada, found that these young people were invested in becoming "black" linguistically and culturally during ESL learning so as to identify themselves with black Americans. In Australia, many refugee youths from Africa reject identification with blackness, not wanting to identify with Australia's indigenous Aboriginals. "Black" is in fact an uncertain and unstable racial identifier. While African refugees, other immigrants, such as Haitians in the United States, Australian Aboriginals, and African Americans may share skin color, they have unique ethnic identities.

Ethnicity. As mentioned above, in many countries such as the United States, ethnicity and race are often used interchangeably. Still others conflate nationality with ethnicity, even when carefully differentiating race and ethnicity (Gollnick & Chinn, 2006). However, this conflation leads to inaccurate descriptions of individuals, especially in immigrant countries where governments seek to define groups. As we saw above, nation-states are not built around one ethnic group. Ethnicity results from opposition and a perceived difference, because people in homogeneous societies do not identify by ethnicity or even consider they have any ethnicity. The oppositional nature of ethnicity results from power differentials in society, differences that are enacted in social interactions. Therefore, ethnicity only becomes salient in people's lives when they and others seek to differentiate them from "the other." For example, in the United States, the Federal Census defines a pan-ethnic group as Hispanic. This category consists of people from a range of different countries, many of whom do identify by their heritage country. It also includes different racial groups. The pan-ethnic category of

Asian and Pacific Islander (also used by the U.S. Census) is problematic because it includes a variety of countries whose citizens would differentiate among themselves, such as Japanese, Lao, Hmong, or Samoan.

Task: Reflect

Now that you have read about the inaccuracies in trying to identify people in terms of nationality, race, or ethnicity, think again about your own identity. In the earlier reflection, did you identify with any nationality, race, or ethnicity? To what extent is that identification one you have chosen for yourself or one that has been imposed? What values, beliefs, and behaviors do you share with others in this category?

Our views of racial and ethnic groups, other than the one(s) we identify with, are often created through the media and through the way our community is perceived by other groups. As language teachers, we need to understand the wider communities' stereotyping and attitudes towards race and ethnicity, as well as the positioning our students adopt, in order to develop inclusive classrooms that give all learners the opportunity to succeed.

Gender

Early work on the relationship between gender and language found differences in speech patterns between men and women, such as women using more hedges (Lakoff, 1975), men interrupting more in mixed-gender conservations (Thorne & Henley, 1975), and men and women being socialized differently, with women focusing on maintaining social relationships (Tannen, 1990). In more recent work on second language learning and gender, Pavlenko, Blackledge, Piller, and Teutsch-Dwyer (2001) criticize the earlier research because it sees gender as a characteristic of individuals, rather than being socially constructed. Further, they demonstrate that gender in and of itself does not necessarily enable (or not) second language learning. However, they note that, as a result of social norms, access to language skills may vary across gender, whether in immigrant countries or where English is being learned as a school subject. However, women are not without agency and can (and do) learn English to improve their conditions and to reject patriarchy in many different settings where English is taught.

They and others have found that English language teaching textbooks often portray stereotypical roles. Similarly, we have seen classrooms where stereotypical roles have been assigned even by teachers who would not consider themselves sexist. For example, they may call on boys more than girls or may accept a husband responding for a wife in an adult education setting.

The concern, then, for English language teachers is to examine their contexts to determine whether males are privileged in ways that deny females opportunities for learning the full range of English, the role portrayals mirror those of the wider society, and the women and girls in their classrooms want to accept or reject those roles.

Family Roles

For many immigrants, moving to a new country can entail a change in family roles. Parent and child roles are often reversed, as young children act as interpreters for their less linguistically proficient parents. Children are often asked to interpret at the doctor's or in service encounters or parent-teacher meetings because their English is more proficient than that of their parents. Such situations, however, place children in an awkward position because they have to take on the role of expert and caretaker.

Adolescent refugees and immigrants, as well as those facing the identification as refugee or immigrant, have to pass through the developmental process from child to adult, a process that is often deemed a crisis or a difficult identity change in English receiving countries, such as Britain, Australia, Canada, New Zealand, and the United States. Yet, these young people may have come from societies where there is no such transitional phase and where young people move from childhood immediately to adulthood. Additionally, their experiences as refugees or immigrants may have forced adult responsibilities onto them while they were still the age of childhood. Some, for example, may have been child soldiers, been raped, or had to support their younger siblings.

Peer pressure on immigrant and refugee students is even greater than on the native-born. Immigrant and refugee adolescents quickly adopt many of the behaviors of their peers, often rejecting the norms of their home community, as we saw in the vignette at the beginning of this chapter. They may reject the language of the home, refusing to use anything but the language of their new country. This extreme acculturation often leads to conflict within families and communities: parents often want their children to retain the values and behaviors of their community. Further, parents may be at a loss as to how to discipline their children if the methods used in their home country are not considered acceptable in their new country.

11

In countries where English is being learned as a school subject, family roles are usually determined by local sociocultural norms. However, a number of factors can impact language learners in these settings. There may be tensions between ascribed roles and those that children and young people want to adopt because of exposure to different social rules they encounter, especially through international media. There may also be tensions between the expectations of an English teacher from another country with different norms. For example, in some cultures, parents leave education to the schools but claim complete control over moral education. A teacher coming from Australia, for example, may see that her role is to introduce her students to social issues that are salient in Australia. Textbooks, similarly, often choose topics aligned to middle-class Western ideas because they are mostly written by middle-class Westerners. Topics such as women's roles in the home or at work may cause conflicts or, at best, discomfort or confusion. For example, in immigrant and refugee families, children may have an important role in the workforce after school so that the family has sufficient income. Such workforce participation may fall especially heavily on teenagers in a family with a single mother parent and many younger siblings. Yet, teachers expect those young people to do extensive homework and engage in after-school activities, the roles that a typical teenager takes in the local culture. Language teachers need to understand what roles learners take outside the classroom because these impact on their motivation and investment in learning English.

Bi- or multilingualism

The majority of countries in the world are multilingual and the majority of people use more than one language. Many countries encourage the learning of one or more foreign languages—sometimes with utilitarian goals, as we saw earlier. Yet, the use of different languages in multilingual societies usually carries societal values and, therefore, positions users according to their language use. For example, while English may be the language for global interaction, learners from countries that were former colonies of English-speaking nations may be ambivalent about, or even hostile to, learning the language of their oppressors (Canagarajah, 2001; Chick, 2001). In many of these former colonies, a local, indigenized variety of English has developed as a lingua franca. (See Chapter 3 for more on this subject.) However, this variety may not be considered prestigious by other speakers of English or even by the government of the country. Singapore, for example, has conducted a series of English language campaigns to encourage Singaporeans to use a "standard" variety, rather than Singapore

English. Liberians, who are immigrating to Australia and the United States, consider themselves to be native speakers of English; yet the wider community in those countries has difficulty understanding them, and they are placed in ESL classes, which they resent and resist.

Having store names and signs in English is perceived as a sign of modernization in many countries, but having Spanish store names and signs in the United States is viewed by many as a sign of rejecting English and, therefore, the United States. Interestingly, the Council of Europe's goal of plurilingualism for all European citizens is that they should learn two languages in addition to their mother tongue—a goal designed to promote a European identity, through greater movement across countries for work, study, and tourism. While *multilingualism* and *plurilingualism* are often used interchangeably, recent scholarship has differentiated between the two terms. Some scholars use "plurilingual(ism) to refer to the unique aspects of individual repertoires and agency and multilingual(ism) to refer to broader social language context/contact(s) and the coexistence of several languages in a particular situation" (Marshall & Moore, 2013, p. 474). One aspect of bi- and multilingualism that expresses identity is the phenomenon of multiple language use in a single context, which is known as code-switching (and more recently as translanguaging).

Code-switching. Code-switching refers to bilinguals in a contact language situation shifting from one language to the other. It has been widely studied and researchers have identified two types of code-switching: situational and metaphorical. Situational code-switching is when the speaker changes language or variety because of changes in the setting or speakers. For example, multilinguals will rarely code-switch during an interaction where a monolingual is present. Metaphorical code-switching is used by speakers to change the tone of the interaction (Blom & Gumperz, 1972). Building and expanding on this work, Myers-Scotton (1993) shows that speakers in multilingual situations know which particular language is expected in which particular situations. So, for example, in multilingual Singapore, in an informal situation, Hokkien speakers would normally use Hokkien. However, they might choose English "to increase social distance, to avoid an overt display of ethnicity, or for aesthetic effect" (McKay, 2005, p. 290). Additionally, they may code-switch to demonstrate their identity as both English and speakers of local languages, Hokkien, Malay, or Tamil. Therefore, teachers can expect their learners to code-switch for a number of different reasons and code-switching should not be considered a sign of a lack of fluency, but rather a way of responding to a situation or a way for learners to mark identities. Furthermore, teachers and learners can decide how to use their multiple languages in the classroom, an issue we discuss in detail in Chapter 3.

Translanguaging. In translanguaging contexts, multilinguals are encouraged to make use of their entire linguistic repertoires. Translanguaging means not just moving backwards and forwards across two languages, but going beyond the boundaries of all the semiotic (meaning-making) systems at one's disposal. These systems may be linguistic or non-linguistic, such as gestures and body language or moving across modalities from a textbook to a whiteboard to an oral discussion. Translanguaging was identified in Welsh schools, where teachers found they were using Welsh, but their students were often responding in English (García & Li Wei, 2014). Translanguaging, then, is the negotiation of meaning across languages and language varieties (Canagarajah, 2013), and it is this negotiation that is the core practice of language teaching because it maximizes all the available resources of both learners and teacher.

The Classroom and Identity Formation

If experiences help shape identity, then the classroom is a place where identities are defined and shaped. Canagarajah (2001), reporting on an ethnographic study of a university-level general English class for Tamil students, found that the learners resisted the content and pedagogy of their U.S. textbook, despite their strong motivation to learn English. They wanted to learn grammar as a product, and pass their examinations, while maintaining their cultural integrity by not internalizing the discourse of the course. Such a rejection of culture associated with language, of course, raises the important question of the relationship between language and culture and the extent to which learning a second language means learning a second culture (a discussion we shall have in Chapters 2 and 3). As we shall also see in Chapter 2, the identity expressed by the teacher impacts on the classroom and how learners position themselves.

However, teachers also position learners through classroom discourse, through the textbooks they use, the activities they choose, and the roles they ask learners to take in the classroom. We briefly discuss each of these influences below. Each topic will be covered in more detail in Volume II.

Classroom Discourse

Here, we are referring only to the talk that takes place in classrooms, even though postmodern and critical approaches to discourse would consider the activities and roles discussed below as part of discourse. Student-teacher inter-actions mostly reflect the dominant societal values, such as those related to gen-der, class, ethnicity, or race.

Classroom discourse, then, can either perpetuate the power imbalances of society or challenge those power relations. In classes with language minority learners in the United States, Canada, and elsewhere, minority learners are more successful when their own cultural and linguistic experiences are legiti-mized (Toohey, Day, & Manyak, 2007; Wong & Grant, 2007). When teachers position learners as capable and motivated, they are more successful learners. Included here is what talk, behaviors, and interactions teachers permit in the classroom. By talk, we embrace both the type of language permitted (such as terms of respect or derogatory expressions) and which language (English or the home language of learners, or translanguaging). In many classroom settings, the home language is highly valued; in others, learners are forbidden to use it, based on the belief that it will prevent the acquisition of English. To deny learn-ers the use of their own language in the classroom is to deny them an essential marker of their own identity and to reduce them (especially if they are adult beginners) to cognitively deficient persons who cannot convey their wants and needs. Not only can the home (and other) language(s) be bridges to learning English (see Chapter 12), but can also actually facilitate the learning of English (Wei, 2018). Teachers need to ensure that the discourse of the classroom is respectful of difference and that no single group of learners dominates interac-tions or is privileged.

Textbooks and Activities

Textbooks and classroom activities also impact learner identities and, therefore, their investment in learning English. Textbooks often reflect stereotypical views of race, gender, ethnicity, or nationality. In addition to the way people are por-trayed in textbooks, we need to consider the way language is portrayed. How is English portrayed? At the 1996 Annual IATEFL (International Association of Teachers of English as a Foreign Language) Conference in Keele, Ron Carter said that:

> The language course book represents a "can do" society in which inter-action is generally smooth and trouble free, the speakers cooperate with each other politely, the conversation is neat, tidy and predictable, utterances are always as complete as sentences and no-one else can interrupt anyone else or speak at the same time as anyone else.

Not only does such textbook English provide unrealistic models for learners, but it also implies that English as a language operates differently from what learners are used to in their own language. They may view their language as untidy and interaction in their language as troublesome, compared with the idealized model of English presented to them. A further consideration is the variety of English provided (a point we will return to in Chapters 2 and 3). One of us (Denise) recalls teaching in the 1970s in Australia, where the only textbooks available were U.S. or British models that were not going to help immigrants to Australia in their encounters with Australian English or aid international students to understand their Australian professors. In addition, using such models gave Australian English a second-class status and, therefore, its users second-class status compared to British or American speakers. Similarly, to what extent do textbooks reflect multilingual/plurilingual practices?

Task: Explore

Select an ESL/EFL textbook that you are using or that is readily available to you. Choose one chapter from the textbook and answer the following questions:

1   How is gender portrayed? What are the roles assigned to males and females? How do these roles reflect the cultural values where you are using the textbook?
2   How is ethnicity portrayed? Is it stereotypical? In what way?
3   How is English portrayed? To what extent is it a language of power and advancement? Is it shown as a "can do" society as described by Carter (1996)? How are other languages portrayed (or not)?

The activities teachers choose also position learners in relation to race, gender, ethnicity, home languages, and in relation to academic success, as well. Are the activities ones in which women always play traditional female roles? Are learners expected to reject their own identity and take on that of a dominant race or ethnicity? Are the activities ones that learners view as trivial or not requiring them to explore or use their own knowledge base, including linguistic ones?

Roles of Teachers and Learners

A currently popular dichotomy concerning the role of the teacher is often expressed as "sage on the stage," compared with "guide on the side." This catchy phrase is meant to capture the difference between teacher-centered instruction and learner-centered instruction or teacher-fronted instruction and peer interaction. While we explore this topic in detail throughout the volumes in this series, it is important to note here that teachers' decisions about their own roles and those of their learners position students to both the teacher and their peers and, therefore, have an impact on their identities. Are learners to be passive recipients of teacher knowledge or active participants in their own learning? Does the teacher acknowledge that learners bring their own understandings to the classroom and value these understandings? Roles are not static. Teachers and learners may adopt different roles for different purposes. It is incumbent on the teacher to ensure that the roles facilitate learning by all students.

Conclusion

Learners bring their identities into the classroom, identities that have been shaped and re-shaped by their experiences, by how they have been evaluated and perceived by others. The classroom and wider school community continue to shape learners' identity. Learners add English to their repertoire of language use, which positions them differently than before they could use English. The values associated with this addition to their linguistic repertoire depend on the context in which they learn and use English. Additionally, the experiences learners encounter in the learning environment itself shape their identity—either reinforcing already held values and beliefs or re-shaping them. Education in general and language learning in particular are not neutral enterprises. Language teachers therefore have responsibility for creating language learning experiences that result in student learning, while valuing learners' self-identification choices.

Task: Expand

Cadman, K., & O'Regan, K. (Eds.). (2006). Tales out of school: Identity and English language teaching. Series "S": Special edition of *TESOL in Context.*

This special edition of the Australian professional journal is devoted to the issue of identity and mostly includes studies from Australia. It presents a variety of theoretical perspectives and settings, including indigenous,

(continued)

(continued)

international students, and refugees. Most chapters focus on what classroom teachers can do.

Norton, B. (Ed.). (1997). Language, identity, and the ownership of English. Special topic issue of *TESOL Quarterly, 31*(3).

This special issue of the international professional journal is devoted to the issue of identity and includes a range of different studies and perspectives.

Norton, B. (2013). *Identity and language learning: Extending the conversation*, 2nd ed. Bristol, England: Multilingual Matters.

This is a revised edition of Norton's seminal ethnographic study of five woman immigrants in Canada. As well as providing rich empirical data on the lives of these women, Norton develops theories about the characteristics of identity and how it is formed and re-formed in second language contexts.

Questions for Discussion

1   What are the various factors that affect identity formation that are mentioned in this chapter? Discuss other possible factors that are not mentioned in this chapter.
2   How does identity formation of English language learners affect their acquisition of English?
3   Explain the differences between ethnicity, race, and nationality.
4   Explain how the classroom affects identity formation of English language learners.
5   Explain how the assignment of gender roles both in and outside the classroom can affect language learning.

Note

1   Language has been changed only for purposes of clarification.

References

Blom, J. P., & Gumperz, J. J. (1972). Social meaning in linguistic structures: Code-switching in Norway. In J. J. Gumperz & D. Hymes (Eds.), *Directions in sociolinguistics* (pp. 407–434). New York, NY: Holt, Rinehart & Winston.

Cadman, K., & O'Regan, K. (Eds.). (2006). Tales out of school: Identity and English language teaching. Series "S": Special edition of *TESOL in Context*.

Canagarajah, A. S. (2001). Critical ethnography of a Sri Lankan classroom: Ambiguities in student opposition to reproduction through ESOL. In C. N. Candlin & N. Mercer (Eds.), *English language teaching in its social context* (pp. 208–226). London, England: Routledge.

Canagarajah, A. S. (2013). *Translingual practice: Global Englishes and cosmopolitan relations.* New York, NY: Routledge.

Carter, R. 1996. Speaking Englishes, speaking cultures. Plenary presented at the 30th IATEFL Conference, April 1996, Keele, England. [A version of the paper was published as Carter, R. (2003) Text 13: Orders of reality: CANCODE, communication, & culture in B. Seidlhofer (Ed.) *Controversies in applied linguistics* (pp. 90–104). Oxford, England: Oxford University Press.]

Chick, J. K. (2001). Safe-talk: Collusion in apartheid education. In C. N. Candlin & N. Mercer (Eds.), *English language teaching in its social context* (pp. 227–240). London, United Kingdom: Routledge.

Fantino, A. M., & Colak, A. (2001). Refugee children in Canada: Searching for identity. *Child Welfare, 53*(5), 587–597.

García, O. & Li Wei. (2014). *Translanguaging: Language, education, and bilingualism.* Basingtoke, England: Palgrave Macmillan.

Gardner, R. C., & Lambert, W. E. (1972). *Attitudes and motivation in second language learning.* Rowley, MA: Newbury House.

Gollnick, D. M., & Chinn, P. C. (2006). *Multicultural education in a pluralistic society,* 7th ed. Upper Saddle River, NJ: Pearson.

Ibrahim, A. E. K. (1999). Becoming Black: Rap and Hip-Hop, race, gender, and identity and the politics of ESL learning. *TESOL Quarterly, 33*(3), 349–369.

Imam, S. R. (2005). English as a global language and the question of nation-building education in Bangladesh. *Comparative Education, 41*, 471–486.

Lakoff, R. (1975). *Language and woman's place.* New York, NY: Harper & Row.

Marshall, S. & Moore, D. (2013). 2B or not 2B plurilingual: Navigating languages, literacies, and plurilingual competence in postsecondary education in Canada. *TESOL Quarterly, 47*(3), 472–499.

McKay, S. L. (2005). Sociolinguistics and language learning. In E. Hinkel (Ed.), *Handbook of research in second language teaching and learning* (pp. 281–299). Mahwah, NJ: Lawrence Erlbaum Associates, Inc.

McKay, S. L., & Wong, S.-L. C. (1996). Multiple discourses, multiple identities: Investment and agency in second-language learning among Chinese adolescent immigrant students. *Harvard Educational Review, 66*(3), 577–608.

Mohan, B., Leung, C., & Davison, C. (2001). *English as a second language in the mainstream: Teaching, learning and identity.* Harlow, England: Pearson.

Murray, D. E. (2018). The world of English language teaching: Creating equity or inequity? *Language Teaching Research,* 1–11. doi.org/10.1177/1362168818777529

Myers-Scotton, C. (1993). *Social motivation for codeswitching.* Oxford, England: Clarendon.

Nieto, S. (1992). *Affirming diversity: The sociopolitical context of multicultural education.* New York, NY: Longman.

Norton, B. (1995). Social identity, investment, and language learning. *TESOL Quarterly*, *29*(1), 9–31.

Norton, B. (2000). *Identity and language learning: Gender, ethnicity, and educational change.* Essex, England: Longman.

Norton, B. (2013). *Identity and language learning: Extending the conversation*, 2nd ed. Bristol, England: Multilingual Matters.

Pavlenko, A., Blackledge, A., Piller, I., & Teutsch-Dwyer, M. (Eds.). (2001). *Multilingualism, second language learning, and gender.* Berlin, Germany: Mouton de Gruyter.

Ryan, E. B., & Giles, H. (Eds.). (1982). *Attitudes towards language variation.* London, England: Edward Arnold.

Schneider, E. W. (2014). New reflections on the evolutionary dynamics of world Englishes. *World Englishes*, *33*(1), 9–32. Retrieved from https://doi.org/10.1111/weng.12069

Schumann, J. (1978). *The pidginization process: A model for second language acquisition.* Rowley, MA: Newbury House.

Tannen, D. (1990). *You just don't understand me.* New York, NY: Morrow.

Thorne, B., & Henley, N. (Eds.). (1975). *Sex roles, interruptions, and silences in conversations.* Rowley, MA: Newbury House.

Toohey, K., Day, E., & Manyak, P. (2007). ESL learners in the early school years. In J. Cummins & C. Davison (Eds.), *International handbook of English language teaching* (Vol. 2, pp. 626–638). New York, NY: Springer.

Wei, L. (2018). *Translanguaging and the goal of TESOL.* Retrieved from www.tesol.org/docs/default-source/ppt/li-wei.pdf?sfvrsn=0

Wong, S.-L. C., & Grant, R. (2007). Academic achievement and social identity among bilingual students in the US. In J. Cummins & C. Davison (Eds.), *International handbook of English language teaching* (Vol. 2, pp. 681–691). New York, NY: Springer.

2

THE WORLD OF ENGLISH

VIGNETTE

My language learning seems to be continuous learning. I was learning English while working. As soon as I finished my bachelor degree, I got a job as an English teacher in a secondary school, where I had an opportunity to work with an American Peace Corps volunteer. Her name was Ann. She taught me some slang and idioms which are often used by native speakers, and other things. But I was very surprised to see that she could not understand some vocabulary I used, like lift *or* ring you up, *despite my clear pronunciation. I ended up learning the differences between American English and British English. Before that I thought that English was English and all native speakers knew all English. I had to thank Ann for that lesson; otherwise, I would continue using inappropriate language despite being an English teacher.* [Thai teacher Nit, from Murray class notes]

Task: Reflect

1   What surprised you about Nit's story?
2   If you learned English in a school setting, what variety of English was used as the model?

(continued)

(continued)

3   If you are a native speaker of English, what variety do you speak?

4   How important is it for language teachers to understand both British and American English? Are there other varieties they need to know?

5   Do you agree with Nit's comment that she would be using inappropriate language? Why? Why not?

Introduction

English has become the global language for commerce, science, technology, media, and international diplomacy. In this chapter, we discuss the varieties of English that have developed and are still developing as a result of historical and current global interactions of peoples. In Chapter 3, we discuss how these trends have affected English language teaching in different contexts. English language teachers need to understand the important roles they play in this spread of English and how global trends affect both their own instruction and the lives of their learners.

We frame both Chapters 2 and 3 in the theoretical and research perspective that was first developed by Kachru (1986) and subsequently built on, re-examined, and refined by many researchers. Kachru developed the concept of World Englishes,[1] identifying three concentric circles of "Englishes"—the *Inner Circle*, the *Outer Circle*, and the *Expanding Circle*. The Inner Circle refers to those countries where English is the dominant language and the one first learned by most of the population (i.e., these are countries of native speakers[2]), used for the discourse of education, politics, business, science and technology, and administration. Such countries include Australia, Anglophone Canada, New Zealand, the United Kingdom, and the United States. The Outer Circle refers to countries where English may or may not be the official language but for historical reasons still plays a role in such discourses. Such countries include former British colonies such as India, Kenya, Malaysia, and Singapore, or former American colonies, such as the Philippines. Linguists describe the variety of English used in the Outer Circle as nativized because they adopt some of the features of the local language(s). For example, in Singapore, *lah*, which is a particle from Malay, is used in Singapore English (Singlish) at the end of words or phrases for emphasis. The Expanding Circle, the outermost of the concentric circles, refers to countries where English is widely used as a foreign language for communication with native English speakers or other EFL speakers, such as Brazil, China, Egypt, Germany, Japan, or Thailand. Building on this concept, others have identified a sub-group within the Inner Circle that they call BANA (Britain, Australasia, and North America).

Task: Reflect

Which circle do you work or live in? Think about the other two circles. How different do you think it would be to teach in those circles? What questions would you want to have answered before you taught there?

Kachru's model has been criticized because it seems to set up false dichotomies. For example, many Outer Circle users of English are native speakers, for example, in Singapore, where many families use English in the home, as well as in education or government. Similarly, the division between Outer and Expanding Circles is fuzzy, with many countries in the Expanding Circle teaching bilingually or even teaching subject areas in English in high school—for example, Germany. Further, English learning takes place outside classrooms. This grassroots (Schneider, 2016) acquisition of English occurs for instrumental reasons, such as tourism or social media, developing a variety of English that Vittachi (2010) has called *Globalese*. However, it is a useful construct to provide a framework for discussing the perceptions of English use and teaching around the world.

To understand the role of English and, therefore, English language teaching in these different circles, we must first unpack the issues around how to define a language. We will, therefore, begin with a discussion of language variety and standard language and, then, move on to discuss who a native speaker is and who can teach English. In Chapter 3, we discuss the context of these circles in terms of the types of English learners and English language program delivery.

Language Variation

All languages vary depending on characteristics of the user—age, gender, region, social class, and ethnicity—and the use to which the language is put—speaking or writing to whom, about what, for what purpose, using what medium of communication: "To the extent that speakers share knowledge of the communicative constraints and options governing a significant number of social situations, they can be said to be members of the same speech community" (Gumperz, 1986, p. 16). The linguistic study of language use in speech communities is called *sociolinguistics*. Speech communities are not homogeneous and speakers can belong to a number of different speech communities. So, for example, you probably belong to a specific regional speech community. Also, overlapping with this community and extending beyond it, you probably belong to a speech community that uses language of your age group, which may not be intelligible to those from a different age group. You also belong to the speech community of English language educators. What delineates a speech community is its members' recognition that they share sufficient rules of communication that they can understand the sociocultural meanings conveyed through their communicative acts.

Some aspects of language variety by user will be discussed here, while variety according to use will be developed in Chapter 9.

Language Variety by User

Dialect is used as an overarching term to describe varieties that vary because of geographical area, social class, gender, ethnicity, or age. In some of the literature, *sociolect* is the term used for varieties that vary because of social class. We will use the general term *dialect* here to refer to all variation according to attributes of the user of the language. First, however, is the issue of how to differentiate a language from a dialect. While people may have folk notions about how they differ, linguistically, there are no definitive rules for identifying a language, only sociocultural conventions. One criterion that has been used is that of mutual intelligibility—if speakers can understand one other, then they speak the same language. However, this criterion does not stand up in practice. Swedish and Danish are mutually intelligible. In fact, speakers who live close to the borders are more easily able to understand speakers of the other language than speakers from the same country who live at great distances. Yet, all agree that Swedish and Danish are two different languages. On the other hand, speakers of different dialects of Chinese are not intelligible to each other; yet they agree that they all speak Chinese. It has, therefore, been said that a language is a dialect with an army and a navy. In other words, determining whether a variety is a language or a dialect depends on sociopolitical history.

Sociolinguists analyze both the linguistic features of varieties and also the conditions of their use. While this is a fascinating area of linguistics, for our purposes here, it is sufficient to note this language universal of variation exists and go on to discuss one particular category of varieties, namely standard varieties, because of its use and misuse in education.

24

THE WORLD OF ENGLISH

Standard Varieties

What is standard English? An extensive literature argues for speakers (and writers) adhering to a standard, with a contesting literature arguing that a standard is a sociocultural construct, not a linguistic one. The former argument is usually made by governments, or the media, abhorring "falling" standards. The latter proponents argue that which variety becomes a "standard" does so because of political and economic power, not because of any inherent status of the language itself. Rather, it is the variety used by the powerful. Kachru argued that the English in the Inner Circle was norm-providing, in the Outer Circle norm-developing, and in the Expanding Circle norm-dependent. So, the English of the Inner Circle became the standard and, therefore, the target for those learning the language. However, the Inner Circle itself includes many varieties—across the BANA countries and within them. Kachru does make an important point because most of the instruments for testing English proficiency are developed in the United States or the United Kingdom and are based on the norms of those countries. Similarly, teachers may or may not be hired based on how closely their variety approaches a norm from the Inner Circle, which we discuss more fully below. (We discuss the issue of standards for large-scale assessment in Volume II.)

In fact, not only do the BANA countries have their own standard/norm, but many of the Outer Circle varieties of English have become established and spoken by native speakers, such as in Singapore mentioned above or South Asia (Kachru, 2004). Some writers have even posited that nativization has occurred in EFL varieties, such as in Europe (Kelch & Santana-Williamson, 2002) and China (Modiano, 2003). Are they sufficiently established to have become norms? This question is the crucial one. While linguists argue against the Kachru circles for these reasons (see, for example, Yano, 2001), within the Outer Circle countries there is still debate and often complete disagreement with linguists as to the validity of the local variety. For example, the Singapore government has frequent campaigns to teach people (including those who are native speakers of Singlish) what they consider to be grammatically correct English. A campaign launched in 2000, called "The Speak Good English Campaign," included lessons in newspapers, on television, and on the web, which identified Singlish features and then provided "Good English" alternatives. For example, the use of the particle *lah* for emphasis is identified as unacceptable because it is a nativized form and does not occur in the Englishes of the Inner Circle, especially Standard British English. The campaign has continued since then and has its own website (goodenglish.org.sg). As recently as March 2017, they launched a free pocket-size book called *Grammar Rules*.

Modiano (1999a), seeking to describe a standard English that was socially, culturally, and politically neutral, developed a model that was not based on history but on language proficiency. He placed at the center those who spoke English proficiently and were comprehensible to other speakers of English, whom he called "proficient in international English" speakers. To be comprehensible, he claimed, they needed to speak a variety that others could understand, and without a strong regional accent. The next circle he called learners, that is, those who are not yet proficient in internationally comprehensible English, with the Outer Circle for those who had no English. But this model raises questions. How much is too strong a regional accent and who decides? Fluent speakers of regional varieties, according to this model, would, therefore, not be classed as proficient. How do we measure comprehensibility? Further, proficiency is a highly contested construct. Our linguistic competencies are dependent on context, where context includes topic and audience of the communication. I might be able to interact in English about computer technology with other computer scientists but not interact socially, for example. Modiano (1999b) later modified his model, making the core "English as an international language," where this language consists of a core of features that are comprehensible to most native speakers and to competent nonnative speakers. But, what are the core features and what are the non-core features? How do we determine these? Jenkins (2000), in an effort to address this issue, conducted a large study of phonological features that are consistent across varieties, calling this core "English as an international language." Agreeing with Modiano, Kachru (2004) himself has argued that we should reconceptualize his construct, with the Inner Circle being those who are proficient in English, no matter how they acquired it, with the Expanding Circle moving out to lower and lower levels of proficiency. This reconceptualization still begs the question of what proficient use of English is and becomes not only an academic question but a gate-keeping question when deciding on answers in large-scale assessments (see Volume II) or when trying to provide statistical data on the number of English speakers in an individual country or compare the numbers in the three circles. Graddol (1997, 2006), in a number of publications, has estimated the number of speakers. In his 1997 work he estimated that, using Kachru's original three circles, by the start of the 21st century the Inner and Outer Circles would both be 375 million, and the Expanding Circle 750 million. Recent data (Lyons, 2017) claim 1.6 billion people use English worldwide, with 360 million using it as their first language. Whether these speakers are proficient or at some early stage of learning English is impossible to determine. The only value in such statistics is that the number of English users is growing rapidly and that growth is in the Expanding Circle.

The work Jenkins began in 2000 has developed across all aspects of English, in addition to phonological features, and has been called English as a Lingua Franca (ELF). For Jenkins and others (e.g., Seidlhofer, 2011) engaged in exploring an ELF model, *ELF* refers to English being used "as a contact language across lingua-cultures whose members are in the main nonnative speakers," whereas *World Englishes* refers to the nativized varieties referred to earlier (Jenkins, 2006, p. 157). Seidlhofer refers to both of these varieties as EIL, with World Englishes being for *intra*national communication and ELF for *inter*national communication.

Another model that helps us understand both how learners use language and what might be an appropriate target for their language learning and for our teaching is that of Leung, Harris, and Rampton (1997). To refine what it means to know and use a language, they developed a different three-part construct: language expertise (linguistic and cultural knowledge), language affiliation (identification and attachment), and language inheritance (connectedness and continuity). What is important, then, about a learner's language is their linguistic repertoire in relation to each of these criteria. Furthermore, how a learner identifies with or is connected with both their home language and English affects their motivation, which is key to their success in acquiring English, as we shall see in Part III of this volume. Norton has identified "investment," in addition to motivation, because language is both a social practice and a linguistic system, and thus identification or identity depends on both the psychological construct of motivation and the social practice of investment:

> If learners "invest" in the target language, they do so with the understanding that they will acquire a wider range of symbolic resources (language, education, friendship) and materials resources (capital goods, real estate, money) which will increase the value of their cultural capital and power.
>
> (Norton, 2013, p. 6)

We shall use Leung, Harris, and Rampton's construct below to discuss the language of learners in both the Inner and Outer Circle.

Who Is a Native Speaker?

Parallel with the controversy over standard language is the issue of who is considered a native speaker. The *native speaker (NS)* is a sociocultural construct, not identifiable linguistically. Yet, it plays a large part in framing how English is taught and by whom in all three circles.

The NS has long been viewed as having a special status with the commonly held definition that a NS is someone who was exposed to a language and learned it from birth. The popularity of the term in linguistics grew as a result of Chomsky's (1957) construct of the ideal speaker-hearer, whose instincts about their language provide a rich source of data about the grammar of a language. However, the creation of the NS allows for the nonnative speaker to be defined against a norm. In the field of ELT, as we discuss below, this norming has led to unsustainable practices in hiring teachers, unsustainable practically and ethically.

If we apply the definition above and Kachru's construct, there are many examples of rich English use in Outer and Expanding Circle contexts, with speakers using the language from birth. A large nativized literature exists in both Africa and Asia, for example. Many of these authors have won international prizes. Scholarly journals debate and research the literature and English language use in these arenas.[3] However, as Kachru and Nelson (1996) note, Britons and Americans are expected to be tolerant of each other's English but not that of South Asians, Southeast Asians, West Africans, or East Africans, or, we would contend, of Australian, New Zealand, or South African English (see example below). In practice, then, the ideal NS has only been someone exposed to and using the language from birth *if* they are from Britain or the United States *and* use a standard variety. Only two countries in the Inner Circle were, therefore, norm-providing, as Kachru had said of the Inner Circle. Being born in a country does not in and of itself result on one learning the language of the country. Most countries are multilingual and the official language is not the home language of many of the population. A child may be born in one country, but the family moves to another; the child may or may not acquire the language of the country of her birth, depending on opportunities to learn it in the new land. Thus, the common definition of NS does not hold up against real language users.

Many scholars have claimed that the NS is myth or fallacy (Brutt-Griffler & Samimy, 1999; Canagarajah, 1999; Phillipson, 1992). One of the earliest was Paikeday (1985), who stated that the native speaker is dead, in response to Chomsky's ideal speaker-hearer: "One would like to be able to assign each and every individual to one class or other (here, to native and non-native speaker), but the situation does not allow it" (Paikeday, 1985, p. 2). It doesn't allow it, because many factors contribute to a person's language use, as we also saw in Chapter 1.

There is still no consensus on a definition of NS. However, there seems to remain a need for such a definition: "We need it as a model, a goal almost as an inspiration" (Davies, 1996, p. 157). Thus, many scholars have sought to clarify and expand the definition so it is ideologically neutral. Several scholars have, therefore, suggested a range of criteria against which a NS can be defined—either one, several, or all (Kubota, 2004; Lee, 2005; Nayar, 1994) of the following criteria:

- first language acquired,
- acculturation through growing up in a speech community,
- linguistic and communicative competence,
- acquisition through formal education or daily use,
- dominance, frequency, and ease of use,
- nationality,
- identification with a speech community or recognition by a speech community,
- ability to differentiate between one's own variety and the standard,
- ethnicity,
- monolingualism, and
- variety used.

If there are so many criteria that can lead to native-like performance, how valuable is the concept for ELT? Further, all of these criteria can be refuted. For example, linguists who may not speak a language may be able to differentiate between varieties. People of the same ethnicity may speak a variety or a different language, depending on their own life experiences. So, all these criteria contribute in some way to the language someone uses, but are not particularly helpful in trying to define NS—it is too broad to meaningfully operate as a means of determining the target learners should be aiming for and that teachers should teach in English language instruction. We therefore consider that the three-part construct of Leung et al. (1997) is the most useful way to think about language and what is the appropriate target of language teaching. What language expertise (linguistic and cultural knowledge) do learners need, what language/variety do they want to affiliate with (identification and attachment), and what language inheritance do they bring to the classroom (connectedness and continuity)?

The Legacy of Colonialism

The use of English in the Outer Circle, consisting as it does of former British (and U.S.), colonies, needs to be examined against the impact of colonialism and the ideologies associated with it. It is in the Outer Circle that the hegemony of English as an international language is interrelated with a former dominant cultural power: "With the spread of English across the empire, the issue of the standardization of English became not merely one of cultural politics within Great Britain [as we saw above] but increasingly one of imperial cultural politics" (Pennycook, 1994, p. 110). Colonialism also has an impact in countries that were colonized by countries other than English-speaking ones. Countries in the Expanding Circle have not been exempt from being colonized, even though that colonization was not by an English-speaking group. Korea, for example, was long colonized by Japan. Kim (2002) has pointed out that the same colonized behaviors as in Inner Circle countries dominate the elite in Korea. The elite value Western thought and scholarship over Korean or other Asian thought and scholarship, leading many Korean students to choose to study in the United States rather than at home.

There are two quite different responses to being colonized. Some postcolonialist scholars have noted the psychological effects of colonialism as a tendency to submit to the colonizers and denigrate one's own heritage, and cultural and societal norms. The alternate response is resistance to linguistic and cultural dominance. We will provide examples of both these responses.

Emulating the Colonial Variety

Despite its association with colonialism, some countries endeavor to maintain a British standard, rather than embracing their local variety. Many African and Asian Anglophones, of course, have a vested interest in maintaining the status quo and rejecting local varieties as emerging standards because it maintains their positions of privilege. As we saw above, Singapore launched the Speak Good English Movement, devoted to a standard different from the local variety. The 1999 press release announcing the campaign stated (Agence France-Presse, 1999):

> SINGAPORE will launch a speak-good-English campaign as part of government moves to discourage "Singlish," the island state's unique version of the language.
> Prime Minister Goh Chok Tong said Singlish—with its bewildering mix of English, Malay, Indian, and Chinese dialects—was unacceptable, describing it as "English corrupted by Singaporeans."

But the positive attitude toward British English goes beyond comparing it negatively to nativized varieties that have developed in the Outer Circle. This attitude is also often applied to varieties in the Inner Circle that are neither British nor American. In an ongoing research study of international students in several universities in Australia, a Sri Lankan respondent recently stated "Australians are fluent in Strine[4] and Ockerish,[5] not proper English. I have nothing to learn from such crude bogans."[6] It does seem, however, that this student has certainly learned some local slang. In a similar vein, one of us (Denise), who is Australian-born, has documented the negative perceptions that native speakers of British and Standard American English (SAE) hold about Australian English. She was refused English teaching jobs in Britain and other parts of Europe because of her Australian variety, and in California, when offered a job, was told to "fix her accent" (Murray, 2010).

Resistance to the Colonial Variety

Resistance can be to learning the language of the colonizers or to resisting other aspects of colonization. At the heart of this potential resistance is the question of why English is taught and which variety is taught in the particular country. For ELT educators, there is the constant dilemma—to both teach English and also help learners develop their own awareness of the effect of colonialism, and even resist that effect.

In a study of KwaZulu schools in South Africa, Chick (2001) found that learners and teachers colluded to maintain traditional teaching approaches of teacher-led classroom interaction. Together they rejected more communicative and interactive strategies. In so doing, they were able to maintain a non-threatening classroom environment, one in which their lack of English proficiency was not revealed. In a study of learners in Sri Lanka, Canagarajah (2001) showed how the learners resisted the content of instruction in order to make the curriculum more related to their own needs and in an effort to reduce threats to their identity. Both responses to the neocolonial imposition of English were designed to save face. As Edge (1996, p. 17) says,

> If what we (and, particularly, we who live in or draw on such centers of TESOL as the United States or Britain) have to offer is essentially methodological and if those methods are subversive and inappropriate, how exactly do we justify our activities? What sort of future are we attempting to build with other people?

Nonnative English Speakers in TESOL (NNESTs)

As well as what variety of English should be the target and in which language instruction should take place, another contentious issue has been who should teach English, partly because of the continuing belief in the notion of native speaker. For many years and still in many Inner Circle contexts, the NS is considered as the only model capable of teaching English. We demonstrated above that this construct has no reality in terms of linguistic features, that there is in fact a blurring of these categories. In addition, the NS as the only credible teacher of English is untenable in practice because the vast majority of ELT teachers are what traditionally would have been called nonnative speakers (Canagarajah, 1999; Matsuda & Matsuda, 2001). While we have exploded the myth of the NS, we have chosen to use the term *NNEST*. In other work, one of us rejected this term, using *multilingual teacher* instead, reflecting Cook's concept of multicompetence, "the knowledge of more than one language in the same mind or the same community" (Cook, 2012, p. 3768). However, several NNS professionals have themselves indicated they prefer to use *NNEST* because it explicitly reminds us of the false dichotomy that still persists in the field.[7] Recent discussions have also centered around how NNEST is used interchangeably to mean *nonnative English speakers in TESOL* or *nonnative English-speaking teachers* (Selvi, 2014). There has been concern that the focus on classroom teachers ignores others in the TESOL professions, such as teacher educators, publishers, and researchers. Even though our focus here is on teachers, we have honored the decision of the professional association (TESOL International), which chose the first definition for the name of the interest section because it was more inclusive.

A number of researchers have found that NNESTs bring strengths and abilities to the language classroom, especially as role models and mentors for students learning English (Braine, 2010; Ellis, 2002; Liu, 1999a; Tatar & Yıldız, 2010). They provide role models because learners can see an example of a successful second language learner. They can be mentors because they, too, have experienced learning another language. In a study of NNESTs' perceptions of their students' views, Amin (2001) found these visible minority teachers in Canada believed their students considered only white teachers to be NSs. These teachers, however, found that it was precisely their NNS positioning that helped them "draw on their experience of otherness to build successful pedagogies" (p. 103), such as building community by using materials that supported inclusiveness, and by disrupting the myth of the NS. In her 2016 plenary, Richardson cited the extant literature that demonstrates that students themselves do not inherently have a bias against NNESTs. Rather, students have nuanced attitudes towards both NESTs and NNESTs, attributing different strengths and weaknesses to each grouping and to their teaching styles (Uzum, 2018).

Several research studies (Brutt-Griffler & Samimy, 1999; Liu, 1999b; McKay, 2000; Murray & Garvey, 2004) have examined NNESTs during their initial training in an Inner Circle country. While they agree that these prospective teachers provide role models and can be mentors to their students, they also raise issues about English proficiency, knowledge of the culture of the Inner Circle country, and their identity dilemma.[8] Some have shown that NNESTs are faced with reconstructing their identity during the practicum experience. Murray and Garvey (2004) found that, although some student-teachers believed that they could not be role models because students would look at them and know they were NNESTs, over the course of the practicum positive feedback from learners led them to reappraise their own views of themselves. NNESTs saw themselves as role models and as motivating learners. Brown and Miller (2006) also found that, while rejecting the claim that only NSs can teach English, the NS competence as the ideal persisted, even if expressed as "near native fluency" (p. 126). These researchers recommended that certification and other training programs should challenge this assumption and deconstruct the NS construct with their student-teachers. In this vein, Brutt-Griffler and Samimy (2006) relate a program in which they deliberately sought to empower their prospective NNESTs through critical praxis. That is, they try deconstructing the construct of nativeness and focus on the struggle NNESTs have as they try to practice as ELT professionals. Both Murray and Garvey and Brown and Miller also found that the prospective teachers struggled with the pedagogical language needed for the classroom, which was also recognized by the supervising teacher. Unlike their NS peers, they had not been exposed to an English-medium schooling and so were unfamiliar with "teacher talk" in English. It seems that for NNESTs to identify as ELT professionals requires rethinking their own values and beliefs about what it means to be such a teacher, but it also means acquiring a pedagogical language.

Despite the research findings, NNESTs are still often denied ELT jobs in the Inner Circle. This situation is especially the case in programs for international students. Ellis (2002) notes that NNESTs are common in the adult ESL sector; however, they are not common in the international student sector, where students often request to be taught by an NS. During our tenures as English language program administrators and teaching assistant (TA) supervisors, we have advocated for the inclusion of NNEST instructors in our own workplaces. If students complained about having NNESTs, we explained our reasons and then asked the student to trial the class or classes. Interestingly, students soon found that they were learning from a qualified teacher, which was more important than whether their teachers were NESTs or NNESTs.

While we have provided examples for the Inner Circle, there is abundant evidence that NSs are preferred over NNESTs in both the Outer and Expanding Circles. Many countries advertise that only people from Britain and the United States need apply, while others employ NSs as adjuncts for conversation classes.

Unfortunately, many of these NSs are hired whether they have training in ELT or not. TESOL International Association has made a concerted effort to denounce such unfair practices through the creation of position statements and by refusing to list job advertisements that required NS teachers.

While the debate continues about which target is appropriate, countries in the Outer Circle have found that they have an economic advantage over those in the Inner Circle and have started to gain a substantial market share of the billion-dollar ELT industry. Singapore and India, in particular, have developed English language programs for international students, especially those from poorer countries, such as China or those in Southeast Asia. This situation will undoubtedly impact materials and pedagogy, and some ELT professionals worry about it. As Wong and Thomas (1993) have observed about Malaysian English, a more fruitful approach is to

> empower our students by building on these nativized items; in doing so, our students will be able to find their own personal and cultural voices, and at the same time will learn to transform their meaning into a language that is understandable to a larger audience. The classroom will therefore become an arena where, through an evolving dialogue with their inner selves, their peers and their teachers, learners will see themselves gradually becoming a part of a larger community whose strength lies not in its homogeneity but in its rich cultural diversity.
>
> (p. 25)

Task: Explore

Conduct a short questionnaire with some of your colleagues or peers. If you are in a pre-service course or in-service workshop, give the questionnaire to ten of your peers. If you are teaching, give the questionnaire to five of your colleagues. Collate your results and share with a colleague or peer.

Questionnaire

Have you ever had a nonnative English-speaking teacher (NNEST)?

Yes   No

　If "yes," on a five point scale, rate the teacher on the following statements.
　1 = Strongly disagree; 2 = Disagree ; 3 = Neutral ; 4 = Agree; 5 = Strongly agree

THE WORLD OF ENGLISH

1   The NNEST promoted learning more effectively. 1 2 3 4 5
2   The NNEST supplied first language equivalents. 1 2 3 4 5
3   The NNEST provided explanations of grammar. 1 2 3 4 5
4   The NNEST focused more on accuracy than fluency. 1 2 3 4 5
5   The NNEST used the first language too much in lessons. 1 2 3 4 5
6   The NNEST had good pronunciation. 1 2 3 4 5
7   The NNEST provided an excellent model. 1 2 3 4 5
8   The NNEST supplied more cultural information. 1 2 3 4 5
9   The NNEST was less strict in classroom management. 1 2 3 4 5
10 The NNEST was easy to understand. 1 2 3 4 5

Conclusion

While applied linguists may conduct research and argue about whether English is an international, global, or world language, educators have practical decisions to make regarding the appropriate target variety for their learners. As we showed above, educators can inform policy makers from governments to school principals to testing agencies. They can advocate on behalf of their learners. However, in their own classrooms, we believe it is important for teachers to engage learners in critical analysis of the role that English plays in the world and in their own lives. They need to examine their own needs and determine which variety(ies) of English best serve those needs.

Task: Expand

Braine, G. (2010). *Nonnative speaker English teachers: Research, pedagogy, and professional growth*. New York, NY: Routledge.
This volume provides a thorough overview of the issues faced by NNESTs.

Kachru, B. B., Kachru, Y., & Nelson, C. (Eds.) (2009). *Handbook of World Englishes*. London, England: Wiley-Blackwell.
This collection focuses on critical aspects and case studies of the theoretical, ideological, applied, and pedagogical issues related to English use around the world.

Seidlhofer, B. (2011). *Understanding English as a Lingua Franca*. Oxford, England: Oxford University Press.

(continued)

(continued)

This is a comprehensive discussion of how and why ELF functions as it does. The volume includes discussion of the globalization of English.

NNEST website for TESOL available at: http://nnest.massou.net/
This website has a variety of resources for those interested in this issue.

Questions for Discussion

1 What has been the effect of colonialism on the teaching and learning of English in the Outer Circle?
2 Why is Kachru's circle model arbitrary for describing the different Englishes in the world?
3 What definition of NS would describe linguistic reality?
4 What advantages do NNESTs bring to the ELT classroom?
5 Why is it difficult to count the number of English speakers in the world?

Notes

1 They began a new journal of the same name, which is now the primary venue for research and discussions about World Englishes.
2 *Native speaker* and *nonnative speaker* are contested terms. We will discuss this in detail later in the chapter. For the purposes of discussing the three circles, it is sufficient for readers to use their own definitions, whether folk ones or ones they know from their readings.
3 For example, *English in Africa* was established in 1974.
4 *Strine* is a colloquial term for Australian English, based on a book called *Let Stalk Strine* by Afferbeck Lauder in 1965. The term is meant to replicate the way Australians themselves pronounce "Australian." The pseudonymous author name is the Australian way of saying "alphabetical order." The actual author was Alastair Ardoch Morrison.
5 *Ocker* is an Australian slang term for an Australian.
6 A *bogan* is an Australian slang colloquial term for a person who doesn't take pride in their appearance and spends their time drinking beer and hanging about.
7 The international professional association, TESOL, has also embraced the term *NNEST*, using it as the name for an interest section.
8 In Chapter 4 we discuss the role of culture in language learning.

References

Agence France-Presse. (1999). *Singapore to launch speak-good-English campaign* [Electronic version]. Retrieved from www.singapore-window.org/sw99/90830afp.htm

Amin, N. (2001). Nativism, the native speaker construct, and minority immigrant women teachers of English as a second language. *The CATESOL Journal*, *13*(1), 89–107.

Braine, G. (2010). *Nonnative speaker English teachers: Research, pedagogy, and professional growth*. New York, NY: Routledge.

Brown, J., & Miller, J. (2006). Dilemmas of identity in teacher education: Reflections on one pre-service ESL teacher cohort. *TESOL in Context, Series "S,"* 118–146.

Brutt-Griffler, J., & Samimy, K. K. (1999). Revisiting the colonial in the postcolonial: Critical praxis for non-native-English-speaking teachers in a TESOL program. *TESOL Quarterly*, *33*(3), 413–431.

Canagarajah, A. S. (1999). Interrogating the "Native Speaker Fallacy": Non-linguistic roots, non-pedagogical results. In G. Braine (Ed.), *Non-native educators in English language teaching* (pp. 77–92). Mahwah, NJ: Lawrence Erlbaum.

Canagarajah, A. S. (2001). Critical ethnography of a Sri Lankan classroom: Ambiguities in student opposition to reproduction through ESOL. In C. N. Candlin & N. Mercer (Eds.), *English language teaching in its social context* (pp. 208–226). London, England: Routledge.

Chick, J. K. (2001). Safe-talk: Collusion in apartheid education. In C. N. Candlin & N. Mercer (Eds.), *English language teaching in its social context* (pp. 227–240). London, England: Routledge.

Chomsky, N. (1957). *Syntactic structures*. The Hague, Netherlands: Mouton.

Cook, V. J. (2012). Multicompetence. In C. Chappelle (Ed.), *The encyclopedia of applied linguistics* (pp. 3768–3774), Chichester, England: Wiley-Blackwell.

Davies, A. (1996). Proficiency or the native speaker: What are we trying to achieve in ELT? In G. Cook & B. Seidlhofer (Eds.), *Principle and practice in applied linguistics* (pp. 145–157). Oxford, England: Oxford University Press.

Edge, J. (1996). Cross-cultural paradoxes in a profession of values. *TESOL Quarterly*, *30*(1), 9–30.

Ellis, L. (2002). Teaching from experience: A new perspective on the non-native teacher in adult ESL. *Australian Review of Applied Linguistics*, *25*(1), 71–107.

Graddol, D. (1997). *The future of English?* London, England: British Council.

Graddol, D. (2006). *English next*. London, England: British Council.

Gumperz, J. J. (1986). Introduction. In J. J. Gumperz & D. Hymes (Eds.), *Directions in sociolinguistics: The ethnography of communication* (pp. 1–25). Oxford, England: Basil Blackwell.

Jenkins, J. (2000). *The phonology of English as an international language*. Oxford, England: Oxford University Press.

Jenkins, J. (2006). Current perspectives in teaching World Englishes and English as a Lingua Franca. *TESOL Quarterly*, *40*(1), 157–181.

Kachru, B. B. (1986). *The alchemy of English: The spread, functions and models of non-native Englishes*. Oxford, England: Pergamon Press.

Kachru, B. B. (2004). *Asian Englishes: Beyond the canon*. Hong Kong: Hong Kong University Press.

Kachru, B. B., Kachru, Y., & Nelson, C. (Eds.) (2009). *Handbook of World Englishes*. London, England: Wiley-Blackwell.

Kachru, B. B., & Nelson, C. L. (1996). World Englishes. In S. L. McKay (Ed.), *Sociolinguistics and language teaching* (pp. 71–102). Cambridge, England: Cambridge University Press.

Kelch, K., & Santana-Williamson, E. (2002). ESL students' attitudes toward native- and nonnative-speaking instructors' accents. *The CATESOL Journal, 14*(1), 57–72.

Kim, Y. M. (2002). *Naneun: yeongeo sadaejuui: ttwieoneomgi*. Seoul: Hankyurae.

Kubota, M. (2004). Native speaker: A unitary fantasy of a diverse reality. *The Language Teacher, 28*(1), 3–30.

Lee, J. J. (2005). The native speaker: An achievable model? [Electronic version]. *Asian EFL Journal, 7*. Retrieved from www.asian-efl-journal.com/June_05_jl.pdf

Leung, C., Harris, R., & Rampton, B. (1997). The idealised native speaker, reified ethnicities, and classroom realities. *TESOL Quarterly, 31*, 543–560.

Liu, D. (1999a). From their own perspectives: The impact of non-native professionals on their students. In G. Braine (Ed.), *Non-native educators in English language teaching*. Mahwah, NJ: Lawrence Erlbaum.

Liu, D. (1999b). Training non-native TESOL students: Challenges for TESOL teacher education in the West. In G. Braine (Ed.), *Non-native educators in English language teaching*. Mahwah, NJ: Lawrence Erlbaum.

Lyons, D. (July 26, 2017). *How many people speak English, and where is it spoken?* Retrieved from www.babbel.com/en/magazine/how-many-people-speak-english-and-where-is-it-spoken/

Matsuda, A., & Matsuda, P. (2001). Autonomy and collaboration in teacher education: Journal sharing among native and nonnative English-speaking teachers. *The CATESOL Journal, 13*(1), 109–121.

McKay, S. (2000). An investigation of five Japanese English teachers' reflections on their U.S. MA TESOL practicum experience. *JALT Journal, 22*(1), 46–68.

Modiano, M. (1999a). International English in the global village. *English Today, 15*(2), 3–15.

Modiano, M. (1999b). Standard English(es) and educational practices for the world's lingua franca. *English Today, 15*(4), 3–13.

Modiano, M. (2003). Euro-English: A Swedish perspective. *English Today, 19*(2), 35–41.

Murray, D. E. (2010). Changing stripes—chameleon or tiger? In D. Nunan & J. Choi (Eds.), *Language and culture: Reflective narratives and the emergence of identity* (pp. 164–169). New York, NY: Routledge.

Murray, D. E., & Garvey, E. (2004). The multilingual teacher: Issues for teacher education. *Prospect, 19*(2), 3–24.

Nayar, P. B. (1994, April). *Whose English is it?* Retrieved from www-writing.berkeley.edu/TESL-EJ/ej01/f.1/html

Norton, B. (2013). *Identity and language learning: Extending the conversation*, 2nd ed. Bristol, England: Multilingual Matters.

Norton, B. (1995). Social identity, investment, and language learning. *TESOL Quarterly*, *29*(1), 9–31.

Paikeday, T. M. (1985). *The native speaker is dead*. Toronto: Paikeday Publishing Inc.

Pennycook, A. (1994). *The cultural politics of English as an international language*. London, England: Longman.

Phillipson, R. (1992). *Linguistic imperialism*. Oxford: Oxford University Press

Richardson, S. (2016). Plenary speech. The "native factor," the haves and the have-nots . . . and why we still need to talk about this in 2016. *IATEFL Online*. Retrieved from https://iatefl.britishcouncil.org/2016/session/plenary-silvana-richardson

Schneider, E. W. (2016). Grassroot Englishes in tourism interactions. *English Today*, *32*(3), 2–10.

Seidlhofer, B. (2011). *Understanding English as a Lingua Franca*. Oxford, England: Oxford University Press.

Selvi, A. F. (2014). Myths and misconceptions about nonnative English speakers in the TESOL (NNST) movement. *TESOL Journal*, *5*(3), 573–611.

Tatar, S., & Yıldız, S. (2010). Empowering nonnative-English speaking teachers in the classroom. In A. Mahboob (Ed.), *The NNEST lens: Nonnative English speakers in TESOL* (pp. 114–128). Newcastle upon Tyne, England: Cambridge Scholars Publishing.

Uzum, B. (2018). Attitudes of students toward NESTs and NNESTs. *The TESOL encyclopedia of English language teaching* (pp. 1–7), John Wiley & Sons, Inc. Retrieved from https://doi.org/10.1002/9781118784235.eelt0008

Vittachi, N. (2010). A short course in Globalese. In D. Nunan & J. Choi (Eds.), *Language and culture: Reflective narratives and the emergence of identity* (pp. 215–222). New York, NY: Routledge.

Wong, L., & Thomas, J. (1993). Nativization and the making of meaning. In M. N. Brock & L. Walters (Eds.), *Teaching composition around the Pacific Rim* (pp. 15–27). Philadelphia, PA: Multilingual Matters.

Yano, Y. (2001). World Englishes in 2000 and beyond. *World Englishes*, *20*(2), 119–131.

3

ENGLISH LANGUAGE LEARNING AROUND THE WORLD

VIGNETTE

In a 2008 issue of the journal Essential Teacher, *Cara L. Preuss, a doctoral student in language and literacy described her identity crisis in becoming a language educator. Already a teacher with lengthy experience in a variety of language education arenas, such as an ESL, EFL, Spanish, general elementary, and bilingual Spanish-English teacher, she is working to continue improving her professional practice. To this end, in addition to studying for her PhD, she knows she should be attending conferences and submitting papers for publication. But, her identity crisis comes as she explores the breadth and depth of the field, uncovering as she goes, a host of acronyms and other types of short forms, representing different aspects and also different points of view and perceptions of her identity as a teacher. She feels as if she's "drowning in alphabet soup." She bemoans these divisions and opaque short forms that, she feels, put both students and teachers into separate boxes and prevent language educators from developing a powerful community of practice. She wants, instead, for teachers to come together with a shared set of concepts (and terminology and acronyms), so they can all speak clearly and with one voice to the policy- and other decision-makers, as well as to the public.*

Task: Reflect

1   Have you also felt as if you're drowning in the acronyms and their short forms in the field of language education? How has this affected your desire to become (or to continue as) a language teacher?

2   In what ways do the labels that we use to describe our learners and our teaching position learners as deficient?

3   How important is it for language educators to be advocates for their learners, their profession, and their field of practice?

4   How important is it for you and the field, for an Argentinian secondary school teacher of English to understand the context and practice of a British teacher who teaches a short, 4-week summer course to rich European teenagers visiting England, and vice versa? What does this example tell you about the cohesion of our field?

Introduction

In this chapter we examine issues around teaching English in each of the three circles delineated by Kachru (1986). In Outer and Expanding Circles, English is perceived to have instrumental value in providing people with greater access to social and economic capital, and therefore the perception is that it is wise and even required for nations to promote English language teaching and learning. Research on Inner Circle countries demonstrates the economic and health advantages of knowing English (Seargeant, Erling, Solly, & Hasan Chowdhury, 2017). However, despite the rhetoric that English is an automatic good for individuals and society, it can also exacerbate inequality. No matter where English language teaching (ELT) teachers work, they are part of the worldwide teaching English to speakers of other languages (TESOL) profession. Therefore, this chapter explores how teaching and learning are shaped in these different contexts.

In the light of the discussion in Chapter 2 about the values attributed to both Inner Circle varieties of English and native-speaker teachers, it is not surprising that English as a medium of instruction (EMI) is a dominant issue in all three circles. In addition, each context has specific issues because of the nature of the learners in that context. However, the Inner Circle differs from the others because these countries have international students coming to study, as well as immigrants and refugees, and they provide special instruction for these different learners. Australia and Canada have long established nationally designed programs for immigrants and refugees—both during compulsory schooling and for adults. Even though the programs in the United States receive Federal funding, they are arranged and delivered locally, leading to large differences across the country. The United Kingdom developed competencies for adult learners in 2001, but it does not have the organized programs at the adult level that Australia and Canada have. In the United States, Canada, and Australia, international students' access to English language instruction is controlled through their immigration departments that offer special student visas. In Britain, while a member of the European Union (EU), students from EU countries have been able to come freely without visas to learn English. In contrast, in Outer and Expanding Circles, the teaching of English is to their own nationals although recently some of the Outer Circle countries have started to offer programs for international students. An issue that is not raised in the Inner Circle for the teaching of English, but is a major issue for the other circles, is the age for beginning second language instruction. We shall, therefore, have a section on the Inner Circle and one on the Outer and Expanding Circles. Each section includes two themes—the nature of the learner and the medium of instruction—while the section on the Outer and Expanding Circles includes a third theme of age to begin second language instruction.

The Inner Circle

While the Inner Circle consists of countries where English is the dominant language, these countries are also characterized by diverse, multilingual/multicultural populations, including indigenous peoples and diverse regional, ethnic, or social varieties of English. Therefore, one of the tensions in English as a second language (ESL) education in these settings is the role of minority languages and varieties. These varieties are either devalued, or they are considered as steps to acquiring the majority language and perhaps are of sentimental value for language minority communities. Most often they are considered as barriers to acquiring the variety of language represented by the majority.

The Nature of the Learners in the Inner Circle

Here we discuss the two major learner groupings—immigrants/refugees and international students.

Immigrants and refugees. In the United States, growth in the enrollment of English language learners (ELL[1]) in K-12 between 1995 and 2004 was 57 percent, with an additional growth between 2004–5 and 2014–15, compared

42

with less than 4 percent growth for all students (NCES, 2018). At 4.6 million in 2014–15, ELLs comprise 9.4 percent of the total student population. In some states, which have traditionally had limited (if any) immigration, growth has been more than 300 percent between 1995 and 2005. While growth has not been as spectacular in Australia, Canada, New Zealand, and the United Kingdom, substantial numbers of immigrant children and young people are in schools in those countries. Additionally, adult immigrants are also learning English in a variety of settings.

Immigrants come to Britain, Australasia, and North American (BANA) countries (see Chapter 2) at various different ages, but they also continue acquiring English throughout their lives. It is, therefore, insufficient to look only at young learners, youth, and adults as if they were homogeneous cohorts. Rather, we have a range of different learner attributes across the spectrum of length of time since arrival in the host country. Even within a time period there are differences, depending on learners' previous educational background and exposure to English.

Young learners have had little previous education in their home country; and if they are refugees, they may have had no education or literacy development in their home language. Recently arrived youth and adults may have already been educated in their home language and be literate in that language. Others may have had little previous education because of poverty or the traumas of being refugees. Some may have come to a BANA country when they were young and have been primarily educated in the BANA country and acquired English through exposure in the community (sometimes called "ear" learners, to distinguish them from "eye" learners, who have studied English as an academic study). They have, in fact, had no formal English language learning. This group of learners has been identified as "Generation 1.5," (Goen, Porter, Swanson, & Vandommelen, 2002, p. 131) in acknowledgement that these students have language backgrounds and educational needs somewhere between those of recently arrived *first generation* immigrants and U.S.-born *second generation* immigrants.[2] The term was first used by sociologists Rumbaut and Ima (1988) in their study of Southeast Asian youth in the United States and was then taken up in the ELT literature. Interestingly, Park (1999) notes that the Korean-American community specifically refers to immigrants who arrive as children as *il cheom o se*, which means "one point five generation."

Young learners or recently arrived youth learners can be accommodated in *newcomer* programs, that is, programs where they can focus on basic English for one or more years before moving into mainstream classes with perhaps additional ESL language support. Such programs are supported by many stakeholders because of the "sheltered"[3] nature of the programs which give learners time to adapt not only to a new language, but also a new culture. There is, however, some controversy over such programs as immigrants may be ghettoized and then suffer an additional disruption when they move into mainstream classes (Feinberg, 2000). Where newcomer programs are not available, learners usually participate in ESL or bilingual programs (see below for a discussion of bilingual programs). Generation 1.5, however, does not fit this mold. If they arrive in the BANA country prior to first grade, they are likely to be placed in mainstream classes.

Often immigrant and refugee young people do not acquire the academic language required in the schools for a variety of reasons, either through lack of access or through lack of investment (see Chapter 1). They may learn the language only through interaction and so acquire only conversational English. They and their families may not have access to the discourses of school, which are largely those of middle-class white communities (Gee, 1996). They may experience racism and other forms of discrimination that lead them to perceive schooling as not giving them opportunities to advance. They may have seen second generation immigrants sometimes achieve less than their first generation parents or professionals in their communities—for example, working as taxi drivers because their qualifications have not been recognized. They may have also been prematurely mainstreamed without language support. This latter is especially the case for Generation 1.5 learners, who are often reasonably fluent orally, so their English needs may be misdiagnosed. At the same time, others are held in ESL classes longer than necessary and are never taught the discourses and subject matter needed for academic success. The language needs of Generation 1.5 students may not be noticed until they reach college level. Thus, particularly in the United States, colleges have large numbers of either remedial or ESL classes, especially in writing, to prepare these learners for their coursework at university.

Similarly, immigrants who arrive at high school age with little or no English rarely have time to acquire sufficient proficiency in English to learn the content that is needed to graduate from high school. This situation is exacerbated because their previous academic learning may have been from a different cultural perspective with different content (especially in subjects such as social studies) or, especially in the case of refugees, may have not existed at all.

Immigrants arriving as adults also have challenges in their efforts to learn English. Some adult learners focus on improving their English to get any job or one in their previous field because English language proficiency has a large positive effect on earnings, occupational status, and workplace participation (Chiswick, Cohen, & Zach, 1997; Chiswick, Lee, & Miller, 2003), with those learners with low proficiency being twice as likely to be employed in unskilled jobs as those with higher proficiency (Batalova, Fix, & Creticos, 2008). Some take English classes to help their children with homework so that they can be more successful in school. However, many have already worked a full day when they come to English class. Often English classes for adults in the United States are full, with long waiting lists. Sometimes class sizes are so large and students are so frequently changing that teachers cannot remember all the names of their students. Government policies in some BANA countries (for example, Australia and the United States) pay ESL providers by the number of hours of instruction or the number of students in a class, which forces these providers to replace learners who leave (for whatever reason) with new learners. Teachers are then faced with a constantly changing, multilevel class of learners in which it is almost impossible to build a positive learning community. Often families have to make choices about which members will learn English, which will be caregivers, and which will work to provide income (Wigglesworth, 2003). Even those with professional qualifications from their own country may have to take unskilled work because their qualifications are not recognized.

Immigration, whether voluntary or involuntary, causes dislocation and identity reevaluation, as discussed in Chapter 1. The dislocation can also lead to health and psychological trauma, especially for immigrants with low levels of English language proficiency who experience more health problems and psychological stress, and are less likely to seek help in these areas (Carrington, McIntosh, & Walmsley, 2007). The refugees in particular have experienced dislocation, trauma, possible persecution, separation from friends and family, or other human rights violations. Survivors of torture experience multiple effects of their trauma (Canadian Centre for Victims of Torture 2018; The Forum of Australian Services for Survivors of Torture and Trauma, 2018). Both of these organizations provide extensive information on their websites, which show that these learners may be overwhelmed by their past experiences, feel anxious because they have no control over their lives, distrust strangers, fear groups, lack meaning in their lives, and often have memory loss and lack concentration. These factors are all barriers to effective English learning. In addition, they may also fear authority figures and so distrust government because of previous state-sanctioned violence. Often these mental health issues are neglected (Fazel & Stein, 2003).

There are also large numbers of refugees who come from Anglophone-influenced countries, such as Liberia or Nigeria, and speak a nativized variety of English (see Chapter 2). They not only reject being considered as colonials, but also reject any identification as non-fluent users of English because their variety of English is a large part of their identity. In placement assessments, they may be assessed as orally fluent. However, because they lack literacy skills in either their home language or English, they are placed in ESL classes. Yet, they do not want to be perceived as needing English instruction (Murray & Lloyd, 2007).

What variety of English do these immigrants and refugees acquire? The appropriate target can be determined through the lens of Leung, Harris, and Rampton's (1997) three aspects of the learners' specific context of language learning referred to in Chapter 2: language expertise, language affiliation, and language inheritance, all of which influence a learner's investment in learning English. Thus, a learner in the United States who lives in a predominantly African-American neighborhood and who interacts with young people from that community may identify with that local community, whose members may speak the variety known as *African American Vernacular English (AAVE)*. As research has shown, such learners in a natural setting, through contact and/or identification acquire features of AAVE, rather than *Standard American English (SAE)*. Goldstein (1987) found that her Hispanic learners, through contact with African-American peers, adopted AAVE. Similarly, Ibrahim (1999) showed that African immigrants to Canada chose to identify with AAVE speakers and developed that variety. Immigrants living in Yorkshire in England acquire a Yorkshire regional variety if they identify with and/or have primary contact with their local community. The question teachers are faced with is what models should be used in the classroom for such learners.

Other learners aspire to identify with the social group that has power and, therefore, identify with them and their variety, often rejecting the local variety used by their peers. What models should be used for the learners? Some immigrants to Australia, Canada, the United Kingdom, or the United States reject English, identifying with their own established ethnic communities. They may consider acquiring English as selling out and giving a perception of denying or betraying their heritage. Such a rejection of English and what it stands for creates a barrier to their acquisition of English. In contrast, many learners perceive that the host society rejects their heritage and home language. This perception can lead to either a total rejection of English and of the cultures of power or to a desire to speak the language of power and change the status of their community once they have gained a position of power. Again, the question teachers are faced with is what models of language use are appropriate for such learners.

International students. While the Inner Circle countries have histories of immigration, and, more recently in Britain of migrant workers, they also have encouraged international students to study high school or university courses, as well as English. Universities have looked to full fee-paying international students to bolster their budgets because governments have reduced funding. The United States, the United Kingdom, and Australia receive the highest number of students, but from 2008, student numbers to the United States have dropped. Countries of origin have fluctuated in all three countries, depending on government policies in sending and receiving countries, such as visa restrictions or reductions in scholarship funding. For both the United States and Australia, China and India constitute the top two countries of origin.

We can identify three categories of international student.

- Students studying English only. Mostly these students are self-supporting and study intensively for short periods. Some may come on government scholarships to improve their English. In some cases, future job promotion may depend on successful completion of such courses.
- Students preparing for a high school or university course. These students have either been accepted conditionally, based on their successful scores on IELTS (International English Teaching System) or TOEFL (Test of English as a Foreign Language) or have been accepted as long as they pass a certified English course. Thus, many of the English courses are preparing students for these tests. Others are preparing them for university and offer content-based courses preparing them for specific courses of study.
- Students taking an English course concurrently with a high school or university course. Many universities have recognized that, despite having met the university's English entrance requirement, international students are not sufficiently proficient in academic literacy to be successful in their university course. Many universities and high schools therefore offer either an adjunct course or stand-alone English course. Adjunct courses are those where the English and subject-matter instructors collaborate and the English course supports the subject-matter course (see Volume II for a thorough discussion of such programs).

There are important questions for English language teachers to ask. Do these learners identify with English? Are they invested in the host country and its culture? In general, these learners are using English as a tool, so they can learn the content for a degree or high school diploma. However, many have recognized that proficiency in English increases their employability on their return to their home country because of English being the *global lingua franca*. For some, this is why they have chosen to study in an English-speaking country. Further, some aspire to stay as immigrants to the country where they are studying. For example, the Australian government made changes to its point system for accepting immigrants in the skilled category such that students graduating with postgraduate degrees in areas of need in Australia (such as accounting) could automatically become permanent residents. For these students, this policy change often meant a change in motivation towards learning English so that they had a greater commitment to it. In other cases, people wanting to immigrate chose to take a degree in a subject they were not invested in learning just to gain permanent residency.

While international students may not have experienced the traumas of refugees, they do experience culture shock as they try to adjust to a new country and its educational system with which they may not be familiar. As we explain in Chapter 4, they may bring different cultural expectations to the language classroom about the role of the teacher and their role as learners.

The scenarios above show that the motivations and, therefore, the investment in acquiring English vary considerably in the Inner Circle. A further aspect of the Inner Circle context that impacts on learners is the medium of instruction used in the English language classroom.

Medium of Instruction

Medium of instruction (MOI) has been contested historically in the Inner Circle. Early in the 20th century, the primary methodology used was grammar translation where grammatical structures were explained in the home language and translation from one language to the other was the goal of instruction. As the field developed in the middle of the 20th century, new theories of language and language learning were proposed. With the development of the audiolingual method, teachers were required to use English only, with learners practicing English through imitation and drilling. The rationale for using only English was that the more learners heard and used English, the faster they would acquire it and that listening and speaking preceded reading and writing. This instructional practice sometimes led to quite farcical applications as teachers tried to explain abstract concepts to beginning learners. When communicative approaches became popular, again the target language was required as the MOI. However, because research showed that selective use of the home language could facilitate the learning of English, the home language was no longer banned from the English classroom, but nor was it the MOI. Rather, it was seen as a tool, to be used to facilitate learning.

At the same time, bilingual programs had developed for immigrants, especially in the United States and Canada in K-12 contexts—in Canada because of its two official languages and in the United States because of the large numbers of learners speaking the same language (see Lessow-Hurley, 2018 for a thorough discussion of Canadian and U.S. bilingual programs). In Australia and

New Zealand, in contrast, bilingual programs were mostly restricted to teaching indigenous learners because most ELT classes consisted of students from a variety of different languages, making English the only viable MOI.

A number of different models have been used to teach bilingually, but in most cases, the goal has been to ensure learners can access and learn the content in the school curriculum. In some cases, the goal has been to maintain the heritage language. Two-way bilingual programs have both native English speakers and native speakers of another language (Spanish, or Chinese, for example, in the United States or French in Canada), where each is learning the other language. School content is delivered in one or the other language. These are also called enrichment programs because language majority students are involved. Other programs have had classes only of nonnative English speakers (but with a common language), one day using the home language and the next day English or using English in the morning and the home language in the afternoon. These can be either maintenance or transitional in nature. The goal of maintenance programs is bilingualism whereas the goal of transitional programs is the acquisition of English by the minority language speakers. Research has shown that well-implemented bilingual programs with proficient and experienced teachers lead to better educational outcomes for K-12 learners (Thomas & Collier, 2003). In some adult education settings in Australia, bilingual programs have also been effective in facilitating English language learning (Murray & Wigglesworth, 2005). However, in many contexts, effective bilingual programs are not possible—either because of insufficient numbers of fluent bilinguals who have training as L2 teachers, and/or contexts where there is no critical mass speaking one language to create a bilingual class. However, in such cases, translanguaging (see Chapter 1) is "an asset to English language teaching that positively influences language outcomes, innovation, and practice" (TESOL International Association, 2018, p. 6).

Another type of bilingual program is the elite bilingual school, such as international schools, European Schools, and immersion programs in the form of two-way bilingual programs. International schools were primarily established to teach the children of expatriates, but they also enroll local children. European Schools do the same but are for families from the European Union. It is notable that, in 2009, one state in Australia began funding bilingual public schools, but not for immigrants; they were to teach native-born Australians languages from Asia, such as Mandarin. Foreign language immersion programs (also referred to as dual language immersion) are becoming more common in K-12 U.S. public school contexts (e.g., see Fortune & Tedick, 2008). These programs primarily support native English speakers in learning a foreign language with the primary goal of creating societal bilinguals. Additionally, there have long been non-public, fee-paying bilingual schools such as Japanese, French, and German. Similarly, the first bilingual state primary school opened in the United Kingdom using a two-way immersion model for French and English. These programs cater primarily to upwardly mobile, highly educated, higher socio-economic status learners of two or more internationally useful languages (De Mejía, 2002).

Task: Explore

Go to the website of TESOL, the professional association (www.tesol.org). Find "Advance the Field" and then choose "Advocacy Resources" from the menu. At the bottom of the list is "TESOL Position Statements." Explore the position statements. How do these statements agree or disagree with positions we have advocated in this chapter?

The Outer and Expanding Circles

The Outer Circle, comprising as it does former British and U.S. colonies, exhibits specific characteristics because of this colonial past. In Chapter 2 we delineated these characteristics, all of which impact on the learners in the Outer Circle. However, each country provides a unique context, and in this brief chapter it is impossible to cover all the former colonies, especially since many of them have not been well studied by applied linguists or ELT researchers. This is particularly the case for much of Africa and the Caribbean. We will, therefore, touch on issues in the countries for which there is more research. Further, as discussed in Chapter 2, there is no clear divide between each of the three circles. In this section we will discuss issues common to both the Outer Circle and the Inner Circle. While it might seem superficially that the Outer Circle should present few issues around English language teaching because English is a language of use in those countries, the Outer Circle shares with the Expanding Circle the issue of MOI and the age to begin formal English instruction. In both circles, the majority of learners are raised in families using a language other than English.

Learners in the Outer and Expanding Circles

Learners in both circles are in compulsory education contexts, higher education, adult settings, and private tutoring schools. Adult settings are usually occupation-oriented. English is usually a required subject for some years during compulsory education. The number of years of instruction and the age at which English instruction begins vary by country. Compulsory education is usually state-funded, with private schools for full-time education often only for the privileged.

In many countries, the focus of instruction has been on primarily grammar, and vocabulary, and literature, and sometimes the culture of English-speaking countries, rather than on communication This focus has begun to change in the last couple of decades. The Japanese Ministry of Education, Culture, Sports, Science and Technology (MEXT) issued a new, communicative curriculum, which took effect in April 2011, in which EFL became compulsory across all grade levels. The curriculum suggested specific classroom communicative practices. However, as in many countries where such changes have been implemented, the taught curriculum does not actually meet communicative guidelines because teachers don't all have sufficient communicative skills, are more comfortable with a grammar-based approach, and national examinations do not assess communication (Mondejar, Valdivia, Laurier, & Mboutsiadis, 2012).

The Council of Europe introduced the common European Common Framework of Reference for Languages (Council of Europe, n.d.), with the goal of "provid[ing] a basis for the mutual recognition of language qualifications, thus facilitating educational and occupational mobility." The framework itself includes "i) the competences necessary for communication, ii) the related knowledge and skills and iii) the situations and domains of communication." Because the Framework is used to develop curricula in the countries of the European Union, the member countries have embraced communication as the primary goal of language teaching.

Thailand introduced a standards-based curriculum in 1999. The standards for language content are based on that of the American Council on the Teaching of Foreign Languages (ACTFL), which has 11 standards around five interconnected areas: communication, cultures, connections, comparisons, and communities (American Council on the Teaching of Foreign Languages, 1996). Despite these changes in stated curriculum goals, in many countries nationwide examinations still prevail and are pen-and-paper tests. Additionally, class size makes it quite difficult for teachers to use a more communicative approach.[4] Consequently, teachers may still prioritize grammar and vocabulary. As a result, many students enroll in private schools to develop their communicative abilities, especially if those schools employ native speakers (NSs); others enroll in private "cram" schools to prepare for the written national tests. For example, "the Taiwanese Ministry of Education reported an increase from approximately 2200 registered private language schools in the year 2000 to over 4500 in 2004, the majority of which are English language cram schools" (Yang, 2006).

For many learners, English is just another school subject and they see no connection with their future lives. They may not expect to work for a multinational company or one in their own country where English is expected. Yet others view English as the only route to future advancement, often to the exclusion of their own first language.

English is often the MOI (see section below) in higher education. In many countries in the Outer Circle, higher education is available to only a small elite—not only because of the MOI, but also because of the cost.

Task: Reflect

Think about your own experiences learning another language. What language was used in the classroom? How did you feel about this? How would you have felt if the choices had been different—if you could only use the target language, how would you have felt about using your first language; if you and the teacher mostly used your home language, how would you have felt if that had been forbidden?

Medium of Instruction in the Outer and Expanding Circles

Closely associated with these different views towards English is the issue of the medium of instruction (MOI), which often is English Medium of Instruction (EMI). The choice is often not only a sociopolitical issue around English and one local language, but around multiple languages. For example, in the Philippines, MOI choice is among English, Filipino, and the more than 300 other indigenous languages, while in Sri Lanka it is among English, Sinhala, and Tamil. In many countries in sub-Saharan Africa, it is among many languages. Any choice has political, social, and cultural implications. Singapore has designated English as the MOI, with Malay, Mandarin, and Tamil all taught in the schools. Malaysia, after more than three decades of using Bahasa Malaysia readopted English as the MOI for science and mathematics. Such English-only policies can be an example of what Phillipson (1992) calls *linguicism*, the continued domination of politics and the economy of the group that speaks English. Every time we successfully teach a learner English, we at the same time disenfranchise those who do not have the opportunity to learn the language of power. As Obondo (2007) has shown for many Outer Circle countries in Africa, local, indigenous languages become denigrated and people reject their use as a MOI. They see the only access to power as through English,[5] yet it is only the elite who have access to English from birth who can truly profit from English as the MOI. In Hong Kong, both English and Chinese are taught with one or the other as MOI for other subjects, depending on the school. The Philippines has clear guidelines about how both English and Tagalog (the two official languages) are taught. English, math, and science are taught in English, while history and civics are taught in Tagalog.

While MOI is a major concern in the Outer Circle countries, it was less so in some Expanding Circle countries—China, Japan, Korea, and Thailand, for example, have their own strong monolingual identifications, so they had resisted adopting English as an MOI until recently, despite calls in both Korea and Taiwan for English to become a second language. There are, however, bilingual schools where the elite send their children. More recently, there has been an explosion of English MOI programs in China and Japan, with a focus on English being used monolingually because students believe that if the teachers translanguage, it means they are not proficient in English. A large study in China and Japan, therefore, called for a reconceptualization of proficiency (Galloway, Kriukow, & Numajiri, 2017).

The situation is more complex in Europe. In the EU, English plus one other foreign language is compulsory. In order to improve their country's English proficiency, some countries, like Malaysia in the Outer Circle, have chosen EMI. Many countries have for long allowed English for theses and dissertations, but some have gone further. For example, some university departments in Denmark switched to EMI because of the large number of international students (Phillipson & Skutnabb-Kangas, 1999). A number of schools in European countries have adopted a *content and language integrated learning (CLIL)* approach largely because "It is an old dream of teachers and learners alike to take all toil and effort out of learning" (Klippel, 2008, p. 29). The belief is that, if content is taught through English and begins at a young age, it will be effortless. As we will explain below, this is not necessarily the case. Further, there has been a backlash against EMI. For example, two universities, along with the Inspectorate of Education, in the Netherlands are being sued for their use of EMI. The association that is leading the lawsuit contends that a core role of universities is the preservation of Dutch and Dutch culture. The switch to EMI has been partly because of the influx of international students, as in Denmark, mentioned previously. The Dutch Education Ministry has responded that, while internationalization of education is a worthwhile goal, it should not be to the detriment of Dutch students or the Dutch language.

There are major concerns about adopting CLIL more broadly, in addition to the devaluation of local languages. Given the global dominance of English,

English would be the language of choice, rather than any other language. As a result, content areas would likely be discussed and written about only in English, with no communities of practice in the home language. Language and schooling are vehicles for the transmission of culture. What culture and values would be transmitted? Further, from a practical viewpoint, most countries do not have sufficient content-area teachers proficient in English, especially the pedagogical language needed to teach their subject area.

Another program similar to CLIL that has become popular since the 1990s is bilingual schools, where the goal is immersion in English. Bangkok has more than 100 bilingual schools, both public and private, while Taiwan has around ten. One group of bilingual schools in Thailand uses a parallel model, where core subjects are taught both in the home language and English.

Age of Commencement of English Language Instruction

Because one of the persistent myths about language learning is that young children learn more easily than youth or adults (see Chapters 11 and 12 for research and theories of second language acquisition), many countries have proposed lowering the age to begin teaching English (for example, see Japan, discussed above). They have done this in the hope that their population will become bilingual and so reap all the economic advantages that accrue to those who can trade and do business in a global economy where English is the *lingua franca*. Many countries have begun teaching English in the early grades. In countries where this is not the case, parents often send their children to private schools to begin their English instruction. One of the largest problems such countries have faced is that elementary school teachers have not been trained in language teaching and may not be proficient speakers of English. Some have, therefore, employed NS teachers, with limited success, as we discussed in Chapter 2. Hong Kong extended its use of NS teachers in 2002, and Taiwan sought to hire 1000 NS teachers in 2003, using competitive salaries, return air fares, and housing stipends as incentives. Often people who have no training are employed, either as teachers or language teachers; often they pay more to NSs, creating tensions with their NNEST colleagues (Boyle, 1997; Luk & Lin, 2007); often they are unable to employ more than one teacher per school, so learners really have little access to the NS.

Although children do have some advantages in language learning, older people also have advantages, such as cognitive development and an already-learned language. It is clear that, in large classes, with teachers who either are not trained in language teaching or are not proficient users of English themselves, there are no advantages for beginning teaching in the young years. Further, there is extensive research that demonstrates the importance of early education being taught in the home language (e.g., Ball, 2011). However, as we saw in Chapter 1, *which* language is complicated by the whole issue of language variety. For example, South Africa, like many countries, has promoted home language (also referred to as mother tongue) education. However, recently, the issue has been raised about which variety of a particular language is being used in education. Krause (2018) demonstrates that the Xhosa (one of the many indigenous home languages in South Africa) being used in education is the variety that the first European missionaries to the country encountered in their immediate environment. However, it differs considerably from the varieties that learners bring with them to the classroom from their community. She, therefore, argues that there should be a discussion about whether it would be more useful for learners to have English as the MOI than another language.

Conclusion

Although there are considerable differences teaching English in the Inner, Outer, and Expanding Circles, two issues are common to all three settings: the medium of instruction and the fact that English can create both barriers and opportunities for learners and their communities. While in the Inner Circle the debate is over whether immigrants should maintain their home language, in the Outer and Expanding Circles the argument is over how best to develop proficiency in the population, which also leads to policies that begin English teaching at young ages. Whether you teach immigrants, refugees, or international students in the Inner Circle or local students in the Outer and Expanding Circles, it is important to remember that learners are individuals, bringing with them their own particular experiences, cultural and personal values, language varieties, and beliefs about the importance of learning English.

Task: Expand

Dave's ESL Café is a well-established website for all things ESL/EFL. The site includes a job center. Read the positions to try to evaluate the types of contexts in which English is being taught around the world (www.eslcafe. com/jobs/).

Questions for Discussion

1   What are the differences and similarities between the immigrant/refugee populations and the international student populations in the Inner Circle?
2   What are the differences and similarities between learners of English in the Expanding Circle and of the Inner and Outer Circles?
3   What medium of instruction is most appropriate in your context? Why? What sociocultural factors influence MOI?

Notes

1   *ELL* is the official title for English-as-a-second-language students in U.S. public schools.
2   Although Goen et al. (2002) refer to immigrants in the United States, the designation *Generation 1.5* is also applicable in the other Inner Circle countries.
3   Sheltered instruction is where content area teachers use various strategies to make the material accessible to second language learners. This concept will be covered in detail in Volume II.
4   However, in Volume II, we will provide a variety of activities that can be conducted in large classes.
5   Because Africa has a long history of colonial occupation by different invaders, English is not the only language competing with indigenous languages as an MOI.

References

American Council on the Teaching of Foreign Languages. (1996). *National standards for foreign language education*. Retrieved from www.actfl.org/i4a/pages/index.cfm?pageid=3392

Ball, J. (2011). *Mother tongue-based bilingual or multilingual education in the early years*. Paris, France: UNESCO. Retrieved from https://unesdoc.unesco.org/ark:/48223/pf0000212270

Batalova, J., Fix, M., & Creticos, P. A. (2008). *Uneven progress: The employment pathways of skilled immigrants in the United States*. Retrieved from www.migrationpolicy.org/pubs/BrainWasteOct08.pdf

Boyle, J. (1997). Native-speaker teachers of English in Hong Kong. *Language and Education, 11*(3), 163–181.

Canadian Centre for Victims of Torture. (2018). Retrieved from CCVT.org

Carrington, K., McIntosh, A., & Walmsley, J. (2007). *The social costs and benefits of migration into Australia*. Retrieved from www.immi.gov.au/media/publications/research/social-costs-benefits/

Chiswick, B. R., Cohen, Y., & Zach, T. (1997). The labour market status of immigrants: Effects of the unemployment rate at arrival and duration of residence. *Industrial and Labour Relations Review, 50*(2), 289–303.

Chiswick, B. R., Lee, Y., & Miller, P. W. (2003). Schooling, literacy, numeracy and labour market success. *The Economic Record, 79*(245), 165–181.

Council of Europe. (n.d.). *The Common European Reference for Languages: Learning, Teaching, Assessment.* Retrieved from www.coe.int/T/DG4/Linguistic/CADRE_EN.asp

De Mejía, A.-M. (2002). *Power, prestige, and bilingualism: International perspectives on elite bilingual education.* Clevedon, England: Multilingual Matters.

Fazel, M., & Stein, A. (2003). Mental health of refugee children: Comparative study. *British Medical Journal, 327*(7407), 134.

Feinberg, R. C. (2000). Newcomer schools: Salvation or segregated oblivion for immigrant students? *Theory into Practice, 39*(4), 220–227.

Fortune, T. W., & Tedick, D. J. (2008). One-way, Two-way, and Indigenous Immersion: A call for cross-fertilization: Evolving perspectives on immersion education. In T. W. Fortune & D. J. Tedick (Eds.), *Pathways to multilingualism* (pp. 3–21). Clevedon, England: Multilingual Matters.

Galloway, N., Kriukow, J., & Numajiri, T. (2017). Internationalisation, higher education and the growing demand for English: A investigation into the English medium of instruction (EMI) movement in China and Japan. London, England: British Council. Retrieved from https://englishagenda.britishcouncil.org/research-publications/research-papers/internationalisation-higher-education-and-growing-demand-english-investigation-english-medium

Gee, J. P. (1996). *Social linguistics and literacies: Ideology in discourses.* London, England: Taylor & Francis.

Goen, S., Porter, P., Swanson, D., & Vandommelen, D. (2002). Generation 1.5. *The CATESOL Journal, 14*(1), 103–105.

Goldstein, L. M. (1987). Standard English: The only target for nonnative speakers of English. *TESOL Quarterly, 21*(3), 417–438.

Ibrahim, A. E. K. (1999). Becoming Black: Rap and hip-hop, race, gender, and identity and the politics of ESL learning. *TESOL Quarterly, 33*(3), 349–369.

Kachru, B. B. (1986). *The alchemy of English: The spread, functions and models of non-native Englishes.* Oxford, England: Pergamon Press.

Klippel, F. (2008). New prospects or imminent danger? The impact of English medium of instruction on education in Germany. In D. E. Murray (Ed.), *Planning change, changing plans: Innovations in second language teaching* (pp. 26–42). Ann Arbor, MI: University of Michigan Press.

Krause, L.-S. (2018). *It's time to rethink what is meant by "mother tongue" education.* Retrieved from https://theconversation.com/its-time-to-rethink-whats-meant-by-mother-tongue-education-96475

Lessow-Hurley, J. (2018). *The foundations of dual language instruction,* 6th ed. New York, NY: Pearson.

Leung, C., Harris, R., & Rampton, B. (1997). The idealised native speaker, reified ethnicities, and classroom realities. *TESOL Quarterly, 31,* 543–560.

Luk, J., & Lin, A. M. Y. (2007). *Classroom interactions as cross-cultural encounters: Native speakers in EFL lessons.* Mahwah, NJ: Lawrence Erlbaum Associates.

Mondejar, M., Valdivia, L., Laurier, J., & Mboutsiadis, B. (2012). Effective implementation of foreign language education reform in Japan: What more can be done? In A. Stewart & N. Sonda (Eds.), *JALT2011 Conference Proceedings: Teaching, learning, growing* (pp. 171–191). Tokyo: JALT.

Murray, D. E., & Lloyd, R. (2007). *Uptake of AMEP provision by youth from Africa: Opportunities and barriers.* Sydney, Australia: NCELTR.

Murray, D. E., & Wigglesworth, G. (Eds.). (2005). *First language support in adult ESL in Australia.* Sydney, Australia: NCELTR.

NCES. (2018). *English language learners.* Retrieved from https://nces.ed.gov/fastfacts/display.asp?id=96

Obondo, M. A. (2007). Tensions between English and mother tongue teaching in postcolonial Africa. In J. Cummins & C. Davison (Eds.), *International handbook of English language teaching part I* (pp. 37–50). New York, NY: Springer.

Park, K. (1999). "I really do feel I'm 1.5": The construction of self and community by young Korean Americans. *Amerasia Journal, 25*(1), 139–163.

Phillipson, R. (1992). *Linguistic imperialism.* Oxford, England: Oxford University Press.

Phillipson, R., & Skutnabb-Kangas, T. (1999). Englishisation: One dimension of globalisation. *AILA Review, 13*, 19–36.

Preuss, C. L. (2008). SOS! I'm having an identity crisis. *Essential Teacher, 5*(3), 22–24.

Rumbaut, R. G., & Ima, K. (1988). *The adaptation of Southeast Asian refugee youth: A comparative study* (Final Report to the U.S. Department of Health and Human Services, Office of Refugee Resettlement, Washington, D.C.: U.S. Department of Health and Human Services). San Diego, CA: San Diego State University.

Seargeant, P., Erling, E. J., Solly, M., & Hasan Chowdhury, Q. (2017). The communicative needs of Bangladeshi economic migrants: The functional values of host country languages versus English as a lingua franca. *Journal of English as a Lingua Franca, 6*(1), 141–166, doi: https://doi.org/10.1515/jelf-2017-0008

TESOL International Association. (2018). *Action agenda for the future of the TESOL profession.* Retrieved from www.tesol.org/summit-2017/action-agenda-for-the-future-of-the-tesol-profession

The Forum of Australian Services for Survivors of Torture and Trauma. (2018). Retrieved from http://fasstt.org.au/

Thomas, W. P., & Collier, V. P. (2003). *What we know about effective instructional approaches for language minority learners.* Arlington, VA: Educational Research Service.

Victoria Foundation for Survivors of Torture. (1998). *Rebuilding shattered lives.* Parkville, Australia: Victoria Foundation for Survivors of Torture.

Wigglesworth, G. (Ed.). (2003). *The kaleidoscope of adult second language learning: Learner, teacher and researcher.* Sydney, Australia: NCELTR.

Yang, K. T. H. (2006). Cross-cultural differences in the perception of an "ideal" language school manager: Comparing the views of local and expatriate ELT staff in Taiwanese schools. Unpublished MA thesis, Macquarie University, Sydney, Australia.

4

THE CULTURAL CONTEXT

VIGNETTE

There was a U.S. Peace Corps[1] teacher in Africa who, on the first day of class, walked into the classroom (the students were all lined up at the door), beckoned the students in and began talking about herself, introducing herself to the class, revealing information about her family, friends, and hobbies in an attempt to break the ice. She wondered why the students did not respect her. In one of my teacher education classes, I had asked students to read an article about such intercultural misunderstandings and discuss it in class. One student, who had taught in Mexico, had not been at the previous class and had not done the reading. As students began talking about cultural differences, she talked about her experience in Mexico. She said, "Oh, Mexicans are not interested in education. The students show no respect for learning or for the teacher." I showed surprise on my face and noted that that had not been my experience, nor was it reported in the research literature. Another student, with great insight asked, "Well, what did you do on the first day of class? How did you teach? What did you say to the students?" The student related a story similar to the one we'd read for homework. This student, after several years of teaching in Mexico still had no idea that her own behavior, values, and attitudes to school had led her students to believe that she was not really a teacher, that she was not someone to respect because she didn't know even the most fundamental things. She didn't know she should have students march into the room, stand, and say good morning politely, and, then, she should take roll. Students thought, "How could we learn anything from such a person? Surely, she was not a real teacher."

(continued)

(continued)

So, they did not treat her with the respect they would give to a teacher who did demonstrate their cultural values regarding how teachers behave in classrooms. [Murray, personal notes]

Task: Reflect

1   Think of teachers you have respected. What in their behaviors led you to respect them?
2   Think of teachers you did not respect. What in their behaviors led you not to respect them?
3   If you had been the young teacher in Mexico, how would you have tried to find out the cultural expectations Mexican students have of teachers?
4   What would you do if learners' cultural expectations violate what you know about how languages are learned?

Introduction

In Chapters 1–3 we discussed aspects of the context around identity formation, World Englishes, and the myth of the native speaker (NS) model. We also need to unpack what is meant by *culture* because this is a term in common usage but with a variety of different meanings. Second, we need to examine the roles teachers and learners can take in the language classroom. As we showed in the vignette above, teacher and learner roles may be culturally determined; and learners may bring to the classroom different expectations of their own and their teachers' roles. Further, teacher and learner roles may be assigned—by the institution and its expectations of what is appropriate behavior for teachers and learners.

What Is Culture?

Task: Reflect

What ideas and words come into your mind when you hear the word *culture*? Brainstorm and list as many words or phrases you can think of. Share this list and compare it with that of a colleague or peer.

By its very nature, ELT is an intercultural[2] enterprise. Learners are learning a language so they can interact with English speakers from around the world. In fact, given the much larger number of learners in the Expanding Circle, it is most likely that learners will interact with NNSs, rather than NSs. The reality of English as a global language is that a Belgian engineer may be working for a Japanese company building a dam in India, or a Chinese company may be building an underground railway line in Colombia. In addition, the ESL classroom is usually multicultural and multilingual. Interactions in the classroom are, therefore, intercultural. In the Expanding Circle, while the teacher and learner often share the same cultural heritage, often an expatriate NS teaches there or is assigned for conversation classes, as we described in Chapter 3.

The Nature of Culture

Approaches to culture vary. On one level, people refer to *big C* and *little c* culture. The former refers to a view of culture as contributions to civilization (architecture, art, literature, music, and so on); the latter to our everyday lives (what we like to call the fiestas, famous people, and food view). Both approaches are content oriented, viewing culture as knowledge that can be examined and taught as a subject. Kramsch (1998) and many other scholars have rejected this culture-as-content view, noting that "culture can be defined as membership in a discourse community that shares a common social space and history, and common imaginings" (p. 10). But how does one join? How are the imaginings shared? In her earlier work, Kramsch had identified the essence of culture as being "a social contract, a product of self and other perceptions" (1993, p. 205) that result in "a common system of standards for perceiving, believing, evaluating, and acting" (p. 127). In other words, culture is more that an accretion of facts; it is a process. Pennycook expands on this, saying, "I am referring to a sense of culture as the process by which people make sense of their lives, a process always involved in struggles over meaning and representation" (Pennycook, 1995, p. 47). This approach sees culture as dynamic, taking place through social action and interaction.

While we take this approach to culture as being more appropriate for ELT, we also notice some of the findings of those who have studied culture and cultural differences as content to be useful in our work as teachers. One of the most useful models is that of Hofstede (2001, 2011), for whom culture is the collective programming of the mind (p. 3), of habitus—that is, the system of permanent and transferable tendencies (p. 4). This definition views culture not only as static, but also as uncontested. Despite this, his extensive research (and that of others using his model) in over 76 countries has uncovered a number of useful continua to describe different cultures, ones that are useful for ELT teachers to consider. These dimensions are

- individualism-collectivism—relations between the individual and his/her fellow
- masculinity-femininity—division of roles and values
- uncertainty avoidance—more or less need to avoid uncertainty about the future
- power (distance)—distance between individuals at different levels of hierarchy
- future orientation—long-term versus short-term orientation to life
- indulgence-restraint—the level of control of gratification

Task: Explore

On a five-point scale, rate yourself and ten of your peers on each of Hofstede's dimensions. What differences did you find? Was there a cultural basis for these differences?

| 1 | 2 | 3 | 4 | 5 |

individualism--collectivism

| 1 | 2 | 3 | 4 | 5 |

masculinity---femininity

| 1 | 2 | 3 | 4 | 5 |

high uncertainty avoidance----------------------low uncertainty avoidance

| 1 | 2 | 3 | 4 | 5 |

high power distance------------------------------------low power distance

| 1 | 2 | 3 | 4 | 5 |

long-term oriented------------------------------------short-term oriented

| 1 | 2 | 3 | 4 | 5 |

indulgence---restraint

These dimensions are self-explanatory, except for masculinity-femininity, which compares the assertiveness and materialism of masculinity with the values around the warmth of social relationships and caring for the weak of femininity. Hofstede has been much criticized for his naming of this dimension and has himself admitted it is problematic but notes that it is not intended to describe individual males or females, but rather societal attributes of each. Other researchers (House, Hanges, Javidan, Dorfman, & Gupta, 2004) have expanded on his findings and have identified gender egalitarianism, assertiveness, performance orientation, and humane orientation as dimensions within the broader category of masculinity-femininity. Hofstede has been further criticized for his overall research because he equates country with culture, which is problematic because the majority of countries are multilingual and multicultural, as we saw in previous chapters. However, his data do show interesting trends. They show how different countries fall on each dimension and then, by graphing them on two dimensions, he shows clusters of countries with similar characteristics. While a country may group with particular ones on two dimensions, it may cluster differently on a different pair of dimensions. His findings also allow for comparisons across countries. So, for example, Thailand is shown to be more collectivist, less masculine, and has higher power distance and uncertainty avoidance than Australia.

If culture is considered as only content, whose culture is to be taught in the language classroom? As we showed in Chapter 2, English is not owned by any one cultural group. Even if an institution chooses British English over American English as the goal for learners, within Britain there are many different cultural groups with different values, behaviors, and ways of viewing the world. Further, if culture is content and uncontested, both language and the pedagogy for teaching it become descriptive and unproblematic. This perception results, for example, in a

> language coursebook [that] represents a "can do" society in which interaction is generally smooth and trouble free, the speakers cooperate with each other politely, the conversation is neat, tidy and predictable, utterances are always as complete as sentences and no-one else can interrupt anyone else or speak at the same time as anyone else.
>
> (Carter, 1996)

However, as we will demonstrate in Chapter 9, real human interaction is more complex, filled with false starts, misunderstandings, and contests over who has the floor. Even pedagogical approaches, such as communicative language teaching, which teach not only the structures of English, but also what is appropriate to speak to whom, and when, have been criticized as treating culture as static:

"There is a danger of reducing the notion of culture even further to a limited concern for appropriateness, especially as taken up in actual pedagogy" (Chen, 1995, p. 159).

Language and Culture

Even if culture is considered as a process of constant struggle over meaning, there is still the issue of the relationship between language and culture, which has immediate bearing on ELT classroom practices. This relationship is also contested. Some take a deterministic view in which language is culturally determined and constrains one's view of the world; others take the view that linguistic knowledge and cultural knowledge are different and can be acquired independently. As we mentioned in Chapter 1, Denise was teaching in Australia in the 1970s when her center was visited by some cadres from China, who were interested in either sending some of their people to Australia to learn English or having Australians go to China to teach. They observed classes and examined the curriculum and materials. They were insistent: "We want Chinese to learn English, not culture." Certainly, which culture is taught depends on which variety of English is being taught, as we discussed in Chapters 2 and 3. But, is it possible to learn another language without some aspects of its culture? Many ELT teacher education programs require that potential teachers learn a foreign language, not only so that they can experience what their learners will go through, but also to get inside another culture, another world view. As Levy (2007, p. 110) notes "This is one reason why learning a language can be such a profound (and worthwhile) experience, because one's core beliefs and values may be challenged, reoriented, and reset."

The deterministic view is best explained through the Sapir-Whorf hypothesis, which claims that the way people think is determined by the structure of their native language. Sapir was a linguist and Whorf (Carroll, 1956) began his working life as an insurance adjuster. On one such job, Whorf was investigating why a fire had occurred even though the workers claimed the barrels were empty. On investigation, he found they were empty of the fuel, but there remained fumes (gases), so the barrels were not really empty. His eureka moment led him to conclude that language constrained how people think, the way people view the world. He went on to study Native American languages, Hopi in particular, and explained that the different views of the world the Hopi had from white mainstream America were because of their linguistic differences. Hopi, for example, does not have tenses that are marked grammatically as does English. Instead, Hopi uses markers to identify whether the statement is an unchangeable truth, a report of an event the speaker has witnessed, or a hypothesis. Consequently, he hypothesized, because Hopi have such markers, they do not have the same notion of time being countable and a commodity as do English speakers. In addition, English speakers engage in hypotheses that the Hopi avoid. Today, the Sapir-Whorf hypothesis is not taken literally, largely because no matter what language people speak they can perceive and express the same concepts; they just have different ways their grammars express it. Further, linguists have identified a number of universal patterns across languages. A weaker version of the Sapir-Whorf hypothesis is proposed: language may have some influence on thought and cultural behavior, but thought and culture may likewise influence language. Scollon and Scollon (2001) show how different discourse practices in different languages can lead to misunderstandings in intercultural communication, a point we explore further in Chapter 9.

A Framework for Explaining Culture

In a discussion of the role of culture in computer-assisted language learning (CALL), Levy (2007) articulates an overarching approach that seeks to encompass all the facets of culture. His framework, like that of Hofstede, provides a useful analytical tool for ELT teachers as they work to understand the contexts in which they work. He describes five key dimensions. These are as follows:

1   Culture as elemental. All people have their own culture, but we are often unaware of our own cultural orientations and may project them onto others. So, in learning another language, learners need to first understand their own culture.
2   Culture as relative. Culture is not absolute. One can understand a culture only in relation to other cultures. So, "the culture learner is almost inevitably drawn towards an approach which contrasts what 'they' do with what 'we' do" (p. 107). He warns, however, that contrasting cultures is problematic and can lead to generalizations and stereotyping. So, a nuanced perspective is needed.
3   Culture as group membership. All people are members of multiple groups, with their own particular culture and language use. So, teachers need to help learners understand these different memberships and the consequences of joining particular groups, and learners need to decide which group memberships they want to aspire to, as we discussed in detail in Chapters 2 and 3.
4   Culture as contested. Cultures are challenged at many levels, from the national (the so-called clashes of civilization) to the individual (culture

shock or the choice of which English to learn or not learn). These contests all take place through language or, as Scollon and Scollon (2001) explore, through discourse.

5   Culture as individual (variable and multiple). "Culture is a variable concept and understandings of ostensibly the same culture will differ from one person to the next" (p. 111). How each person represents their culture is personal and individual. So, learners need to explore their representations and share them with other learners.

Task: Reflect

Using Levy's characterization of the dimensions of culture, think about your own language learning experience(s). In what ways did each of these facets play out as you learned a second or other language? Share your reflections with a colleague or peer.

Learners' Culture

Despite the amount of research and discussion about the role of culture in language learning, some (Frazier, 2002; Spack, 1997) have argued that teachers can become overly sensitive to cultural differences and ascribe cultural explanations to learner behavior when, in fact, its basis is quite different, and the learner as an individual gets overlooked. They (and we) are concerned that learners will be stereotyped. While we agree that it is vital for the teacher to view each learner as an individual, an understanding of one's own culture and how culture frames and is framed by our seeing, being, behaving, and communicating is important if teachers are to be sensitive to their contexts and avoid the types of behavior of the teacher in the vignette.

This understanding is particularly important because teacher expectations of learners may be socioculturally based. Research (Good, 1981; Jussim & Eccles, 1992; Marzano, 2003; Stronge, 2002) has shown that what teachers expect results in just such outcomes from learners (often called TESO or TESA—teacher expectations/student outcomes/achievement). While this research has focused on issues, such as gender or race or low-income learners, it is clear that if teachers have preconceptions about some learners' abilities to succeed, they treat them differently and that different treatment can lead to different outcomes for learners. So, it is important for teachers to examine their own beliefs and attitudes and, then, to investigate their classroom to uncover how these beliefs and attitudes are enacted. (We provide tools for the exploration of beliefs and attitudes in Volume II.) Such different treatment can include calling on only those students that the teacher expects will achieve or singling out for special tasks only those students who are of the same race, gender, or class as the teacher.

Roles of Teachers and Learners

Task: Reflect

Think of a classroom situation (not necessarily a language one) in which you felt uncomfortable with the teaching/learning process. What made you feel uncomfortable? What was it about the teacher that conflicted with your beliefs about teaching and learning? What was it about your classmates that conflicted with your beliefs about teaching and learning? Did the teacher behave differently from other teachers? Did some learners control the floor, not letting anyone else participate? Did some learners seem bored?

In some teaching contexts, teachers have the freedom to adopt roles and give learners roles depending on the teaching goals. In other contexts teachers are constrained by the institutional requirements or broader cultural expectations of appropriate roles. Additionally, learners themselves may have preconceived notions of appropriate roles based on their own previous experiences and cultural values. So, in order to explore the contexts in which you teach, you will also need to understand what roles are and what the possibilities are.

Materials also play a role in the teaching-learning enterprise. The roles played by these three players—teacher, learner, and materials—in the classroom are interdependent and are both work-related and interpersonal. We shall discuss the role of materials in Volume II. Roles are work-related because teachers and learners have expectations about what learning tasks are appropriate in the language classroom and how learners should perform the tasks. For example, learners take quite different roles if they are imitating utterances the teacher makes and repeating them as a whole class than if they are working in groups to solve a problem. Roles have interpersonal attributes because teachers and learners bring with them to the classroom beliefs about and attitudes towards status and position, and all the participants have their own value systems and personalities.

Some of the roles that teachers have traditionally adopted are as

- transmitter of information (about language)
- manager of learning—both content and activities
- manager of classrooms—including discipline
- a subject matter expert
- model of language use
- a monitor of progress.

These roles have been questioned as being too narrowly focused on teacher control. Instead, many educators advocate for social constructivist and learner-centered approaches because such approaches lead to greater learner autonomy. Constructivism is a theoretical approach to education that is inquiry-based. Learner-centered approaches include those in which learners contribute to the development of learning goals and activities, and in which teaching methodology and activities are aligned to learners' preferences. Learner autonomy refers to learners taking responsibility for their own learning, making decisions about content, pace of learning, modes of learning, and the extent of self-direction or teacher-direction. In such a view, the teacher is a facilitator or coach of student learning, providing opportunities to learners so they are motivated and empowered or, as researchers in CALL have said, the teacher becomes the guide on the side rather than the sage on the stage (for example, Corbel, 2007). In Chapters 1–3, we discussed the issue of the hegemony of English and linguistic and cultural imperialism. The roles teachers adopt and what they expect of their learners can either empower learners (see the examples we gave of Chick, 2001 and Canagarajah, 2001) or maintain the status quo. As McLaren notes (1998),

> When teachers accept their role as technicians and fail to challenge the ways in which educational curricula correspond to the demands of industry or the means by which schooling reproduces existing class, race, and gender relations in our society, they run the risk of transmitting to subalternized student populations the message that their subordinate roles in the social order are justified and inviolable.
>
> (p. 2)

The roles that teachers adopt as evaluators of student learning play out in actions in the language classroom, as well as in formal and informal assessments. As teachers and learners interact in the classroom, teachers provide feedback to learners. How teachers provide feedback can influence student learning. For example, teachers often, in taking the role of empowering learners and expecting them to become autonomous learners, relinquish the role of coach. Perhaps they do not want to discourage some learners and so provide generic feedback on their performance, feedback that learners are not able to act on. Or, teachers focus on their role as monitor of progress and accentuate the negative, rather than the positive, and so discourage learners. Research (Jensen, 1998, 2007) shows that to be effective and promote learning, feedback needs to be timely, specific, and under some control of the learner. While we will discuss feedback more fully in Volume II, Chapter 11, here it is important to note that how teachers provide feedback is intimately tied to the roles they adopt.

Other roles that teachers may adopt are the following: needs analyst, curriculum developer, materials developer, counselor, mentor, team member, researcher, and professional (Richards & Lockhart, 1994). We discuss the role of teacher as needs analyst and curriculum developer, as materials developer in Volume II, and as researcher in Volume II and as mentor and professional in Chapter 14. However, teachers may also be asked to identify learners with emotional needs and refer them for counseling and work with other teachers on curriculum or other school activities. As teachers develop as professionals, they will develop their own roles as teachers, based on their own beliefs about teaching and learning and the impact of the context in which they teach.

Conclusion

Neither culture nor roles are static. Furthermore, they interact because different cultures have different expectations about the roles teachers or learners play. The vignette at the beginning of this chapter demonstrates how a mismatch between learner and teacher expectations can affect teaching and learning. Yet, educators must be careful not to stereotype learners based on their cultural background. Learners are individuals, who act because of the sum of all their experiences, which differ from learner to learner. However, it is vital for language teachers to understand the role culture plays in language learning and the roles they and their learners adopt or have imposed on them in the language classroom.

"The language should be taught as a means of intercultural exchange, so that the language and culture of learners will be valued alongside English" (Erling, 2009, p. 43). Our goal should be for learners to be able to engage in intercultural interactions, to create an intercultural space (Liddicoat & Crozet, 2000) where they and their interlocutor can successfully negotiate meaning, regardless of who that interlocutor might be. Elsewhere (Christison & Murray, 2009, p. 17), we have proposed strategies teachers can adopt to develop such a space for their learners. These strategies include the following:

- explicit instruction in linguistic codes and text types for success;
- explicit instruction in the arbitrariness of, and power attributed to, different codes and text types;
- presentation of authentic culturally specific language;
- focus on intercultural communication rather than multicultural education;
- explicit instruction in the relationship between the culture of the first and second languages; and
- learning how to relate to otherness.

Task: Expand

Holliday, A., Hyde, M., & Kullman, J. (2017). *Intercultural communication: An advanced resource book for students*, 2nd ed. Abingdon, England: Routledge.
This is a very useful discussion that considers all the concepts and arguments about language, identity, and sociocultural contexts that have been discussed in Chapters 1–4.

Scollon, R., & Scollon, S. (2001). *Intercultural communication: A discourse approach*, 2nd ed. Oxford, England: Blackwell.
As the title suggests, Scollon and Scollon use a specific approach to understanding intercultural communication and culture. They show that often intercultural communication is not a question of different cultures, but of different discourse systems, of different ways of using language.

Wright, T. (1987). *Roles of teachers and learners*. Oxford, England: Oxford University Press.
Although this book is three decades old, it presents the most extensive discussion on teacher and learner roles. As well as discussing the roles, with cogent examples, it also provides the reader with many suggestions and tools so teachers can investigate roles for themselves.

Questions for Discussion

1 Pennycook's definition of culture indicates that it is "a process always involved in struggles over meaning and representation" (1995, p. 47). What does Pennycook mean by this? Think of some examples to illustrate.
2 In what ways are the cultures of your schools' students and those of the community similar and dissimilar?
3 We indicated that sometimes learners reject the particular roles teachers adopt and require the learners to adopt. How do you think teachers should

respond if the learners in their class have different expectations about teacher and learner roles?

4   What roles do teachers take in your institution? In what ways are these roles a result of the wider community's views of teacher behavior?

Notes

1 The Peace Corps is a U.S. Federal Government volunteer program that has operated since 1961: "The Peace Corps is a service opportunity for motivated changemakers to immerse themselves in a community abroad, working side by side with local leaders to tackle the most pressing challenges of our generation" (Peace Corps, n.d.).
2 We prefer the term *intercultural* to *cross-cultural* because the latter implies failures in communication, but not all interaction across cultures leads to misunderstandings.

References

Canagarajah, A. S. (2001). Critical ethnography of a Sri Lankan classroom: Ambiguities in student opposition to reproduction through ESOL. In C. N. Candlin & N. Mercer (Eds.), *English language teaching in its social context* (pp. 208–226). London, England: Routledge.

Carroll, J. B. (Ed.). (1956). *Language, thought and reality*. Cambridge, MA: MIT Press.

Carter, R. (1996). *Speaking Englishes, speaking cultures.* Opening plenary presented at the 30th IATEFL Conference, April, 1996, Keele, England. [A version of the paper was published as Carter, R. (2003) Text 13: Orders of reality: CANCODE, communication, & culture in B. Seidlhofer (Ed.) *Controversies in applied linguistics* (pp. 90–104). Oxford, England: Oxford University Press.]

Chen, S. (1995). Cultural components in the teaching of Asian languages. *ARAL Series S, 12,* 153–168.

Chick, J. K. (2001). Safe-talk: Collusion in apartheid education. In C. N. Candlin & N. Mercer (Eds.), *English language teaching in its social context* (pp. 227–240). London, England: Routledge.

Christison, M. A., & Murray, D. E. (Eds.). (2009). *Leadership in English language education: Theoretical foundations and practical skills for changing times.* New York, NY: Routledge.

Corbel, C. (2007). Teachers' roles in the global hypermedia environment. In J. Cummins & C. Davison (Eds.), *International handbook of English language teaching* (pp. 1113–1124). New York, NY: Springer.

Erling, E. (2009). The many names of English. *English Today, 21*(1), 40–44.

Frazier, S. (2002). The trouble with cross-cultural oversensitivity. *The CATESOL Journal, 14*(1), 283–291.

Good, T. L. (1981). Teacher expectations and student perceptions: A decade of research. *Educational Leadership, 38*(5), 415–422.

Hofstede, G. (2001). *Culture's consequences,* 2nd ed. Thousand Oaks, CA: Sage.

Hofstede, G. (2011). Dimensionalizing cultures: The Hofstede model in context. *Online readings in psychology and culture*, *2*(1). Retrieved from http://dx.doi. org/10.9707/2307-0919.1014

Holliday, A., Hyde, M., & Kullman, J. (2017). *Intercultural communication: An advanced resource book for students*, 2nd ed. Abingdon, England: Routledge.

House, R. J., Hanges, P. J., Javidan, M., Dorfman, P. W., & Gupta, V. (Eds.). (2004). *Culture, leadership, and organizations: The GLOBE study of 62 societies, Vol 1*. Thousand Oaks, CA: Sage.

Jensen, E. (1998). *Teaching with the brain in mind*. Alexandria, VA: Association for Supervision and Curriculum Development.

Jensen, E. (2007). *Introduction to brain-compatible learning* (2nd ed.). Thousand Oaks, CA: Corwin Press.

Jussim, L., & Eccles, J. S. (1992). Teacher expectations II: Construction and reflection of student achievement. *Journal of Personality and Social Psychology*, *63*(6), 947–961.

Kramsch, C. (1993). *Context and culture in language education*. Oxford, England: Oxford University Press.

Kramsch, C. (1998). *Language and culture*. Oxford, England: Oxford University Press.

Levy, M. (2007). Culture, culture learning and new technologies: Towards a pedagogical framework. *Language Learning & Technology*, *11*(2), 104–127.

Liddicoat, A. J., & Crozet, C. (Eds.). (2000). *Teaching languages, teaching cultures*. Melbourne, Australia: Applied Linguistics Association of Australia and Language Australia.

Marzano, R. J. (2003). *What works in schools: Translating research into action*. Alexandria, VA: Association for Supervision and Curriculum Development.

McLaren, P. (1998). *Life in schools: An introduction of critical pedagogy in the foundations of education*. New York, NY: Longman.

Peace Corps. (n.d.). Peace Corps. Retrieved from www.peacecorps.gov/about/

Pennycook, A. (1995). English in the world/the world in English. In J. Tollefson (Ed.), *Power and inequality in language education* (pp. 34–58). Cambridge, England: Cambridge University Press.

Richards, J., & Lockhart, C. (1994). *Reflective teaching in second language classrooms*. Cambridge, England: Cambridge University Press.

Scollon, R., & Scollon, S. (2001). *Intercultural communication: A discourse approach*. Oxford, United Kindgom: Blackwell.

Spack, R. (1997). The rhetorical construction of multilingual students. *TESOL Quarterly*, *31*(4), 765–774.

Stronge, J. H. (2002). *Qualities of effective teachers*. Alexandria, VA: Association for Supervision and Curriculum Development.

Wright, T. (1987). *Roles of teachers and learners*. Oxford, England: Oxford University Press.

5

LEARNING ABOUT IDENTITY AND SETTING

VIGNETTE

A teacher of adult immigrants in the United States had her learners complete a language use profile, in which each weekend they recorded when and where they spoke English, to whom they spoke, where they were, and what happened. Learners were asked to list seven samples of English use. Learners were hesitant at first, providing limited information. But, after sharing in class, they soon became enthusiastic as they realized that what they had heard would be explained by the teacher in class. At last they would understand what was happening around them. The dialogues they recorded became longer and longer and more accurate. One learner related a conversation with a neighbor that began with the usual greetings, but then recorded that he had said to his neighbor "Your dog came into my backyard. Please keep him at your house. Please repair the fence. Your dog came into my backyard two time."[1] According to the student, the neighbor agreed. However, it was a great opportunity for the teacher to teach polite requests and also teach what is appropriate culturally in the American context to deal with such a situation.

Another learner reported how she had helped her grandchildren with their homework: "I always help them to made homework . . . Jamie want learned 11–20. I took some number card want she pronounce. If 16 she say sixty. I say sixty is 60 isn't 16. A little while she can say sixteen" (Murray, 2005).

Task: Reflect

1 Why do you think the learner wanted to share the dialogue about the dog?
2 How could you use the dialogues that learners overheard?
3 If you were the teacher of the grandmother, how would you use this information in your classroom?
4 Why do you think the grandmother was concentrating on teaching pronunciation to her grandchild?

Introduction

Teachers have "a fundamental need for cogent analysis and self-understanding within the social, cultural, and political contexts" (Freeman & Johnson, 1998, p. 407) in which they work. As we have shown in Chapters 1–4, the context shapes learners' attitudes, motivations, beliefs, values, and therefore their learning. The contexts in which teachers in ELT work vary across time and space. Few teachers stay in the same context throughout their lives, even if they stay in the same country. Learners change. A teacher of international students will find over time that the countries of origin of students change, or their motivation to learn English as instrumental or integrative changes (see Chapter 1). Immigration patterns change—different age groups, different gender balance, different educational levels, and different countries of origin, to name a few possibilities. Even when teaching English in the Expanding Circle, learners' goals may change—from English being a required course of study to be endured, to investment in using English on social media. It is impossible for us to provide an understanding of all the contexts in which you might work. Some may not even exist yet. For example, teachers who were trained in the 1970s or 1980s had no notion that they would need to integrate information and communication technology (ICT) into their practice. Those of us who were trained in the audiolingual method, which required repetition of grammatical structures, had no idea we would be required to develop activities and materials for a more communicative approach. In recent research in Australia, one of us (Denise) found that teachers were disconcerted by the influx of refugees from Africa who had minimal education and had experienced traumatic situations. Some of these refugees were born in refugee camps and had spent their lives there. While superficially these refugees may have seemed like some of those from Southeast Asia who, in the 1970s, came with similar traumatic experiences and lack of education, they brought very different cultural values, beliefs, behaviors, motivations, and approaches to learning (Murray & Lloyd, 2008). Therefore, teachers need to develop skills in how to understand their context—from the broad cultural context in which they work, to the local context of their own classrooms. This context can be considered like an onion, with layer upon layer and with the learner embedded in the center, then the classroom, the institution, the local community, the educational system, the country (and its economic, cultural, political systems), and finally the globe. However, this often-used metaphor is misleading because in reality the layers themselves are cross-hatched and are influenced by and influence one other. The local community may have direct connections to a diaspora across the globe.[2] The school may be part of an international chain, and so on. Therefore, it is better to conceive of the different aspects of the context in which teachers work as corners of a three-dimensional matrix.

We now provide you with some tools to be able to conduct your own analyses, so you can understand any context of teaching and learning you may find yourself in. We expand on this point further in Volume II, where we provide tools for exploring your own instruction, including the roles you adopt and what roles you ask your learners to adopt. In this chapter we will focus on understanding your institution, community, and learners.

Getting to Know the Institution

In order to teach effectively in any institution, you need to understand how it functions. How is it structured? How does information flow? What is the curriculum? What resources are available?

Organizational Structure

The organizational structure of a school or other institution reveals how formal power is distributed and what expectations the school has for its various employees and the organization's culture. The structure should facilitate the flow of information and decision making: "Within an English language education context, the structure needs to facilitate curriculum development, teaching and non-teaching staff discussion, services to students, and communication with all stakeholders, whether parents, recruiting agents, deans, or textbook suppliers" (Christison & Murray, 2009, p. 126). It may also reflect its context, particularly the national culture or the culture of a parent organization if it is a franchise or part of a multi-site institution. Hofstede (2001), for example, shows "that Confucian values of harmony, order, control, and building relationships support formal and clearly articulated organizational structures, along with centralized authority, with leadership ascribed by role rather than achieved through merit"

(Christison & Murray, 2009, pp. 126–127). As already discussed, national culture is not unitary but in most countries is diverse. However, there is often an overarching culture that guides most institutions in a particular country. As well as the national culture, the organizational structure may also reflect governmental accrediting agency regulations through which certain roles may be required, such as counselor or finance officer.

Overall structures can be flat or hierarchical. In flat organizations, there is no fixed hierarchy in the school, individual teachers have a large degree of autonomy, and roles, such as coordinating programs, may rotate. In hierarchical organizations, the structure is pyramidal, with each layer reporting to the next layer higher on the pyramid. Each person in the hierarchy has a specific role, with job descriptions delineated, even if not in writing. Usually the curriculum is handed down, as are rules and regulations. Each of these two structures has its own set of problems. It is quite difficult to maintain a flat structure in a very large organization without creating either anarchy or silos of different groups working on different areas of instruction. Communication then becomes difficult. Similarly, hierarchical structures have been found to be harder to change and are resistant to innovation.

As well as the formal structure, every organization has an informal structure, which is much harder to ascertain, but essential for getting your work done. In many organizations the informal structure is more powerful than the formal one. In other words, there are people without official management or leadership positions who wield power. Power may come from a person's charisma, their knowledge base, or their contacts. For example, a senior member of staff who is admired for her wisdom and experience, but who chooses not to be head of department or serve on influential committees, may influence decisions as she talks with staff members and persuades them to take particular positions on issues.

Task: Reflect

Think about an organization you have been involved in. How were decisions made? Who had the most influence? Whose point of view was usually followed? Why? Did this lead to disharmony among staff? How did the appointed (or elected) leaders respond?

In addition to the formal structure of an organization, its prevailing culture impacts on both teachers and learners. There are many models that describe organizational culture, but one of the most commonly used is that of Handy

(1985), who identifies four types of culture operating in organizations. These types are as follows;

- Power or club culture. These cultures have strong leaders who select people to implement their own agendas.
- Role culture. In this type of organization, people's positions/jobs are carefully described and the functions of the role are more important than the person who fills it.
- Task culture. This type of organization is project-driven. Groups come together to complete specific projects.
- Person culture. Stars dominate in person cultures. They achieve their star status because of their individual skills.

Task: Reflect

Think about an organization in which you have been involved. Which of Handy's descriptors best describes that organization? What specific events and behaviors and attitudes of management and other staff led you to this conclusion?

Collecting Information

Below we provide a list of information to collect about the organization in which you work and, then, questions that will help you understand your organization's structure and culture. If you are assigned a mentor teacher to help in your orientation, you can use these questions to guide your discussions. If you don't have a mentor, try to find answers informally.

Information to collect

- an official organization chart (if there isn't one, draw one for yourself and fill in names to match the roles),
- a website,
- reports to boards or parents,
- newsletters,
- brochures,
- a strategic plan,

- job descriptions, and
- union contracts.

Questions to ask

- Is the structure flat or hierarchical?
- How does information flow? What committees are there? How are committee members chosen? How do committees reach their decisions? How are their decisions conveyed to staff?
- Does the organizational structure impede or facilitate information flow?
- What roles do non-teaching staff have in decision making? In information flow?
- How is change brought about?
- Do people work primarily as teams or as individuals?
- Who are the stakeholders—that is, the people who have an investment in the work your school does? What roles do they play? For example, do teachers have regular meetings with parents? Do other departments influence decisions of your department?
- How is teaching evaluated? By whom? Are there instruments you can see?
- What responsibilities do teachers have in addition to teaching?

Curriculum

The structure of an organization should, but does not always, facilitate the work of the organization. A key part of ELT work is curriculum. In Volume II, we explain how to develop curricula, and Volume III is completely devoted to curriculum design. However, most teachers work in settings where the curriculum is set by others. Therefore, you need to ask a variety of questions to understand your role in relationship to the received curriculum. Such questions include the following:

- What is the theoretical framework on which the curriculum has been developed? (See Volume II and Volume III, Parts III, IV, and V,)
- What are the goals of the curriculum?
- How specific is the curriculum? Is it a framework or a syllabus?
- Are specific textbooks required (see below)? What methodologies are expected to be used?
- How do students progress from level (class) to level? What types of assessments are used? What are individual teachers' responsibilities for assessment of learning?

- Who develops the curriculum? How?
- How often is the curriculum revised?
- How much autonomy do individual teachers have regarding how to implement the curriculum?
- Do you have specific reporting to conduct, e.g., attendance?

Resources

Once you understand the structure of the organization and the curriculum that will guide your instruction, you need to know what resources are available to you. Resources are both human and non-human. Answers to the following questions will tell you what resources are available and what you need to provide for yourself. Some of these questions may seem basic, but many ESL teachers have gone to unfamiliar contexts and found they have to provide all materials themselves, with no preparation about where they might find the materials they need.

Human resources

- What support staff are there? Do teachers have access to them? How? For example, do teachers have to make appointments with counselors for students? Do clerical staff make photocopies for teachers? Do technicians repair computers or teach how to use applications?
- How are teachers paid? Who do you ask if there's an error?
- Are there mentor teachers for new teachers? How are they assigned? What are their duties?
- Who disseminates the institution's policies, such as smartphone use in class or homework requirements?

Nonhuman resources

- Is there flexibility in choosing textbooks? Can teachers choose their own or supplement with other materials? Who pays for additional materials?
- Do students provide their own textbooks or does the school provide them?
- Do students bring their own writing materials or does the school provide them?
- Do students provide their own devices such as tablets?

- Are there whiteboards or blackboards or smartboards? Who provides the markers/chalk?
- Are there audio tapes? Tape recorders? What procedures are there to use them?
- Are there videotapes or DVDs? Videotape recorder or DVD player?
- Are there CALL programs? Computers for learners? Data projectors? Where?
- Are there visuals such as maps and charts, models or other realia[3]?
- Are there stipulated holidays? Vacation time?
- Is there support for professional development? What type? How does one apply?
- Are teachers provided with an office? A phone? A computer/tablet? Can your professional mail (e.g., journals) be sent to the school?
- Can you access the site out of school hours? Who has the keys?

Getting to Know the Community

Educational institutions are situated in communities. In some settings, the learners come directly from the local community and in other settings, learners are living temporarily in the local community and staying in local homes or student housing. Whatever the situation, the local community impacts on learners and the institution. We provide two sample scenarios below to illustrate how the local community and an ELT program interact. These scenarios are based on teachers we have worked with.

Scenario 1	Scenario 2
Susana is teaching ESL in a middle school in California. Her students come from a variety of different language and cultural backgrounds. It is time for parent-teacher conferences but only a small number of parents show up. It is not because they are not committed to their children's education. Some don't come because they	Fabrizio is a teacher in an intensive English program in a private language school in Australia. His students are mostly planning to go on to university, although some are in Australia only to learn English. They come from all over the globe although the majority are from China. The ones who are coming to learn English are all staying with Australian families,

80

think their English is too weak to be able to talk to her. Others think it is impolite to ask Susana, the expert, questions about their children. Others have had no schooling and feel intimidated by even a school building. Yet others have no cultural frame in which to place the concept of teacher-parent conferences. And, others hold down several jobs to get sufficient money to feed their families. They are working in the evening. Some mothers have many younger children and have to stay home to look after them.

Susana remembers a program from her previous school, where three women from the community, Maria, Juanita, and Han—who themselves were from immigrant families (Mexico, Guatemala, and Vietnam respectively)—acted as official liaisons for the school. They spent hours talking to parents in their own languages, telling them about vaccinations, about how they could rearrange their shifts so they could go to parent-teacher conferences, and about the school's expectations for parental involvement. Susana decides to try to implement such a program in her school.

the home stay arranged through the language center. Australia is a multicultural country, and many of the home-stay families are immigrants or descendants of immigrants, speak languages other than English, and follow many of the customs of their homeland. Some of the international students are surprised about their home-stay family assignment and protest that they want to stay with Australian families (by which they mean Anglo families who speak only English). The home-stay coordinator reminds them that what they are experiencing *is* Australia—perhaps different from their perceptions.

Additionally, Fabrizio himself is a NNEST,[4] having come to Australia from Brazil to join his extended family already in Australia. Some students request to move to a class with an NS[5] teacher, but the center refuses, telling the students that Fabrizio is an excellent teacher and suggests they give the class a try. They are told that if they are still unhappy after a week, they can get a refund and go to another language center. Fabrizio is embarrassed by these students' requests, but the center director reassures him that their policy is to employ teachers based on their teaching expertise, not whether they are native speakers of English.

In each of these scenarios, the local community, its demographics, and its culture affect learners and their learning. How can you, as a teacher in a new community, find out about the community, its values, beliefs, composition, and behaviors that might impact on your learners? In the scenarios described in the box, Susana had her school implement a community liaison program. In Fabrizio's case, the center director developed an additional module in the student orientation package. In that module, she had local leaders discuss Australia's multicultural heritage. She also brought in two former students to speak about their experiences in home stay and with NNESTs. She also added information to their brochures and website, including pictures showing the variety of people living in Australia. Fabrizio wrote the story of his language learning experiences, which was posted on the website. The home-stay coordinator hosted a coffee morning for the home-stay families, having them share their experiences living in the community and hosting international students—what worked and what was problematic.

Other teachers have found the following activities useful sources of information:

- visiting local cafes, libraries, youth centers, community centers, churches, synagogues, temples
- participating in local community events such as fairs
- participating in local ethnic festivals
- arranging after-school activities for students
- having schools invite the local community to concerts, information fairs (perhaps with interpreters available), open days, in addition to the more focused parent-teacher conferences
- finding key members of local ethnic (or other key) groups and asking for their help.

Many educators have conducted mini-ethnographies, with the learners in their class as the ethnographers of their communities. Ethnography is a research methodology that was first used by anthropologists, who examined exotic cultures (and sometimes languages) and attempted to "make the unfamiliar familiar." Ethnographers usually focused on small groups or ones with clear boundaries within a larger society. Over time, it has been used by anthropologists, sociologists, and educators in their own settings. The goal of ethnography is to uncover the insider's view of reality. The underlying question, then, is "What do these people see themselves doing?" rather than "What do I see these people doing?" (Spradley & McCurdy, 1972). To do this involves a study over a long period of time in which the researcher is a participant observer, which means that the researcher is not just an objective observer of the group under study but participates in all the activities of the group. As well as observing, the researcher also informally interviews a key informant, someone who is knowledgeable about all aspects of the culture. Ethnographers also collect community artifacts, take extensive field notes of their observations, and conduct interviews (which may be audiotaped). Another characteristic of ethnography is triangulation—that is, the collection from multiple data sources that are used to compare and confirm patterns. So, for example, the researcher cross-checks artifacts against field notes of observations and transcripts of interviews. Key to ethnography is that researchers do not start with a hypothesis that they try to prove. The findings emerge from the data.[6] The ethnography is written primarily as a narrative and description, helping the reader to get into the lives and culture being described. An example in ELT is that of Norton (2000), whose work on the construction of identity by adult immigrant women in Canada we referred to in Chapter 1, and who spent two years deeply involved in the lives of these five immigrant women. By using many quotations, her book presents the women's own voices. Ethnographies, such as hers and those of Chick (2001) and Canagarajah (2001), referred to in Chapter 2, have shown that the process of learning a second language is not just that of acquiring a set of skills but is the result of complex sociocultural interactions that shape learning and learner identities. The mini-ethnographies that learners have conducted are not extensive but adapt this overall approach.

While a number of people have had their learners use an ethnographic approach, Damen (1987) proposes a model that she calls *pragmatic ethnography* because it is not designed to be scientific research: "the procedures used are to serve personal and practical purposes and not to provide scientific data and theory" (p. 63). Her approach has a clear and systematic methodology that can be used by learners as well as teachers. The following steps are modified from her proposed methodology as follows (see also Roberts, Byram, Barro, Jordan, & Street, 2001):

1   Choose a target group or issue that interests you. Try to ensure that the group is bounded, that is, with clear boundaries; otherwise, you get outliers or people who are not central members.
2   Choose one or more informants who can represent the group and you can work with easily. While the informants need to be knowledgeable, you need to think of people who are easy to locate and willing to speak with you. If possible, try to choose a representation of gender and age, because in many groups different ages and different genders have access to different cultural practices and may have different views of cultural practices.
3   Conduct Internet or library research on the group where possible.
4   Interview two or three informants once, or the same informant at least several times. Ethnographic interviews are open-ended, with no set questions. The goal is to find out as much information as possible, without constraining it.

Table 5.1 Exploring language in the community

Who spoke?	*To whom?*	*About what?*	*Where?*	*What they said*	*In what language?*

5   Analyze the data to observe patterns, developing hypotheses about the group. The hypotheses should come from the data. So, it is important first to look for recurring patterns across your data sets before you think you have a hypothesis.

6   Compare those patterns with your own beliefs, values, etc.

As a result of such mini-ethnographies, learners and teachers can uncover information about their local community(ies), information that impacts both language and learning (as we saw in Chapters 1–3).

An even more reduced form of mini-ethnography is to have learners observe specific language use in their local community. They can observe which language is used, by whom, with whom, and for what purposes. Learners with limited English proficiency can be asked to complete a table, such as Table 5.1.

This exercise can be practiced in class so that learners understand what is expected of them. They also need to be told that in most countries they cannot tape-record without the permission of the speakers. However, they can overhear conversations at the bus stop, on the train, at the market, or even around their school. In some contexts in the Expanding Circle, only the home language may be used between people. But this still gives the teacher some sense of whether the learner is exposed to any English outside the classroom and if so, for what purposes English is used, such as advertisements, names of stores, on social media, or on T-shirts.

The Classroom As Resource

As we showed above, learners can be encouraged to participate in finding out about their (new) communities. The classroom can be used more broadly as a resource for also finding out about the learners themselves. In Volume II, we discuss the formal needs analysis method for determining what learners already know about English and what they need to know. However, the classroom is a rich resource for learning about learners' lived experiences, including their identities. You can use a number of classroom activities that combine language learning with expanding your knowledge of the learners and their individual needs. It is important to remember, however, that often learners' lives have been traumatic and teachers should be alert to signals that a learner is reluctant to share experiences or may be in need of professional counseling. For example, a common classroom activity is to have learners draw a family tree so they can be taught the names for different family members. For many learners, this is a traumatic activity because it brings up memories of loved ones who have died, been tortured, or have abandoned them. The activities we describe below have been successfully used in a range of ELT situations.

Learner Questionnaires

Because learners' and teachers' beliefs about teaching and learning may differ, teachers need to uncover learners' understandings as well as reflect on their own. In Volume II, we provide tools for you to reflect on your own teaching and learning beliefs. Below is a brief questionnaire you can ask your learners to complete. You can then compare their beliefs with your own. This will help you plan your content and also classroom activities. For learners whose English is not proficient enough to read and understand these items, you can adapt them.

Learner belief inventory. Read the following statements about language learning. On a five-point scale, say if you agree or disagree with the statement:

1 = *Strongly disagree*

2 = *Disagree*

3 = *Neutral*

4 = *Agree*

5 = *Strongly agree*

1 Children learn a foreign language more easily than adults. 1 2 3 4 5

2 Some languages are easier to learn than others. 1 2 3 4 5

3 People from my country are good at learning languages. 1 2 3 4 5

4 Perfect pronunciation is important.1 2 3 4 5

5 I should try to avoid making errors in English. 1 2 3 4 5

6 I should learn to speak English before learning to write in English. 1 2 3 4 5

7 To learn English, I need to memorize and repeat a lot. 1 2 3 4 5

8   To learn English, I need to speak to people in English. 1 2 3 4 5

9   We should only use English during English lessons. 1 2 3 4 5

10   Grammar is the most important part of English. 1 2 3 4 5

11   It is easier to learn English if you have already learned other languages. 1 2 3 4 5

12   Reading and writing in English are easier than listening and speaking. 1 2 3 4 5

13   Vocabulary is the most difficult part of English to learn. 1 2 3 4 5

14   Everyone can learn to speak a foreign language. 1 2 3 4 5

15   English is an easy language to learn. 1 2 3 4 5

16   Teachers should control the lesson. 1 2 3 4 5

17   We should not discuss controversial issues in class. 1 2 3 4 5

18   I do not like working in groups. 1 2 3 4 5

19   I expect the teacher to be an expert and know all the answers. 1 2 3 4 5

20   I do not want to learn about culture. 1 2 3 4 5

Ethnography

We discussed ethnography briefly above, but scholars working in the cultural dimensions of ELT (Corbett, 2003; Holliday, 1994, 1996) have suggested that each time teachers encounter a new class of students, they need to become ethnographers to uncover the hidden agendas of their learners. In this way, they know not only what language their learners need to know, but also what beliefs, values, and attitudes towards learning and formal classroom education that the learners bring with them. They can adjust their teaching activities accordingly.

One mini-ethnography that learners enjoy and that also helps the teacher understand the community in which learners live is to have them select and write about a family member or a member of their community that they admire. The steps in the activity are the following:

- The learner interviews the person they chose and makes audio recordings of the interviews. They need to be reminded that they need permission from the people they chose to interview. The interviews can be conducted in the home language.

- The learner loosely transcribes the interviews.
- The learner writes a summary of the interview (in English), including direct quotations (with translations if necessary) from the interviewee.
- The learner draws the person or takes their photographs.
- The learner makes a poster for each interviewee with the photo and the summary.
- Posters are posted on the walls of the classroom for other learners to read. The teacher can prepare questions for learners to answer about one another's stories.

Narrative

"To study identity means to explore the story of identity . . . the way we tell ourselves and others who we are, where we came from, and where we are going" (Muñoz, 1995, p. 46). Teachers can try to support this complex process in a variety of ways. Narrative has recently become more accepted as a research tool (Nunan & Choi, 2010) and is especially valuable for learning about learners' experiences and especially their language learning histories. Although there are objections to its use because it presents only one version available at that point in time, it is just such a version that is useful for language teachers. Depending on the language level and developmental level of learners, the narrative can be only a story or can include critical reflections. In the two samples (excerpts from longer narratives), we illustrate this type of enquiry. They are excerpted from narratives learners wrote in our classes.

Excerpt from narrative 1: Chou from China	Excerpt from narrative 2: Gordon from Burundi
In that university, my experiences of English listening learning occurred both during the class in a language lab under a teacher's guidance and after class on the campus on my own.	I was born in Burundi, that was my country and at the age of 17, I was obliged to leave the country due to the war and I went to Tanzania. I lived there for almost 7 years in a refugee camp and there I think I completed my secondary school.

(continued)

(continued)

During the class in a language lab under a teacher's guidance, I could, by using headphones, listen to the cassette tapes played by the teacher about English sentences, dialogues, short passages, stories, and news based on the teacher's course goals and objectives.

After class on the campus, when I learned listening on my own, what I could do was to listen to the radio by tuning in VOA[7] or BBC[8]. And because the signals were not strong enough, I needed to move myself from one place to another, trying to get a better place where I could listen well. Besides, I listened to some tapes by using a Walkman. And on weekends, if time allowed, I could go out with my classmates to watch some English movies on VCD.

I can say that I didn't learn English from my teachers. I used most of the times books, I was really a good reader. I remember one, which really had me, was written by a Kenyan author and he tried his best to write every word how to pronounce it and the meaning, in my native language, in Swahili. So I could read the word because there was the phonetic and the meaning and I spent almost three months sitting and learning from that book and before those three months I had not even a single word of English. But after three months I could speak English and read even an article.

I could already speak Swahili, Kirundi and French. For instance French really helped me to understand English.

In both of these narratives, the learners reveal their own personal language learning strategies, ones that their teachers can build on as they construct lessons and activities for their classrooms.

Language Experience Approaches

Language experience approach (LEA) (Dixon & Nessel, 1983) is a specific approach to using learners' lived experiences in the classroom, while helping them with their reading and writing in English. LEA involves the following steps:

- Learners audio-record events in their past or current lives.
- Advanced learners write their stories; the teacher helps less advanced learners to write their stories.
- The stories are distributed to the class, without correction.
- The learners' stories then become the class reading material. As learners read one another's stories, they can ask for clarification or more details from the author because the author is present in the class.

As well as facilitating the teaching of reading and writing, this approach helps the teacher better understand learners' lives.

Dialogue Journal Writing

Dialogue journals have been used extensively in ELT classrooms (Peyton, 1995). They are a variation of other types of journals that many teachers have their learners keep. "Dialogue journals are written conversations in which a learner and teacher (or other writing partners) communicate regularly (daily, weekly, or on a schedule that fits the educational setting) over a semester, school year, or course" (Peyton, 2000, p. 1). Learners can do their writing at home or in class. The topics may be assigned by the teacher or chosen by the learners, and specific topics can be chosen so that the teacher can learn about the lived experiences of their learners. Topics might include the immigrant experience, colonization, their experiences at work, their interactions with neighbors or friends, or their experiences in other classes at school, which they can share with the teacher or with a classmate. Often "[l]earners may find that different aspects of their identities emerge when they are writing with a classmate as opposed to the teacher, or that they can explore a certain topic better with one classmate than another" (Ullman, 1997, p. 1).

Conclusion

The context of ELT encompasses learners, the school and its staff, the community, the nation, and the global village. Learners' experiences, beliefs, and attitudes all contribute to their English language learning as do the experiences, beliefs, and attitudes about the school, the community, nation, and global village. In this chapter, we have provided you with some tools to explore these different aspects of your own context or contexts you may encounter in the future. As you engage in such explorations, it is important to situate them within the discussions we presented in Chapters 1–4 concerning identity formation, World Englishes, the debates over the NS, the process of understanding culture, and the roles of teachers and learners.

Task: Expand

Nunan, D., & Choi, J. (Eds.). (2010). *Language and culture: Reflective narratives and the emergence of identity*. New York, NY: Routledge.
This is an edited collection of 29 personal narratives written by a variety of linguists, L2 teacher educators, as well as ESL teachers and researchers. The narratives illustrate both the technique of auto-narrative and the complexities of language teaching and learning as these writers tell of their own personal experiences.

Roberts, C., Byram, M., Barro, A., Jordan, S., & Street, B. (Eds.). (2001). *Language learners as ethnographers*. Clevedon, England: Multilingual Matters.
Ethnography as a research methodology is explained. This volume also provides many examples of language learners, using ethnographic techniques in a variety of different settings around the world.

Questions for Discussion

1 Organizations have both formal and informal structures. How would you go about discovering the informal structures? Think of examples to illustrate (they may not necessarily come from ELT situations).

2 Explain how to have learners conduct a mini-ethnography in the local community.

3 If you were Chou's teacher how would you use this information from his language experience narrative?

Notes

1 Texts are as in student's original work.
2 Refugees settle in a range of countries around the world and often maintain communication with their friends and extended families around the world. Such communication has been greatly facilitated through the Internet.
3 Realia refers to props teachers take to the classroom to facilitate and motivate learners —such as knives, spoons, forks, chopsticks, plates, and bowls—for teaching the language of eating.
4 Nonnative English-speakers in TESOL—see Chapter 2.
5 Native speaker—see Chapter 2.
6 We will provide more detail of ethnography in Volume II. For the purposes of having learners exploring the community, this brief introduction is sufficient.

7 Voice of America, a radio broadcast from the United States throughout the world.
8 British Broadcasting Corporation, radio and television broadcast from the United Kingdom throughout the world.

References

Canagarajah, A. S. (2001). Critical ethnography of a Sri Lankan classroom: Ambiguities in student opposition to reproduction through ESOL. In C. N. Candlin & N. Mercer (Eds.), *English language teaching in its social context* (pp. 208–226). London, England: Routledge.

Chick, J. K. (2001). Safe-talk: Collusion in apartheid education. In C. N. Candlin & N. Mercer (Eds.), *English language teaching in its social context* (pp. 227–240). London, England: Routledge.

Christison, M. A., & Murray, D. E. (Eds.). (2009). *Leadership in English language education: Theoretical foundations and practical skills for changing times.* New York, NY: Routledge.

Corbett, J. (2003). *An intercultural approach to English language teaching.* Clevedon, England: Multilingual Matters.

Damen, L. (1987). *Culture learning: The fifth dimension in the language classroom.* Reading, MA: Addison-Wesley.

Dixon, C. N., & Nessel, D. (1983). *Language experience approach to reading (and writing).* Hayward, CA: Alemany Press.

Freeman, D., & Johnson, K. (1998). Reconceptualizing the knowledge-base of language teacher education. *TESOL Quarterly, 32,* 397–417.

Handy, C. B. (1985). *Understanding organisations,* 3rd ed. Harmondsworth, England: Penguin.

Hofstede, G. (2001). *Culture's consequences,* 2nd ed. Thousand Oaks, CA: Sage.

Holliday, A. (1994). *Appropriate methodology and social contact.* Cambridge, England: Cambridge University Press.

Holliday, A. (1996). Developing a sociological imagination: Expanding ethnography in international English language education. *Applied Linguistics, 2*(1), 234–255.

Muñoz, V. (1995). *Where "something catches": Work, love, and identity in your youth.* Albany, NY: State University of New York Press.

Murray, D. E. (2005). Use of L1 in adult ESL settings. In D. E. Murray & G. Wigglesworth (Eds.), *First language support in adult ESL in Australia* (pp. 12–23). Sydney, Australia: NCELTR.

Murray, D. E., & Lloyd, R. (2008). Uptake of the Special Preparatory Program by African communities: Attitudes and expectations. *Sydney: AMEP Research Centre.* Retrieved from http://www.ameprc.mq.edu.au/docs/research_reports/research_reports/Uptake_report.pdf

Norton, B. (2000). *Identity and language learning: Gender, ethnicity, and educational change.* Essex, England: Longman.

Nunan, D., & Choi, J. (Eds.). (2010). *Language and culture: Reflective narratives and the emergence of identity*. New York, NY: Routledge.

Peyton, J. K. (1995). *Dialogue journals: Interactive writing to develop language and literacy*. *ERIC Digest*. Washington, DC: National Clearinghouse for ESL Literacy Education.

Peyton, J. K. (2000). *Dialogue journals: Interactive writing to develop language and literacy*. *ERIC Digest*. Washington, DC: National Clearinghouse for ESL Literacy Education.

Roberts, C., Byram, M., Barro, A., Jordan, S., & Street, B. (Eds.). (2001). *Language learners as ethnographers*. Clevedon, England: Multilingual Matters.

Spradley, J. P., & McCurdy, D. W. (1972). *The cultural experience: Ethnography in a complex society*. Chicago, IL: Science Research Associates.

Ullman, C. (1997). *Social identity and the adult ESL classroom*. *ERIC Digest*. Washington, DC: National Clearinghouse for ESL Literacy Education.

Part II

LANGUAGE AWARENESS

Part II is entitled *Language Awareness* and contains four chapters that help English language teachers develop a knowledge of language structure and its application to teaching. This domain of teacher knowledge is known in the literature as *teacher language awareness (TLA)* (Andrews, 2003), and it is at the forefront of concerns about English language teacher development, particularly for native speaker (NS) teachers who often rely on subconscious knowledge of language and who may not be able to explain language structure effectively to their English learners (Temple Adger, Snow, & Christian, 2018; Wong-Fillmore & Snow, 2000). TLA is not the same as teacher language proficiency, but is, rather, the ability to demonstrate a knowledge of language from a language learner's perspective. It is an essential component of knowledge for teachers in all disciplines who are responsible for educating English learners, especially considering the changing demographics in public schools, increases in migration, together with the growth in international students in universities in North America and elsewhere.

In order to develop subject matter expertise in language, we believe that English language teachers need specific knowledge about language systems and how they work. To this end, we include four chapters on English and its structure. Chapter 6 focuses on the sound system of English and how the properties of consonant and vowel phoneme classes are determined by the articulatory features of sounds. Chapter 7 introduces the system of words and covers such topics as types of morphemes, how they differ in function, form, and effect, and the relationship between spelling and morphology. Chapter 8 introduces the sentence system in English, the role of subconscious knowledge, and the ways in which words combine to form sentences. Chapter 9 focuses on the differences between spoken and written language, as well as cohesion, coherence, register, genre, and the types of methodologies that are used for analyzing both forms of language— that is, spoken and written—such as conversation and discourse analyses.

References

Andrews, S. (2003). Teacher language awareness and the professional knowledge base of the L2 teacher. *Language Awareness*, 12, 81–95.

Temple Adger, C., Snow, C. E., & Christian, D. (2018). *What teachers need to know about language*, 2nd ed. Bristol, England: Multilingual Maters.

Wong-Fillmore, L., & Snow, C. E. (2000). What teachers need to know about language. *Special Report*. ERIC Clearinghouse on Languages and Linguistics. Washington, DC: U.S. Department of Education and Center for Applied Linguistics.

6

THE SOUND SYSTEM

VIGNETTE

I am observing ESL 4300/6300, which is a course for nonnative English speakers who have been admitted to the university. The course is titled "Advanced Pronunciation Skills." There are both graduate and undergraduate students in the class, making it a large class with an enrollment of 27 students. Most students are in the class as an elective option in order to improve their English pronunciation; a few graduate students are in the class because their respective departments have made the course mandatory, and improving their spoken English (i.e., becoming more comprehensible to native speakers) is a requirement for employment at the university as lab or course instructors. It seems that the respective departments believe a semester-long course on English pronunciation will result in dramatic improvements, so there is considerable pressure on the course instructor. Given the large number of students in the class, it is a challenge to provide as much individualized tutoring and support as most students expect. Consequently, the teacher is trying to use group and pair work in addition to the short demonstrations, individual exercises in the pronunciation workbooks, and one-to-one tutoring. The students are mostly from China and Japan, but there are two students from Thailand and three from Mexico. Because of an overlap in teaching schedules, I arrive about 30 minutes into the class. Homework has already been checked and submitted, the short demonstration on the specific sounds that are on focus has just ended, and the students are ready to begin a paired activity.

(continued)

(continued)

Students are participating in an activity called "Dictation Pairs," and the teacher has targeted specific sounds for the students to practice. They each have a handout with four columns; minimal pair word lists have been written in each column, with two columns containing bold-faced words, and partners have complementary handouts. The task is for one student to read the boldfaced words in the minimal pair sets while the other student circles the word she or he hears. When all of the words in the column have been read, students check their own work and switch roles. I mill around as the students dictate their words—class/crass, bland/brand, fright/flight, steam/esteem, sport/ support, please/police, rope/roped, stare/Astaire, bus/busts, class/ clasp, and soak/spoke. [Personal notes, Christison, spring 2002]

Task: Reflect

Before you begin this chapter, take a few moments to reflect on the vignette above and what you already know about the sound system of English.

1 What do you notice about the pairs of words the teacher selected?
2 Why do you think the teacher selected these particular words for the dictation activity?
3 What do these words tell you about the sounds the students may be having difficulty with?

Introduction

Before we begin this chapter on the sound system of English, we want to explain a few of the conventions that we will use for talking about the sounds of English. When we refer to a word as the word itself (as opposed to using the word to represent something), the word will be italicized. *Transcriptions* can be representations of what words sound like in the abstract, or they can be representations of sounds that are actually produced in speech. Abstract sounds and words will appear in slashes (i.e., / /) and actual sounds that a speaker might produce will appear in brackets (i.e., [ ]).

A *phoneme* is a speech sound. It is the smallest unit of sound that makes a difference in meaning. For example, /s/ and /f/ are different phonemes in

96

English, because in words such as *fat* and *sat* exchanging /s/ for /f/ changes the meaning of the word. The sounds in the word *fat* and *sat* can be recorded or transcribed using the symbols [fæt] and [sæt]. A *minimal pair* is made up of two words that contain the same number of sounds, display only one phonetic difference that occurs in the same place in both words, and differ in meaning. In the vignette that introduces this chapter, the teacher selected some minimal pair sets for the students, which were based on the difficulties students were having in their spoken English. For example, based on the words she selected, we might assume that some learners were having difficulty with the /r/ and /l/ distinction in English, while others could be having trouble with initial /s/. Mastering the phonemic inventory of English is particularly important for English language teachers, who must understand the phonemic inventory to assist English learners in producing intelligible language and diagnose production problems when they arise.

In this chapter, we will help you develop expertise in working with the sound system of English. We begin by providing you with a brief introduction to the human vocal tract. Then we will turn our attention to the systems for describing the English phonemes (i.e., consonant and vowel sounds). We will also introduce a consistent set of symbols as a means of recording or transcribing English speech sounds as a way of helping learners work with sounds as they occur in spoken language. Finally, we will focus on the *suprasegmental* features of English (e.g., stress) and some phonological processes that affect English learners.

Sounds and Symbols

English spelling is inconsistent when it comes to the relationship between a word's spelling (i.e., the letters or *graphemes* used in writing conventions) and its sound. For example, consider the words *beard/heard, bleak/break*, or *low/how*. These word pairs look like the minimal pairs *sat* and *fat* above, but in fact they are not. Spelling is often not helpful in determining the pronunciation for English words, because, unlike other languages that have an almost perfect sound/symbol correspondence English sounds can be written in more than one way. For example, the first sound in the word *cat* is the phoneme /k/. It can be written in at least 10 different ways, such as in the words *kick, queen, quai, accomplish, khaki, clique, choir, cow*, or *McLaughlin* (Curzan & Adams, 2006). In order to further illustrate this point, the famous Irish writer George Bernard Shaw said that *fish* should be spelled GHOTI—*gh* as in *laugh, o* as in *women*, and *ti* as in *action*.

97

The *International Phonetic Alphabet (IPA)* is a consistent set of symbols for representing sounds in all known languages. The IPA originated in France in 1886 with a group of language teachers who formed an association called the Phonetic Teachers Association. About a decade later, in 1897, the group changed its name to the International Phonetic Association (Rowe & Levine, 2006) and has retained that name to this day. The IPA provides a way to record the sounds we hear using the principle of one-to-one correspondence between a sound and a symbol. Although linguists use systems other than the IPA for representing English sounds, the systems all follow this principle. In addition, the term *IPA* is often used generically when referring to any system that follows the one sound/one symbol correspondence. The system that we use to represent English sounds in this textbook uses symbols from the IPA, but it also uses symbols from other systems. We have tried to use as few unfamiliar symbols as is possible, thereby making it easier for teachers to learn the system. In addition, the system we use is simplified and intended only to give teachers a basic understanding of English sounds. Table 6.1 provides a list of symbols for the consonant and vowel sounds in English, as well as key words in which the sounds occur. Each sound will be introduced later in this chapter as you learn a system that will help you organize and classify the sounds.

Because there is considerable variation among mother tongue speakers of English worldwide with respect to vowels (as is characterized by the authors themselves!) and because this chapter is intended as a mere introduction to the sound system of English, we have had to make some decisions about the speech we are describing. Table 6.1 represents a rather idealized version of the English sound system for many North American users of English and is often referred to as Standard American English (SAE), as already discussed in Chapter 2. We recognize that not all speakers pronounce the words in Table 6.1 using the same vowels, even within the United States. For example, in U.S. West Coast speech, the vowel in the words *cot* and *caught* are *homophones* (words that sound the same but have different meanings and spellings) and both are transcribed phonetically as /kat/. However, in U.S. Midwestern speech, the vowels sounds are different, so the words are not homophones. The words would be transcribed as /kat/ for *cot* and /kɔt/ for *caught*.

Task: Explore

Identify six words that you pronounce differently from other English speakers. Write them down and share them with a partner or your instructor.

For more information about using IPA, such as with British or Australian English, access the following websites.

The International Phonetic Alphabet
www.internationalphoneticalphabet.org/ipa-sounds/ipa-chart-with-sounds/
Writing the phonetic symbols on your computer:
www.phon.cl.ac.uk/home/wells/eureka-ipa.doc

Table 6.1 Phonetic symbols and key word associations

Vowels and Diphthongs		Consonants	
Symbol	Key word	Symbol	Key word
/a/	caught	/b/	boy
/ɔ/	cot	/d/	day
/æ/	cat	/dʒ/	just
/aɪ/*	high	/f/	face
/aʊ/*	how	/g/	get
/ɔɪ/*	toy	/h/	hat
/e/	name	/k/	car
/i/	beat	/l/	light
/ɪ/	bit	/m/	mine
/o/	go	/n/	no
/ʊ/	book	/p/	pen
/u/	boot	/r/	right
/ɛ/	bet	/s/	see
/ə/	about	/t/	tea
/ɚ/	bird	/ʧ/	cheap
/aɚ/*	bar	/v/	vote
/iɚ/*	beer	/w/	west
/ɛɚ/*	bear	/ʍ/	which
/oɚ/*	four	/y/	yes
		/z/	zoo
		/ð/	they
		/θ/	think
		/ŋ/	sing
		ʃ	shoe
		ʒ	vision

* = diphthongs

Even though the information in Table 6.1 is not detailed enough to account for variability among speakers (see Chapters 1–5), it is a good starting point, giving you a systematic introduction to English sounds and providing you with a way to describe your own speech stream, as well as the speech of your learners.

Task: Reflect

Before you begin reading the remainder of this chapter, try to answer the questions below by thinking about what you may already know about the sound system of English.

1   What parts of the vocal tract do you use in making English sounds?
2   How many consonants are there in English? How many vowels?
3   How are consonants and vowels different from each other?
4   How would you describe the difference in the vowels in the words *pin* and *tool*?

Articulatory Phonetics

Articulatory phonetics is the study of how humans produce the speech sounds that make up language in everyday communication. In order to learn how speech sounds are made and to diagnose problems in speech that may interfere with successful communication, English language teachers need to understand how speech sounds are made and become familiar with the parts of the vocal tract that are used to make speech sounds.

English speech sounds are made by altering the stream of air as it is expelled from the lungs. Sounds that are made in this way are known as *egressive* sounds. Air moves through the *trachea* (windpipe) and into the *larynx* (the voice box). After air passes through the larynx, it is altered by the shape of the *pharyngeal* (throat), *nasal* (nose), and *oral* (mouth) cavities. Although the airstream is modified by all of these structures, it is the structures in the oral cavity that offer the most potential for alteration. As you read about the oral cavity, look at Figure 6.1 and try to locate each of the places of articulation. The position of the tongue, the part of the tongue that is used (e.g., *tip, blade,* or *back*) as well as what it touches—the *alveolar ridge* (the ridge behind the teeth), the *hard palate* (the bony part of the roof of the mouth), or the *soft palate* known as the *velum* (the fleshy part of the roof of the mouth)—can alter the quality of the sound. In addition, the teeth and lips are also involved in making speech sounds in English. The *uvula* (the fleshy structure hanging down at the back of the roof of the mouth) is involved in making speech sounds in other languages, but not in English. In order to describe the sounds of English for learners, it is important to understand how these articulators are used to modify the airstream and produce English sounds.

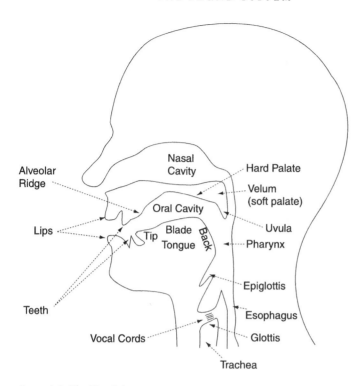

Labels in figure:
Alveolar Ridge, Nasal Cavity, Hard Palate, Velum (soft palate), Oral Cavity, Lips, Tip, Blade, Back, Tongue, Uvula, Pharynx, Teeth, Epiglottis, Esophagus, Vocal Cords, Glottis, Trachea

Figure 6.1 The Vocal Apparatus.

Describing Consonants

A *consonant* is a sound that is produced when the airstream is either stopped or restricted in the vocal tract. We describe consonants based on three features: (1) voicing (whether the vocal cords are vibrating or not), (2) place of articulation (where the air stream is impeded), and (3) manner of articulation (how the sound is impeded).

Voicing

The larynx is called the voice box because it contains two membranes known as the *vocal cords* (see Figure 6.2). The space between the vocal cords is called the *glottis*. The vocal cords can move to create narrow or broad pathways through which air can flow. They function very much like a small elastic or rubber band. When the membranes are tightened, the pathway is narrowed or constricted, and the vocal cords begin to vibrate. The sounds that result are known as *voiced sounds*. When the membranes relax, the vocal cords move apart so that the

101

airstream flows smoothly through the space between the vocal cords, and the vocal cords do not vibrate. The sounds that result when the vocal cords are far apart are *voiceless sounds*. Consonant sounds are classified as either voiced or voiceless. The initial sounds in the words *dim, gone*, and *zebra* are all voiced sounds. The initial sounds in the words *tin, can*, and *see* are all voiceless sounds. The voiced (vd) and voiceless (vl) sounds in English have been identified for you in Table 6.2.

The larynx is engineered specifically to accommodate language in humans so that there is a flap that covers the glottis, which is called the *epiglottis*. During swallowing this flap covers the glottis so that food does not enter the trachea, but instead is routed through the *esophagus* (the passage through which food moves from the throat to the stomach).

Place of Articulation

There are eight different places of articulation for English sounds—bilabial, labiodental, interdental, alveolar, palatal, velar, labiovelar, and glottal. *Bilabial* sounds are produced with both lips together, such as the initial sounds in the words *pet, bat*, and *mice. Labiodental* sounds are made by raising the lower lip until it comes near the top front teeth, such as the initial sounds in the words *fine* and *vine*. Some sounds are articulated using the tongue and the teeth. In English, we call these sounds *interdental* because the tongue goes between the top and bottom teeth. The two interdental sounds in English are found in the initial sounds in the words *think* and *then*. The *alveolar ridge* is behind the upper front teeth. Alveolar sounds are made by placing the tip of the tongue on or behind

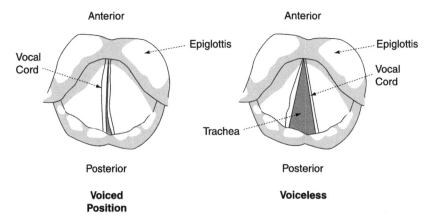

Figure 6.2 The Vocal Cords.

this ridge. The initial sounds in the words *ten, den, neat, sigh, zen, leaf,* and *reef* are all alveolar sounds. *Palatal* sounds are formed when the blade of the tongue touches the hard palate. The initial sounds in *sheet* and *cheap* are palatal, as well as the sounds in medial position in *measure* and *gadget,* and the initial sound in *you. Velar* sounds are created when the blade of the tongue touches the soft palate. The final sounds in the words *tack, tag,* and *song* are velar. *Labiovelar* sounds are created by rounding the lips while the back of the tongue touches the velar region. The initial sounds in words *which* and *witch* are labiovelar. The final place of articulation for English sounds is *glottal.* The sound is sometimes used in place of a [t] sound in the words *button* and *mountain* and initially in the words *hem* and *hop.* It is produced when air is impeded in the glottis. A summary of the places of articulation for English consonants appears in Table 6.2.

There are other places of articulation in the vocal tract that are used in other languages, such as the uvula and the pharynx. *Uvular* sounds are found in Hebrew, Arabic, and French, and *pharyngeal* sounds are common in Arabic, as well as some indigenous languages of North America and Eastern Europe.

Manner of Articulation

So far, we have learned that consonants differ from one another based on whether the vocal cords are vibrating or not (i.e., voiceless and voiced sounds) and on where the sound is made in the articulatory tract (e.g., with the lips or

Table 6.2 English consonants

Manner of Articulation		Bilabial	Labiodental	Interdental	Alveolar	Palatal	Velar	Labiovelar	Glottal
Stop	vl*	p			t		k		ʔ
	vd**	b			d		g		
Fricative	vl		f	θ	s	ʃ			h
	vd		v	ð	z	ʒ			
Affricate	vl					ʧ			
	vd					dʒ			
Nasal	vl								
	vd	m			n		ŋ		
Liquid	vl								
Lateral	vd				l				
Liquid	vl								
Retroflex	vd				r				
Glide	vl							ʍ	
	vd					y		w	

*vl = voiceless and **vd = voiced

on the alveolar ridge). There is one more way in which consonants are different from one another. Consider the following information. There are five alveolar sounds in English that are all voiced—/d/ as in the first sound in the word *dog*, /n/ as in the first sound in *no*, /z/ as in the first sound in *zebra*, /1/ as in the first sound in *little*, and /r/ as in the first sound in *red*. Even though these five sounds are all made on the aveolar ridge and are all voiced, they do not sound alike. What other feature makes these sounds different from one another? The answer to this question is the manner of articulation. *Manner of articulation* refers to how the airstream is constricted and/or released within the vocal tract.

Nasals. Consonants can be produced in both the nasal and oral cavities; however, most sounds in English are produced in the oral cavity. Oral sounds occur when the velum (or soft palate) is raised so that the airstream is blocked from going into the nasal cavity and is forced through the oral cavity. When the velum is lowered, air can move into both the oral and nasal cavities, and the resulting sounds are called *nasals*. There are three nasal consonants in English. The initial sound in *mad* is bilabial, the initial sound in *no* is alveolar, and the final sound in *song* is velar. All nasal sounds in English are voiced.

Stops. *Stops* are sounds that are created by momentarily halting the flow of the airstream, creating pressure behind the point of articulation. There are seven stops made in the oral cavity in English—three voiced and four voiceless. The bilabial stops are [p] and [b], the alveolar [t] and [d], the velar [k] and [g], and the glottal [?]. The first sound in each pair is voiceless, as well as the glottal stop. Technically, nasal sounds in English are also stops, but we differentiate nasal stops from oral stops here in order to demonstrate that nasality is an important feature in describing English sounds. For example, /d/ and /n/ are both voiced alveolar stops, but they are different sounds in English because [n] is made in the nasal cavity and [d] in the oral cavity.

Aspiration. refers to the air that is produced when a stop is released. Stops in word initial position in English are normally accompanied by aspiration. For example, if you put a small piece of paper in front of your mouth and say the word *pin* several times, you will notice that the paper moves when you say the word. This is because of the release of air after the /p/ sound. However, if you place an /s/ before the word *pin* to form the word *spin* and say it several times, you will notice that the paper does not move, meaning that the /p/, when preceded by an /s/, is not aspirated. Aspiration is one way in which sounds can vary. In order to show that a sound is aspirated we can use a superscript *h* [pʰ] to indicate aspiration. Although mother tongue speakers of English (see the Chapter 2 reference to the Inner Circle) use aspiration with stops in word-initial position, many nonnative speakers do not; nevertheless, the speech is intelligible because the presence or absence of aspiration alone does not make a difference in meaning in English; but it does in other languages.

Fricatives. *Fricatives* are produced when the airstream is constricted but not completely stopped. The constriction creates a sort of hissing sound. The labiodental fricatives are the initial sounds in /f/ and /v/, the dental fricatives are /θ/ and /ð/, and the alveolar fricatives /ʃ/ and /ʒ/. The first sound in each set is voiceless. We also have one voiceless glottal fricative /h/, as in the initial sound in the word *help*.

Affricates. Technically, *affricates* are really two consonant sounds that we perceive as one sound—a stop and a fricative together. For example, the initial sound in the word *church* begins as a voiceless alveolar stop /t/ and is followed by a hissing sound characteristic of fricatives. We describe this sound as a voiceless alveolar affricate, and it is written as /ʧ/. The other affricate in English is also alveolar, but it is voiced. It begins with a voiced alveolar stop /d/ and is followed by a hissing sound as in the initial sound in the word *judge*, and it is written as [ʤ]

Liquids. This class of sounds is different from other consonants in English because there is minimal obstruction of the airstream and the friction or hissing sound, which is characteristic of fricatives, is not produced. The tongue is flattened and air moves over the sides of the tongue, much like liquid falling off of a flat surface. There are only two liquids in English—[l] as in the initial sound in *limb* and [r] as in the initial sound in *run*. The sound [l] is known as a *lateral liquid*. We make this sound in English by placing the tip of the tongue in the center of the alveolar ridge and allowing the airstream to escape along one or both sides of the tongue. We make the [r] sound in English by curling the tip of the tongue back and placing it just behind the alveolar ridge, without touching it. Because the tongue moves back (*retro*) and bends (*flex*), we call this sound a *retroflex liquid*. In Table 6.2, you will see that the liquid sounds are presented under the headings *Lateral* for the /l/ and *Retroflex* for /r/.

105

Glides. There are three glide sounds in English, as represented in the initial sounds in the following words: /y/ as in the word *yes*, /w/ as in the word *witch*, and /ʍ/ as in the word *which*. Glides have characteristics of both consonants and vowels, so they are in a sense semi-consonants or semi-vowels, depending on how you want to look at it. The obstruction or constriction of the airstream is less than in most consonants, but it is not as free as in vowels. Glides are preceded or followed by a vowel.

You have likely realized that not all languages have the same phonemic inventory. For example, /q/ represents a voiceless uvular stop that is used in a number of indigenous languages, such as Quechua (an indigenous language of Peru and other countries in South America in the Andean region) and in Inukitut (a language used in northern areas of North America), but not in English. A voiceless velar fricative is represented by /x/ and is found in Spanish in the medial sound in *baja* (as in *Baja California*—the peninsular part of Mexico that extends below the State of California in the United States) and in German as the final sound in the word *Bach*.

Other Terms to Classify Consonants

There are a number of other ways to classify the consonant sounds of English. Although we will not focus on the terms that follow in this section, we introduce them so that you will be familiar with them when you come across them in the literature or in your interactions with your colleagues. Fricatives are sometimes referred to as *sibilants*, a reference to the hissing sound. The term *sibilant* is derived from the Latin verb *sibilare*, meaning *to hiss*. *Continuant* refers to all consonant sounds except stops because the airstream continues in all consonant sounds except stops. *Obstruent* refers to oral stops, fricatives, and affricates. In contrast, all other consonant sounds—nasals, liquids, and glides—are called *sonorants*.

Task: Explore

Give the phonetic symbol for each sound described below and at least two example words in which each sound is used. Try to complete the task without referring to Tables 6.1 or 6.2. Check your work with a partner or refer to the tables.

	Phonetic symbol	Example words
Voiceless bilabial stop	_____	_____
Voiced velar stop	_____	_____
Voiceless dental fricative	_____	_____
Voiceless palatal affricate	_____	_____
Voiceless alveolar stop	_____	_____
Voiced alveolar lateral	_____	_____
Voiced velar nasal	_____	_____
Voiced palatal glide	_____	_____

Describing Vowels

Dimensions

When most people are asked how many vowels there are in English, they usually give the same answer: *a, e, i, o, u*, and sometimes *y*. While it is true that we use the graphemes or letters *a, e, i, o, u*, and *y* to represent the vowel sounds in English (i.e., the spelling), there are actually 12 vowels in SAE. Just as we use a three-dimensional system for describing consonants (i.e., voicing, place of articulation, and manner of articulation), we will use a three-dimensional system for describing vowels. However, the dimensions used for describing vowels will be different from those for consonants. The dimensions for vowels are based on the height of the tongue, the part of the tongue used, and whether the lips are rounded or not. Table 6.3 presents a summary of the vowels in English in terms of their placement within the oral tract. You will see the terms used to differentiate the tongue height are *high, mid*, and *low*, while the terms used to describe the part of the tongue that is used are *front, central*, and *back*. The terms to describe lip roundedness are *rounded* and *unrounded*. All back vowels are rounded, while other vowels are unrounded. If you look at Table 6.3, you can see that the vowel /i/ can be described as a high, front, unrounded vowel (as in the word *beat*) and /u/ as a high, back, rounded vowel (as in the word *boot*). Table 6.1 provides you with example words for each of the vowels in SAE.

Table 6.3 A traditional representation of English vowels in Standard American English

		Front	Central	Back
		Part of the Tongue Used		
Tongue Height	High	i		u
		ɪ		U
	Mid	e		
		ɛ	ɚ ə	o
	Low	æ	a	ɔ

Other Features of Vowels

In the variety of Standard American English (SAE) that we are describing in this chapter, there are two vowels that are made in the center of the oral tract. These vowels are represented by the symbols /ə/ and /ɚ/. The symbol [ə] is called a *schwa*. It can be used as a variant of a full vowel, such as in the initial sounds in *about* and *alone*, in medial position in multisyllabic words, such as *conservatory*, and in final position in words such as *rumba*. The same sound can also occur in words as a full vowel, as in the words *but* and *cut*. The symbol /ɚ/ is called a schwar, and it is the vowel sound in the word *bird*. There is a great deal of variation in central vowel sounds among varieties of English and also variation in how the sounds are represented in linguistic analysis.

There are also a number of different ways to describe vowels in English. Although we will not focus on the terms *tense* and *lax* in the tasks within the chapter and in the questions for discussion at the end of this chapter, we introduce you to the terms so that you will be familiar with them when you come across them in the literature and will be knowledgeable in your interactions with your colleagues. The two categories, tense and lax, are based on the degree of tension in the lips and the degree of constriction in the vocal tract when making vowel sounds. In addition, the terms also have to do with the quality of duration (i.e., how long it takes to make the vowel sound). Tense vowels are produced with more tension in the lips and constriction in the vocal tract than lax vowels, and they are usually of longer duration. There are only four tense vowels in English. They are [i], [e], [u], and [o]; all other vowels in English are considered lax. The difference between the vowel in the word *beat* (/i/) and the vowel in the word *bit* (/ɪ/) is one of tenseness because both vowels can be described as high, front, and unrounded.

Single vowel sounds in a syllable are called *monophthongs* (*mono* = *one* + *phthong* = *sound*), while two vowels in sequence in the same syllable are called *diphthongs* (*di* = *two* + *phthong* = *sound*). Diphthongs begin with one vowel and gradually glide into the second vowel with the emphasis on the first vowel. If the glide is to the front of the mouth, it is represented by /ɪ/, if it is to the back, it is represented by /ʊ/), if it is to the center, it is represented by /ɚ/. There are three common diphthongs that glide front and back in English— /aɪ/ as in the English word *buy*, /aʊ/ as in *how* or *bow*, and /ɔɪ/ as in *boy*. There are four common diphthongs that glide to the schwar vowel in the center— /aɚ/ as in *bar*, /ɪɚ/ as in *beer*, /ɛɚ/ as in *bear*, /oɚ/ as in *bore*. Most vowels in English have some gliding or *diphthongization* as compared to other languages, such as Spanish, which has little (if any) gliding.

Task: Explore

List five English words that contain the following English vowels, but do not rhyme.

The highest front vowel _____

The lowest back vowel _____

Mid-front unrounded vowel _____

High back rounded vowel _____

List four words with diphthongs.

Suprasegmental Features

Suprasegmental features of sounds (sometimes called prosody or prosodic features) help speakers distinguish words, phrases, or even sentences that are otherwise identical in their phonetic segments. Sounds in English can be altered in terms of three suprasegmental features, *stress, pitch,* and *length*.

Stress

Stress refers to the different ways in which we can give a phonetic segment more emphasis. For example, stress distinguishes the verb *constrúct* (with an emphasis on the second syllable) from the noun *cónstruct* (with an emphasis on the first syllable). The options for creating stress are changing the pitch, increasing the length, or increasing the relative loudness of the phonetic segment. The smallest units of speech that contain stress are syllables. In some languages, like Italian and Spanish, the rules that govern sentence and syllabic stress are straightforward and predictable. In English, sentence stress is not predictable but is governed by the propositions.[1] Syllabic stress, to a large degree, is regular and predictable, but it is far more complicated. Changing stress from the first syllable in the word *súbject* to the second syllable, *subjéct* changes the part of speech from a noun to a verb and, of course, changes the meaning of the word. English learners who are speakers of languages with predictable stress often have difficulty with English stress patterns because failure to supply appropriate stress patterns can result in lack of intelligibility even if the pronunciation of the individual phones is comprehensible.

Pitch

Fundamental frequency is the rate at which the vocal cords vibrate and is another word for pitch. Pitch allows listeners to position a sound on a scale from high to low. In many languages of the world, such as Thai and Mandarin, syllabic pitch can change meaning, and it is used to distinguish words made up of the same sound. The classical example of this phenomenon in Mandarin is exemplified with the segmental string /m/ + /a/ or [ma]. By changing the pitch, [ma] can have four different meanings—*mother, hemp, horse*, and *scold*. Languages that function in this way are called *tone languages*. In other languages, such as English, a change in syllabic pitch can change the syntactic function as in the example with the word *construct*. In addition, a change in pitch at the sentence level can change the sentence *The class has been cancelled* from a question to a statement, from a statement to an expression of surprise, from an expression of surprise to a statement of doubt, or any combination of these. Languages that function in this way relative to pitch are called *intonational languages*.

Length

Sounds can be brief or comparatively long. The length of a sound is known as its *duration*. The position of the tongue in the mouth can influence the length of a vowel (e.g., high vowels generally have a shorter duration than low vowels). In addition, vowels that come before voiced consonants are of longer duration that vowels before voiceless consonants. In some languages, such as Hindi and Japanese, lengthening a consonant can change the meaning of a phonetic stream.

A lengthened sound is called a *geminate* sound and is usually about twice the length of an individual sound, called a *singleton*.

Syllables

Most adults are able to identify syllables and determine how many syllables are in a word quite easily, yet defining exactly what a syllable is requires a more detailed answer.

Parts of a Syllable

A *syllable* is a unit of pronunciation (Honig, Diamond, & Gutlohn, 2000), and linguists identify three parts to the unit—*onset* (optional), *nucleus* (obligatory), and *coda* (optional). The nucleus is obligatory, and it is always a vowel. In English it is the only required part of a syllable. Table 6.4 shows the syllable structure for four common words and illustrates the obligatory nature of the vowel and optional nature of the onset and coda. All syllables contain vowels (or consonants that function as vowels, such as in the final syllables in the word *sudden* and *little*).

There are constraints on what sounds can appear in onsets and codas, and there are constraints on what sounds can appear next to each other. For example, we have already discussed aspirated stops in English /pʰ/, /tʰ/, /kʰ/, and have learned that they occur in initial position and that /ŋ/ as in the word *song* can only appear in coda position in English. These constraints are known as *phonotactic constraints*.

If you are teaching in public school contexts, you will likely work with literacy and reading specialists, who may use a slightly different paradigm for syllable structure with two parts—an onset and a rime. In this paradigm, the *rime* is the vowel and everything that comes after it, while the *onset* is the

Table 6.4 Syllable structure*

Word	Onset	Nucleus	Coda
I	—	I	—
at	—	a	t
pan	p	a	n
train	tr	ai	n

*Words are written as spelled, rather than as spoken, for illustrative purposes.

111

Table 6.5 Onset and rime in English syllables

Word	Onset	Rime
I	–	I
at	–	at
pan	p	an
train	tr	ain

*Words are written as spelled, rather than as spoken, for illustrative purposes.

consonant or consonant blend that may come before the rime. The onset is optional. Because the audience for this book includes English language teachers who have a primary concern with literacy, we include the two-part syllable structure in Table 6.5.

Syllable Patterns in English

The most common syllable type in English is consonant/vowel (CV), meaning that English words break into CV syllables whenever possible (McMahon, 2002). English has four main types of syllables, which are defined by the characteristics of sounds contained in the rime. In *closed syllables*, the vowel is followed by a consonant sound, such as in the words *pan, picnic, shape*, and *cube*. When a syllable ends in a single vowel, such as in the words *see* and *veto*, it is called an *open syllable*. Some syllables contain two vowels (i.e., a diphthong), such as in the words *high, boy*, and *now*, and are called *diphthong syllables*. The last syllable type is called a *syllabic consonant syllable* and occurs in words ending in /ņ/ as in the word *sudden*, /ļ/ as in the word *little*, or /m̦/ as in the word *consortium*. The diacritic mark under these phonemes is used to indicate that the consonants are functioning as vowels in terms of syllable structure.

There are some basic patterns that determine where *multisyllabic* or *polysyllabic* words (i.e., words with more than one syllable) in English split into syllables. English words follow one of five basic patterns, and these patterns appear in Table 6.6 below.

In Pattern 1, we see that if there are two vowels (not diphthongs) in the middle of a word the syllable divide is between them. In Pattern 2, with VCV combinations, there are two options—either before or after the consonant. If there are two consonants in the middle of a word, as in Pattern 3, the syllable divide is between the consonants. Patterns 4 and 5 are a bit

Table 6.6 Syllable patterns in English

Patterns	Syllable Division	Key Word
Pattern 1: VV	V/V	du-al
Pattern 2: VCV	V/CV	di-gest
	VC/V	clos-et
Pattern 3: VCCV	VC/CV	pic-nic
Pattern 4: VCCCV	VC-CCV	com-plain
Pattern 5: VCCCCV	VC/CCCV	in-struct

more complicated; however, if a word contains three or more consonants in medial position, there is almost always a closed first syllable and generally a consonant blend.

Word Families or Phonograms

A *phonogram* is a letter or a sequence of letters that represents a sound, a syllable, or a series of sounds. Another word for a phonogram is a *word family*. For example, the words *bank*, *blank*, *sank*, *tank*, and *thank* belong to the same *-ank* word family; -ank is also the rime for the syllable/word in the two category paradigm. Thirty-seven common phonograms can generate over 500 primary or basic English words, so they are useful in helping English learners identify words, see relationships among words, and acquire vocabulary (see Table 6.7). For example, the phonogram *-ash* can be used to generate *bash*, *cash*, *clash*, *crash*, *dash*, *flash*, *gash*, *gnash*, *hash*, *mash*, *rash*, *sash*, *slash*, *smash*, *splash*, *stash*, *thrash*, and *trash*.

Table 6.7 Common phonograms in English

ack	ail	ain	ake	ale
ame	an	ank	ap	ash
at	ate	aw	ay	eat
ell	est	ice	ick	ide
ight	ill	in	ine	ing
ink	ip	ir	ock	oke
ump	unk			

Phonology

Identifying Phonological Rules

Phonology is the study of how speech sounds are combined into larger units and what the rules are that govern the combinations of sounds. Phonological rules are discovered by conducting a phonetic analysis to determine what these rules are. In English and other majority languages, phonetic analyses have already been done; consequently, there is a *corpus* from which to work. A corpus is a collection of written or spoken texts that can be used to help discover rules, such as the rules that govern the sound system. However, when linguists work on endangered languages for which no phonetic analysis has been done, the first task is to conduct a phonetic analysis in order to create an inventory of speech sounds (i.e., a corpus) and determine which sounds are *distinctive* and comprise the phonemes or sounds of the language (i.e., its phonemic inventory). Once linguists have identified the phonemic inventory, they can begin to study its phonology.

Allophones

Some sounds occur in *complementary distribution;* in other words, they occur in different phonetic contexts. For example, in this chapter you learned that the aspirated, voiceless bilabial stop [pʰ] occurs in word-initial position and the unaspirated, voiceless bilabial stop [p] occurs after the sound [s] (see the Aspiration section in this chapter). The two sounds never contrast, and minimal pairs do not exist for the two sounds because the sounds occur in complementary environments (i.e., in contrasting environments) and not in the same environment. Essentially, [pʰ] and [p] are variations of the same phoneme /p/ in English. Variations of the same phoneme are called *allophones.*

For native speakers (NS), the use of [pʰ] and [p] allophones in the specified environments is obligatory, not optional. NSs do not switch one allophone for the other. However, the situation is different for L2 learners. The phonemic inventory of each language is different and learners are likely to be influenced by the phonemic inventory of their first or home languages. There is no perfect match between phonemes and allophones in the first or home language and English (or any second or foreign language). For example, /r/ and /l/ are allophones of the same phoneme in Japanese, but in English they are different phonemes. In addition, /z/ and /s/ are distinct phonemes in English, but in Spanish they are allophones of the same phoneme. These are just a few of the challenges that English learners face. First language (L1) interference is one of the chief contributors to foreign accent; the reverse is true for L1 speakers of English learning the languages mentioned above.

114

Complementary distribution should not be confused with free variation. *Free variation* is a condition in which phonetically different sounds (phonemes or allophones) alternate with each other without changing meaning. An example of this phenomenon is the two options for pronunciation of potato (i.e., [potato] vs. [poteto]). Although each option has the same number of segments, and each item differs from the other one by only one sound; the items of each pair do not differ in meaning. When one meaning is represented by more than one phonemic form (i.e., two different pronunciations), the phenomenon is known as free variation.

Task: Explore

For more information on possible reasons why L2 learners have trouble with English, see www.fact-index.com/n/no/non_native_pronunciations_of_english.html. Identify one additional source of difficulty for English learners not covered in this chapter and share your example with a partner.

Phonological Processes

Native speakers subconsciously know the phonological rules of their first language (L1) because they execute these rules in their everyday speech; nevertheless, few would be able to explicitly state the phonological rules that govern their speech. Phonological processes are for the most part executed without L1 speaker awareness; however, English learners and their teachers can often benefit from consciously knowing about some of these processes. An exhaustive list of phonological processes is beyond the scope of this introductory chapter, but there are four processes that we believe are especially useful in explaining phenomena in the speech of English learners.

Assimilation. *Assimilation* is a phonological process that accounts for variation in pronunciation. Obligatory phonological assimilation is a process that native speakers apply to a string of phonetic units in order to make them easier to perceive and pronounce. An example of assimilation in English is vowel nasalization. Although vowels are generally not nasalized in English, there are phonetic environments when vowel nasalization does occur. For example, when native speakers pronounce the word *ham*, they pronounce it as [hæ̃m] (the ~ over the [æ] means a nasalized sound) rather than [hæm] because the [m] in *ham* is a nasal sound. The speaker subconsciously begins to lower the velum, which results in opening the nasal cavity before the /m/, thereby creating a nasalized vowel.

The vowel is influenced by the nasal sound that follows it. This type of assimilation is called *manner assimilation*, because it involves a change in a feature associated with manner of articulation. *Voice assimilation* also occurs when a sound changes to agree with a surrounding sound relative to its voicing, and *place assimilation* occurs when adjacent sounds are made to agree in their place of articulation.

Deletion. *Deletion* is a phonological process in which sounds or syllables are omitted in words, particularly in unstressed syllables. An example of deletion occurs in the word *laboratory* in some varieties of English. The vowel in the second syllable is deleted in SAE, creating the cluster /br/, making the word four syllables long instead of five. Some speakers of English create a consonant cluster for the word *police* and pronounce it /plis/, thereby deleting a vowel. When deletion occurs between words, it is called *elision*. It occurs at the end of one word when the next word begins with a vowel, such as in *th'apple*.

Insertion. *Insertion* is a process wherein sounds are added to words. For example, when you pronounce the word *length*, you most likely add a /k/ sound, thereby pronouncing the word as [lɛŋkθ] rather than as [lɛŋθ]. The /k/ serves as a transitional sound, because it is voiceless like /θ/ and velar like /ŋ/.

Metathesis. *Metathesis* occurs when sounds reverse their order in words. The word *ask* in some varieties of English is often pronounced as /æks/ by an increasing number of English speakers. You may have also heard children say *pasghetti* for *spaghetti*.

Task: Explore

Describe the phonological process that would explain why there are two forms of the prefix meaning *not* in the following words *immoral*, *indistinct*, *immodest*, *imbalance*, and *insoluble*.

Conclusion

In this chapter we have provided you with some basic tools for understanding the sound system of English and have introduced you to a consistent set of symbols for representing the sounds in English. In addition, we have given you a system for describing speech sounds, such as voicing, place, and manner of articulation to describe consonants and roundedness, height of the tongue, and the part of the tongue to describe vowels. We have discussed the importance of

116

the suprasegmental features in determining meaning and offered a brief over-view of the challenges that learners face.

Task: Expand

Bassano, S. (2017). *Sounds easy: Phonics, spelling, and pronunciation.* Palm Springs, CA: Alta English Publishers.

This book contains photocopiable resources for teaching the sound system of the English language through simple, clear pictures. The exercises are designed for beginning English language learners who have little academic background and who are learning the English alphabet while concurrently building their vocabulary, listening, and speaking skills. The book is especially helpful for English language teachers who are new to teaching English pronunciation.

Murphy, J. (2017). *Teaching the pronunciation of English: Focus on whole courses.* Ann Arbor, MI: University of Michigan Press.

This volume fills a gap by introducing teaching to courses that focus on teaching the pronunciation of English as a second, foreign, or international language. It is designed to support more effective pronunciation teaching in English language teaching in as many different parts of the world as possible. The book demonstrates that pronunciation teaching is compatible with communicative, task-based, post-method, and technology-mediated approaches to language teaching.

Questions for Discussion

1 What are phonemes? What are allophones? Give examples of each in English.
2 Use the system of symbols introduced in Table 6.1 to broadly transcribe each word listed below. Share your list with a partner and discuss the differences you have.

    a   pat _____

    b   pressure _____

    c   motion _____

    d   fun _____

    e   eye _____

    f   put _____

    g   fatigue _____

h   list _____

i   enjoy _____

3   Place an acute accent (i.e., [′]) over the one word that receives primary stress in the following sentences. What do you think determines where stress belongs?

a	Sally had a little boy.	(Surprise over the fact that she gave birth to a boy.)
b	He saw the White House.	(The house where the President of the USA lives.)
c	He saw the white house.	(Not the beige one.)
d	Did he pick up the hot rod?	(The hot stick.)
e	Did he pick up the hot rod?	(The car.)

Note

1   We use the term *proposition* generally to refer to the *content* or *meaning* of a declarative sentence. A proposition can also refer to the pattern of symbols, marks, or sounds that make up a declarative sentence. In addition, the meaning of a proposition also includes that it has the quality or property of being either true or false. In this sense, two meaningful declarative sentences containing different words can express the same proposition if the two sentences mean the same thing. Linguists, writers, and philosophers have not always made it sufficiently clear whether they are using the term *proposition* in the sense of the words or the meaning expressed by the words. Two sentences with the same propositions could have different truth-values, e.g., I am Secretary Clinton as said by Hillary Clinton herself and as said by Mary Smith. A number of linguists claim that all definitions of a proposition are too vague to be useful. For them, it is just a misleading concept that should be removed from the study of semantics.

References

Bassano, S. (2017). *Sounds easy: Phonics, spelling, and pronunciation*. Palm Springs, CA: Alta English Publishers.

Curzan, A., & Adams, M. (2006). *How English works*. White Plains, NY: Pearson Education.

Honig, B., Diamond, L., & Gutlohn, L. (2000). *Teaching reading sourcebook for kindergarten through eighth grade*. Novato, CA: Arena Press.

McMahon, A. (2002). *An introduction to English phonology*. New York, NY: Oxford University Press.

Murphy, J. (2017). *Teaching the pronunciation of English: Focus on whole courses*. Ann Arbor, MI: University of Michigan Press.

Rowe, B. M., & Levine, D. P. (2006). *A concise introduction to linguistics*. White Plains, NY: Pearson Education.

7

THE SYSTEM OF WORDS

VIGNETTE

I am observing a sheltered ESL class[1] on American history. The students should have read the chapter as homework and are working in small groups, answering questions and completing vocabulary worksheets. I have moved my chair to the side of the room. From this location, I can easily listen to the content of the conversation in the group at the back of the room. The group is composed if five eighth grade boys; all are second language learners from at least two different language backgrounds. They are trying to speak English. One young man has clearly emerged as the leader. He has tried to explain the meaning of a number of specific vocabulary items in the chapter, including kayak, igloo, squash, ancestor, descendant, teepee, tribe, fence, oil lamp, seal, beaded dress, *and* adobe. *I am impressed with his knowledge of the vocabulary specific to the chapter and, like a typical teacher, I assume he has been studying diligently.*

When I share my observations with the teacher after class, she is stunned by my revelations, stating that the young man is most often unprepared in class and is seldom able to help others. I find the discrepancy curious enough that I decide to return to class the next day to talk to the young man. Carlos (pseudonym) tells me several things I find interesting. His uncle is a kayaker, and Carlos has seen his uncle's boat in the garage and talked to him about kayaking on numerous occasions. In addition, his aunt and uncle took him on a small trip last summer to the four corners region—a part of the United

(continued)

(continued)

States where the corners of the states of Utah, New Mexico, Arizona, and Colorado meet. They bought him a large picture book that he frequently looks at and reads. Because a large population of Native Americans live in this area, the book contains historical information about these groups and is full of colorful pictures depicting past and present-day life. [Christison, research data, 3/30/2006]

Task: Reflect

Write a short essay (one page) describing the content of your own vocabulary in English. Explain how the vocabulary you know is a reflection of who you are. Be certain to provide some examples of specific vocabulary items. What words do you know that others may not know because of your work, background, hobbies, education, geographical location, family, and travel? What slang words do you know in English? What words might you use in the different contexts in which you use English? Share your essay with a colleague.

(Adapted from Clark, 2004, p. 7)

Introduction

If you completed the reflection activity above, you probably discovered some interesting facts about your own vocabulary in English that may have surprised you. For example, you may have been surprised to learn that you know vocabulary that other people do not know or that you have specific vocabulary for use in different contexts, such as at home, at work, or at school. As in the case with Carlos in the vignette that introduces this chapter, you may have realized that your own vocabulary reflects what you know and what you focus on in your life; it is through vocabulary that you convey the knowledge you have and the levels of your expertise to others. Carlos knew vocabulary his peers did not know because he had life experiences that were different from theirs. If you study music, read about it, spend time playing a musical instrument, and talk about music with your friends and family, you will acquire vocabulary associated with music. By the same token, if you play soccer, garden, or ride horses, you will acquire vocabulary associated with these activities.

Acquiring vocabulary in a second or foreign language is one of the most challenging tasks for English learners, particularly those who must rely almost solely on their experiences in classroom contexts. Nevertheless, control over a broad range of vocabulary items in oral communication is critical for participation in most modern societal endeavors outside of the classroom and is crucial for second language (L2) literacy development because vocabulary knowledge is fundamental to reading comprehension. The amount of reading that we engage in is an indicator of the size of the vocabulary we recognize and use in any given language (Fielding, Wilson, & Anderson, 1986). Consequently, it follows that if learners are to develop strong reading skills in English, they need to increase the number of words they know. This fact is true for children and adults in English as a second language (ESL) and English as a foreign language (EFL) contexts.

L2 vocabulary development is a complex process that involves English learners in making use of both their background knowledge and their cognitive abilities. Vocabulary development involves far more than memorizing lists of vocabulary words or looking words up in a dictionary, although these are the most common classroom tasks for L2 vocabulary development. Memorizing vocabulary lists of 10–15 words a week (or even double that) might not get you very far when you consider that unabridged English dictionaries have between 500,000 and 600,000 entries (Clark, 2003, p. 7), and each of these entries has many different subentries. Learning a sufficient number of words well enough to be able to participate comfortably in both face-to-face communication and in written discourse can seem like a formidable task.

Most of us would agree that by the time children reach school age they can communicate comfortably in their native language(s). Beck and McKeown (1991) estimate that first graders have vocabularies in their first language (L1) of between 2,500 and 5,000 words. Lorge and Chall (1963) give us estimates that are slightly higher, suggesting that they use and understand about 6,000 oral words but, of course, have a very limited reading vocabulary. However, by the time they reach second grade, Graves, Juel, and Graves (1998) note that reading vocabularies increase to between 2,000 and 5,000 words. Nagy and Anderson (1984) also indicate that, by the time learners have reached the end of secondary schooling, they know about 45,000 words in their L1. Other researchers have suggested numbers ranging from 5,000 to 17,000 words (D'Anna, Zechmeister, & Hall, 1991; Hirsh & Nation, 1992). Even though these numbers are considerably fewer words than the 500,000 to 600,000 in an unabridged dictionary, they still represent an overwhelmingly large number of words for beginning proficiency-level English learners and make us rethink the effectiveness of the most common instructional techniques for vocabulary development, such as

121

memorizing word lists, using dictionaries, and other direct instruction method-ologies for learning L2 vocabulary.

Both teachers and materials and curriculum development specialists have to decide which words to teach and which words should be incorporated into classroom instruction. The decision-making process is based on the needs of learners in the particular context or a group of learners for whom the materi-als are intended. Developing an understanding of the English word system is critical in making instructional and curricular decisions. For example, Nagy and Anderson (1984) estimate that there are roughly 85,000 word families used in books up to the end of secondary instruction in the United States. A *word fam-ily* is a group of related words, so someone knowing one of the words (in the family) could guess or infer the meaning of the others when encountering them during the process of reading, such as *subtract, subtraction, subtractive, subtracting* (Stahl, 1999). English language teachers who have developed a sophisticated understanding of the English word system will be able to identify word families that are critical to the texts on which their learners are focused and can develop a a manageable system for L2 vocabulary development.

If you are an L1 speaker of English, most of what you know about the English word system is subconscious. However, the types of questions that English learners have about the English word system require a conscious knowledge of this system. In this chapter we want to help you develop a conscious understand-ing of the word system of English so that you can help L2 learners on their path toward demonstrated proficiency. We believe it is essential for language teach-ers to develop a sophisticated understanding about the system of words in order to make appropriate instructional choices for English learners. In this chapter we will introduce you to language families to show you how vocabulary devel-ops and how words can be related across languages. We then give you some history and background information about English to help you appreciate the complicated nature of the English lexicon. We introduce English morphology and revisit the relationships among morphology, spelling, and literacy develop-ment. Finally, we present information to help you understand how new words are formed in English.

Language Families

Proto-Indo-European

Historical linguistics is the study of how languages change over time and the rela-tionship among different languages (Rowe & Levine, 2006). Historical linguists

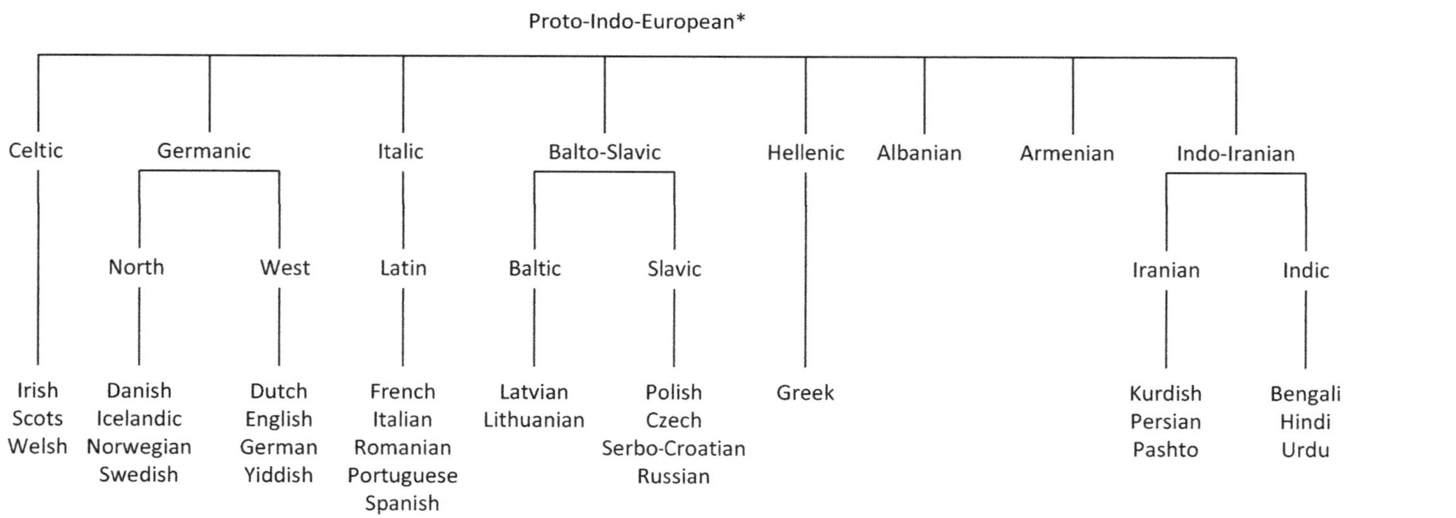

Proto-Indo-European*

Celtic | Germanic | Italic | Balto-Slavic | Hellenic | Albanian | Armenian | Indo-Iranian

Germanic: North, West

Balto-Slavic: Baltic, Slavic

Indo-Iranian: Iranian, Indic

Celtic
Irish
Scots
Welsh

North
Danish
Icelandic
Norwegian
Swedish

West
Dutch
English
German
Yiddish

Italic — Latin
French
Italian
Romanian
Portuguese
Spanish

Baltic
Latvian
Lithuanian

Slavic
Polish
Czech
Serbo-Croatian
Russian

Hellenic
Greek

Albanian

Armenian

Iranian
Kurdish
Persian
Pashto

Indic
Bengali
Hindi
Urdu

* This chart is not meant to be an exhaustive list of all languages in the Indo-European Family. Historical linguists have identified 144 languages in this family.

Figure 7.1 The Proto Indo-European Language Family.

Table 7.1 Some word comparisons among selected Indo-European languages

English	Gothic[2]	Greek	Latin	Sanskrit[3] (Indic)
brother	brother	phrater	frater	bhrater
father	fadar	pater	pater	pita
foot	fotu	poda	pedem	padam
three	thri	tris	tres	trayas

study the process of language change in order to discover relationships among languages and classify them into language families. Historical linguists believe that English is a member of the Indo-European language family and that it descended from an ancient language called *Proto-Indo-European*. It is believed that this language was spoken about 4500 BCE near the borders that Europe shares with Asia. The linguistic descendants of this ancient language are evident in countries throughout Europe as well as in Iran, Pakistan, and northern India. Figure 7.1 shows some of the languages in the Proto-Indo-European language family and how they are related.

The knowledge that we have about Proto-Indo European has been obtained by studying the languages that descended from it. By looking at the relationships of selected words among these languages, we can hypothesize about their relationship and about the structure of the parent language (see Table 7.1).

The similarity of sound and meaning among the words presented in Table 7.1 and the fact that the changes in question occurred in predictable ways (Rowe & Levine, 2006) suggest that these languages diverged from a common parent language (i.e., Proto-Indo-European).

Another way in which relationships among languages is determined is by studying Proto-Indo-European roots. For example, many Proto-Indo-European roots,[4] such as *agro-, ant-, dwo*, and *mdhyo*, can be recognized in English words, such as *agriculture, antidepressant, dual*, and *middle*. As Proto-Indo-European spread over a large geographical area, speakers had less contact with one another; consequently, the language began to change. A more recent example of this language change phenomenon is evident in how the spoken languages of French, Italian, Portuguese, and Spanish all developed from the same Latin origins. So, for example, *pater* in Latin became *père, padre, pai*, and *padre*.

Proto-Indo-European is only one of many different language families. It is beyond the scope of this chapter, both in terms of its introductory nature and its focus on English, to offer a more in-depth discussion of language families. For a more comprehensive list of language families and the languages that belong to each family you may wish to visit www.ethnologue.com/family_index.asp or consult *The Atlas of Languages* (Comrie, Matthews, & Polinsky, 2003).

History of English

The history of English can be divided into three general periods—Old English (449–1100), Middle English (1100–1500), and Modern English (1500–present), and events in each of these periods influenced the way in which English vocabulary developed (Curzan & Adams, 2006).

Old English

Old English was a dialect of Proto-Germanic, a language that was spoken by three Germanic tribes living in northern Europe, and a member of the Germanic language group. If you look carefully at Figure 6.1, you will see that English is most closely aligned to German, Dutch, and Yiddish,[5] so the grammar of Old English (spoken between 449 to 1100) was much like that of modern German. The remnants of Old English vocabulary are still evident in many monosyllabic words in Modern English, such as *eat, drink, house, man*, and *strong*. Also evident in Old English are words from Latin (resulting from contact with Romans) and Old Norse (resulting from Viking[6] invasions). Some Latin words that were adopted into English during this time are *angel, school*, and *wine*, and it is not surprising that many of the adopted Latin words had religious connotations. Old Norse words, such as *dirt, sister, skirt*, and *sky*, were also adopted into English during this time period. Old English is so different from Modern English that, at first glance, it seems like a foreign language and requires specific training in order to be able to read it well. The most famous example of an extant text in Old English is *Beowulf*.

Middle English

The *Middle English* period extended from about CE 1100 to 1500. The invasion of England by the Normans in CE 1066 changed the English language significantly. The Norman invaders, as the conquerors, assumed important governmental and church positions in England; consequently, French became the language of the English aristocracy and continued as such for about 300 years. During this time period many French words were adopted into English and most of the words were related to government, law, and religion, such as *treaty, parliament, tax, baptism, faith*, and *prison*. Chaucer's *Canterbury Tales* is the best-known example of a Middle English text.

Modern English

The *Modern English* period began when the printing press was brought to England in 1475. As a result, books began to be printed and some common people began to learn to read and write. The most famous examples of early Modern English are the works of Shakespeare, his sonnets and plays. Shakespeare is not easy to read because the grammar of Shakespeare's English is different from the Modern English of the 21st century (e.g., Shakespeare's English contained inflectional forms that we no longer use, such as *doth* for *does*, used many vocabulary words that we no longer use, and used vocabulary words familiar to us today in different ways); nevertheless, the Modern English of the 21st century and the Modern English of the 16th century contain both Old English and Norman French words.

Late Modern English

In the late 20th century, English emerged as a world language. It is not just the language of England any more, but is also a national language in Australia, Canada, New Zealand, and the United States. Additionally, it is an official second language or a lingua franca in many other countries, such as India and Nigeria, and one of the official languages in Singapore. There are currently, at the beginning of the 21st century, and according to current estimates, about 1,500 million people speaking English worldwide (Crystal, 2003a, 2003b; Noack & Gamlo, 2015), and nonnative speakers of English outnumber mother tongue speakers about 4:1. As we explained in Chapter 2, the spread of English worldwide and the emergence of World Englishes make English vocabulary even more complex and diverse.

Historical Origins of Words

English has a huge vocabulary of words, which have been borrowed from other languages and which have come into English in the following ways: (a) Latin and Greek (into Old, Middle, and Modern English), (b) Old Norse (into both Old and Middle English), (c) Old French (into Middle English), and (d) modern spoken languages. In addition, many words were borrowed from languages in the British colonies—for example, *amok* (Malay), *bungalow* (Hindi), and *rogue* (Sinhalese).

The historical origin of a word is known as its *etymology*. Dictionaries can give us the etymology of English words and tell us where the word came from and when the word came into English. This information can be a useful point of connection to English for many language learners.

The words below are examples taken from the *American Heritage Dictionary*. Etymological entries in other dictionaries may differ slightly, but the explanations that follow the entries below should provide sufficient clarification, so that you can adapt the information from your dictionary to a slightly different system and can understand the types of information that dictionaries provide relative to etymology.

The word *ear* is a native English word. Its etymology is listed as [<*OE eare*].

This entry tells us that *ear* was derived from Old English (OE) as the word *eare*. Because no other language is listed, we can assume that it was not borrowed from any other language but is a native word.

Sometimes etymological entries give you other historical information about a word, such as the following: [<OE *eare* = D *oor*, Icel., *eyra*, Dan., *ore*, G, *ohr*, L *auris* and Gr, *ous*].

This entry tells us that *ear* is related to words in other languages, such as *oor* in Dutch, *eyra* in Icelandic, *eyra* in Danish, *ohr* in German, *auris* in Latin, and *ous* in Greek, and is the sort of evidence that linguists use to establish hypotheses about a common parent language, such as Proto-Indo-European.

We have borrowings from Old French (OF) into English, such as *chair [ME chaire* < *OFr.* < *Lat. cathedra, chair* < *Gk. kathedra*]. This entry tells us that *chair* was adopted into Middle English from Old French. It also tells us that the word came into Old French from Latin and into Latin from Greek, going beyond the scope of how the word came into English. We also have borrowings from modern spoken languages into Modern English, such as the following: *sherbet* [Ar. *sharbat*] and *patio* [Sp.] These entries tell us that *sherbet* is a direct borrowing into Modern English from the Arabic word *sharbat*. *Patio* is a direct borrowing from Modern Spanish into Modern English.

Task: Explore

The following words are all English words borrowed from modern spoken languages. Guess which language you think they were each borrowed from. Then, find the true etymology in your dictionary.

   kayak, karate, ginseng, hummus, maestro, rouge, salsa, sauté, tortilla

Share your answers with a colleague or partner.

Classifying Morphemes and Words

Defining Morphemes

The study of the structure and classification of words and the units that make up words is known as *morphology*. The minimal unit in morphology is a *morpheme*, the smallest unit of meaning in a language. The emphasis in this definition is on the word *smallest*, since a morpheme cannot be broken down into other units and still carry meaning. For example, the word *pan* /pæn/ is a morpheme because none of its individual units (i.e., [p], [æ], or [n]) carry meaning, nor do any combination of units carry meaning related to the word *pan*. You may have noticed that *pan* has the unit combination *an*, but *an* has nothing to do with the meaning of the original word *pan*, so it is not a separate morpheme in this context. However, the word *pans* /pænz/ is made up of two morphemes. *Pan* refers to a cooking pot and *-s* means plural or "more than one pan." Therefore, the word *pans* is made up of two morphemes. *Pan* is a morpheme and a word; *-s* is a morpheme, but not a word.

In the context of English morphology, there are two ways in which meaningfulness can be defined. The first is the traditional way described above with the word *pan*. Morphemes can refer to things or actions or qualities or quantities of things or actions (Rowe & Levine, 2006). Morphemes can also be said to have meaning if they have a grammatical function. For example, *-s* in the word *pans* is a plural marker. It would be hard to define *-s* in the same sense that we define the word *pan*, but the function of *-s* is very clear.

In general, morphemes fall into two categories—free and bound. A *free morpheme* is a meaningful unit of language that can occur alone and can have other morphemes attached to it. For example, the word *pan* is a free morpheme. A *bound morpheme* is a meaningful unit of language that cannot occur alone. For example, in the word *pans*, *-s* is a bound morpheme. It does not occur alone, but it does carry the meaning of plurality, of more than one.

In addition to being a free morpheme, the word *pan* can also function as a *root*. A root forms the core of a word in the sense that other morphemes can be attached to it. It also carries the meaning of the word and is usually a free morpheme. In the word *unfriendly*, *friend* is the root and carries the meaning of the word; *un-* and *-ly* are bound morphemes that are attached to the root.

Bound morphemes that are attached to roots are referred as *affixes*. More specifically, they are called *prefixes* if they are attached to the front of a root and *suffixes* if they are attached to the end of a root. In the example given above, *un-* is a prefix and *-ly* is a suffix. *Infixes* are affixes that are added to the middle of a root. Although English does not have infixes, they are common in other languages, such as Turkish and Tagalog (a language of the Philippines). Another type of affix is called a *circumfix*. This type of affix is common in Semitic languages, such as Arabic, Hebrew, and Persian. These affixes enter a root in different places. For example, *ktb* is a root in Arabic that means the act of writing. The *ktb* root appears in many Arabic words associated with writing—*katab* (write), *kutubii* (booksellar), and *kataba* (he writes), to name just a few. The word *enlighten* in

English is an example of a circumfix (the root *light* is surrounded by the affixes *en-* and *-en*), but circumfixing is not a common morphological process for creating words in English. English uses principally prefixes and suffixes.

Types of Bound Morphemes

Derivational morphemes. As mentioned previously, bound morphemes can be classified on the basis of their function. Morphemes that change the lexical category (i.e., the part of speech—for example, noun, verb, adjective) of a word or change the meaning of a word are known as *derivational morphemes*. Examples of derivational morphemes are *un-* and *-ly* in the word *unfriendly*. The function of *-ly* is to change a word from an adjective to an adverb. *Un-* means *not* and changes the meaning of a word from negative to a positive.

The most frequently used derivational morphemes (both prefixes and suffixes) in English, along with their meanings, appear in Table 7.2. This list can be useful in helping English learners develop vocabulary systematically.

Table 7.2 Most frequent derivational morphemes

Prefixes		Suffixes	
Morpheme	Meaning	Morpheme	Meaning
anti-	against	-able, -ible	can be done
de-	opposite	-al, -ial	having characteristics of
dis-	not, opposite of	-ed	past-tense verbs
en-, em-	cause to	-en	made of
in-, im-, il-, ir-	not	-er	comparative
inter-	between	-er, -or	one who
mid-	middle	-est	comparative
mis-	wrongly	-ful	full of
non-	not	-ic	having characteristics of
over-	over	-ing	verb form/present participle
pre-	before	-ion, -tion, -ation, -ition	act, process
re-	again	-ity, -ty	state of
semi-	half	-ive, -ative, -itive	adjective form of a noun
sub-	under	-less	without
super-	above	-ly	characteristics of
trans-	across	-ment	action or process
un-	not	-ness	state of, condition of
under-	under	-ous, -eous, -ious -y	possessing the qualities of characterized by

Inflectional morphemes. English also has a limited number of *inflectional morphemes*. These morphemes serve a grammatical function, but they do not change the meaning of the word. For example, the *-s* in *pans* is a plural marker and changes the word *pan* to *pans*, but it does not change the basic meaning of the word. English has only eight inflectional morphemes, and they are all suffixes (see Table 7.3)

Allomorphs

Variations of morphemes are called *allomorphs*. For example, the *-s* suffix, meaning more than one, has three allomorphs because it can be pronounced three different ways: (1) [s] as in the word *cats*, (2) [z] as in the word *pans*, and (3) [əz] as in *churches*. In each case, the meaning is the same. The process of attaching one of the three is not a random process but is governed by rules known as *morphophonemic rules* because of the relationship between phonology and morphology inherent in the rule.

Compound Words

Not all words in English are created by adding affixes to roots. English words can also be created by putting two roots together. These words are called *compound words* or *compounds*. Examples of compound words would be *textbook, birdcage, schoolhouse*, and *bluegreen*. In compound words, one of the morphemes must function as the *head* and determine both the meaning and grammatical category for the word. The morpheme to the right of the other morphemes is the root in a compound word. In the example words above, *book, cage, house*, and *green* are the roots. The root also determines the *part of speech* or the *lexical category*

Table 7.3 English inflectional morphemes

Morpheme	Example	Sample Sentence
Progressive	*-ing*	He is going home tomorrow.
Past tense	*-ed*	She arrived late.
Past participle	*-en*	He has taken all of the money.
Third person present singular	*-s*	She runs every morning.
Plural marker	*-s*	The books are on the desk.
Comparative	*-er*	You are taller than he is.
Superlative	*-est*	She is the tallest of the three girls.
Possessive	*-'s*	Mary's car is in the driveway.

(see Parts of Speech in Chapter 8). In the compound words given above, *birdcage* would function as a *noun*, but *bluegreen* would function as an *adjective*. English uses compounds as nouns, verbs, prepositions, and adjectives.

Stress is important in understanding compound words and can help L2 learners know the intention of the speaker as well as communicate their intended meaning to a listener. In the examples given above, the stress is on the first syllable—*text, bird, school*, and *blue*. This stress pattern is predictable and helps listeners understand important differences in meaning, for example, the difference between a blackbird (a specific type of bird, with stress on the first syllable) and a black bird (any bird that is black, with stress on the second word).

The example compound words listed above are all examples of *closed-form compounds* because the two individual morphemes within these words are fused together. There are also *hyphenated compounds*, such as *sister-in-law* and *open-form compounds*, such as *real estate*.

Task: Explore

Circle the individual morphemes in each word below. Label the morphemes as bound (B) or free (F). Underline words that are compounds, mark the root, and identify its lexical category. Share your results with a partner.

bookworm

takeover

into

farmers

download

empty-handed

performers

adequately

concept

Morphology and English Spelling

In Chapter 6 we discussed the difficulties with English spelling in terms of its one-to-one relationship to English sounds. In spite of the fact that English spelling is irregular and is not directly phonetic, it is consistent with its morphology. Even though affixes and roots often change their pronunciation from one word to another, the spelling remains constant. This is helpful for English learners both with derivational and inflectional morphemes. It is easy to recognize that *receive* and *receipt* are related to each other, as well as *reception* and *receptivity*. If the spelling changed to be consistent with the pronunciation, it would be more difficult to see the relationships and more difficult to decipher meaning. Consider also the inflectional suffix for past tense *-ed*. Even though this morpheme has three distinct pronunciations—[ɪd] as in *waited*, [d] as in *blogged*, and [t] as in *talked*—the spelling remains consistent (i.e., *-ed*). The same is true for the plural suffix.

Morphological Typology

Morphological typology is the study and classification of language based on how morphemes create words. In order to appreciate the difficulties that language learners have in learning English, it is useful to consider some major classifications. There are two main types of languages—*analytic* and *synthetic*. In a purely analytic language all words would be free or root morphemes. Mandarin and Vietnamese are examples of languages that demonstrate this principle. The second type of language is synthetic. Synthetic languages use bound morphemes to create meaning or mark the grammatical function of a free morpheme. There are three different types of synthetic languages. In *fusional* or *inflectional* languages, such as Russian, one bound morpheme may convey several pieces of information, such as gender, plurality, and case. *Agglutinating* languages, such as Hungarian, add one specific meaning to the root morpheme for each bound morpheme. In *polysynthetic* languages, a word is equivalent to an entire sentence. A number of indigenous languages of North America display morphological principles of polysynthetic languages. Of course, this system of classification is based on ideal languages; the reality is not so black and white. Rather, languages display tendencies and generally combine features from more than one type. Nevertheless, knowing more about the different ways in which languages use morphemes to create words helps English language teachers understand the challenges their learners may face with English morphology, especially if an English learner's L1 displays an entirely different system.

How New Words Are Created

There are certain categories of words that grow and change. These categories are known as *open word classes* because new words in these categories are continually being coined. Open-class words include nouns, verbs, adjectives, and adverbs. *Closed word classes* are words such as conjunctions and prepositions. This class of words is stable and new words are rarely added to these categories. *Neologisms* (new words) are open-class words that are new to a language. They are formed by a number of different processes.

Acronyms

An *acronym* is formed by taking the first letter or letters of words. Acronyms are pronounced like words. For example, *radar* is an acronym made from the words in **ra**dio **d**etecting **and r**anging; *USA* is made from the words in **U**nited **S**tates *of America*, but it is not an acronym because it is not pronounced as a word. It is an abbreviation, because we say the individual letters when we come across it in print.

Back formation

Some words look as if they have come about by way of a derivational process (a root to which a morpheme has been added), but in fact they have not. For example, the word *television* appears as if it was derived from the root *televise*. In actuality, the word *televise* was created from the word *television* and is not the root for it; consequently, *televise* is a *back formation*. Other examples of back formations in English are *donate* (from *donation*) and *edit* (from *editor*).

Clipping

Clipping involves snipping a part of a word to create a shortened form—for example, *tats* from *tattoos, phone* from *telephone, gas* from *gasoline,* or *petrol* from *petroleum.*

Blending

Blending is a form of compounding that occurs when parts of two or more words are clipped off and blended to form a new word. For example, *brunch* is a blend of the words *breakfast* and *lunch*.

Compounding

We have already discussed this process related to combining roots. Compounding is a common way to label a new thing or activity, such as *cross-trainers, veggie-burger*, or a *mallrat* (Rowe & Levine, 2006, p. 98).

Derivation

A word is a *derivation* if it has been created by adding a derivational affix (see Table 7.2), such as (*mis*)understand and (*re*)construct. New affixes are rare.

Foreign word borrowing

As we have learned in this chapter, English has a history of borrowing words from other languages, beginning with Latin and Old Norse. Borrowing from other languages continues into the present with such common vocabulary as *yogurt* (Turkish), *casino* (Italian), and *kindergarten* (German).

People's names

Some of the most common adoptions are based on the names of people. For example, the word *sandwich* (for the fourth Earl of Sandwich, who put pieces of roast beef between two slices of bread), *Braille* (for Louis Braille who developed a system of writing for the blind), *malapropism* (after Mrs. Malaprop, a character in the play *The Rivals* by Sheridan), and *saxophone* (named for Adolphe Sax).

Trade names

When new products are created, new words are often coined to label the new products. For example, the machine that makes copies is often called a *Xerox* machine even if the machine is not made by the Xerox Company. The same sort of phenomenon is true of such words as *Kleenex, Jell-O*, and *aspirin*.

Technology

As a result of technological advances, new words are constantly being formed. Words such as *blog, webpage, eBay, email, boot up, download, upload, texting, wifi*, and *thumb drive*.

Greek and Latin roots and affixes

There are numerous Greek and Latin roots, suffixes, and prefixes that are frequently used in science and technology, particularly in medical terminology.

Common and easily recognizable prefixes include *bi-*, *bio-*, *chlor-*, *crani-*, *derm-*, *di-*, *duodeno-*, and *hydro-*. The list is extensive for roots and suffixes as well. New words in science and in medicine are often combinations of these Greek and Latin roots and affixes.

Conclusion

An understanding of the English word system is important in teaching and working with English learners, who may be either children or adults. In this chapter we have given you a brief introduction to specific historical developments in English, such as where English came from and how it is related to other languages, so that you can begin to appreciate the relationship between how English is characterized today and its historical foundations. In order to do this, we characterized English into three different periods of time and discussed specific changes that occurred during these time periods. In presenting this brief overview of English morphology, we have also included types of morphemes and the processes that govern the creation of new words in English.

Task: Expand

Gordan, T. (2012). *The educator's guide to linguistics.* Charlotte, NC: Information Age Publishing.

This book provides an accessible and reader-friendly overview of linguistic research. The book combines theory and practice and brings theoretical discussion to life by including familiar bits of language from daily life, such as names of popular business establishments, recognizable song lyrics, and famous adages. The book is meant to help future teachers in the classroom explore the practical significance of linguistic research.

Questions for Discussion

1 English has been classified as an analytic language. What analytic patterns does English display? Provide at least two different examples. Does English display characteristics of other language types? Provide specific examples. Discuss your analysis with a partner.

2 Work with a small group. What languages have your group members studied or what languages do they know? How would you classify these

languages in terms of their morphological typology? Give examples to support your decisions.

3 The following English words belong to particular lexical categories, such as nouns, verbs, and adjectives. When a prefix or a suffix is attached to one of these words, the meaning changes and so does the category to which the word belongs. Study the words below. Then determine (a) the part of speech for each word, (b) the words that can combine with the affixes, (c) the meaning of each affix, and (d) the new category to which each new word belongs. Discuss your results with a partner.

Affixes: -ful, -ly, -ity, -ion, -en, dis-, en-, in-, and re-.
Words: help, mother, quick, happy, sane, invent, cheap, honest, camp, tangle, adequate, think, consider, hope, hostile, narrate, short.

Notes

1 *Sheltered instruction* is a term used to refer to instruction in content areas (e.g., math, history, or biology) that is specifically intended for, or includes, English learners (ELs). Instruction focuses on providing a framework for the integration of content and language.
2 The Gothic language was spoken until the 8th century by the Goths in Italy and in the Iberian Peninsula in what is now Spain and Portugal.
3 Sanskrit is one of 22 official languages of India. In terms of its influence on the languages and culture in South and Southeast Asia, it is similar to Greek and Latin in Europe.
4 A root is a part of another word that serves as a building block for other words.
5 *Yiddish* literally means "Jewish." It is a High German Language that originated in the 10th century in Germany. Yiddish is written with the Hebrew alphabet as opposed to the Latin/Roman one.
6 Vikings were Norse (Scandinavian) explorers, warriors, and sometimes even pirates, who raided and colonized parts of Europe in the late 8th century. The Vikings also sailed most of the North Atlantic and even reached North America and set up settlements in present-day Newfoundland.

References

Beck, I. L. &, McKeown, M. G. (1991). Conditions of vocabulary acquisition. In R. Barr, M. L. Kamil, P. B., Mosenthal, & P. D. Pearson (Eds.). *Handbook of reading research* (Vol. 2, pp. 789–814). White Plains, NY: Longman.
Clark, M. M. (2003). *The structure of English for readers, writers, and teachers.* Glen Allen, VA: College Publishing.
Comrie, B., Matthews, S., & Polinsky, M. (2003). *The atlas of languages*, rev. ed. New York, NY: Face on File.

Curzan, A., & Adams, M. (2006). *How English works: A linguistic introduction*. New York, NY: Pearson Education.

Crystal, D. (2003a). *The Cambridge encyclopedia of the English language*, 2nd ed. Cambridge, England: Cambridge University of Press.

Crystal, D. (2003b). *English as a global language*, 2nd ed. Cambridge, England: Cambridge University Press.

D'Anna, C. A., Zechmeister, E. B., & Hall, J. W. (1991). Toward a meaningful definition of vocabulary size. *Journal of Reading Behavior, 23*, 109–122.

Fielding, L. G., Wilson, P. T., & Anderson, R. C. (1986). The new focus on free reading: The role of trade books in reading instruction. In T. Raphael & R. E. Reynolds (Eds.), *The contexts of school-based literacy* (pp. 149–160). New York, NY: Random House.

Gordan, T. (2012). *The educator's guide to linguistics*. Charlotte, NC: Information Age Publishing.

Graves, M. E., Juel, C., & Graves, B. B. (1998). *Teaching reading in the twenty-first century*. Needham Heights, MA: Allyn & Bacon.

Hirsh, D., & Nation, P. (1992). What vocabulary size is needed to read unsimplified texts for pleasure? *Reading in a Foreign Language, 8*, 689–696.

Lorge, I., & Chall, J. S. (1963). Estimating the size of vocabularies of children and adults: An analysis of methodological issues. *Journal of Experimental Education, 32*(2), 147–157.

Nagy, W. E., & Anderson, R. C. (1984). How many words are there in printed school English? *Reading Research Quarterly, 19*, 304–350.

Noack, R. & Gamlo, L. (2015). *The world's languages in 7 maps and charts*. Retrieved from www.washingtonpost.com/news/worldviews/wp/2015/04/23/the-worlds-languages-in-7-maps-and-charts/?utm_term=.a7909508448b

Rowe, B. M., & Levine, D. P. (2006). *A concise introduction to linguistics*. New York, NY: Pearson Education

Stahl, S. A. (1999). *Vocabulary development*. Cambridge, MA: Bookline Books.

8

THE SENTENCE SYSTEM

VIGNETTE

I'm struggling in my advanced grammar class in Spanish and am no doubt the worst student in the class. If all of my classmates took a vote on who should be acknowledged as the worst language learner, it's the one award I am confident I would win. I have to pass this class in order to satisfy the foreign language requirement for my MA degree, so I'm feeling under considerable pressure. Everyone else but me has lived in a Spanish-speaking country either as a study abroad student or as a missionary. In addition, we even have some native Spanish speakers in the course. I have only had two years of Spanish at the University. At the teacher's suggestion, I hire a tutor. She is a fellow MA student, a native Spanish speaker from Venezuela, and is my neighbor. Although I like her very much and believe she is trying to help me, I am frustrated. When I ask her why I have to say something in Spanish a particular way, she tells me that it's just the way Spanish works and cannot give me a reason or a rule. The depressing thing is that I study more for this class than any other class. I'm having such a hard time. I make embarrassing mistakes and cannot keep up with the other students. My tutor's own Spanish is beautiful; she is also a graduate student and an educated native speaker. When she returns to Venezuela she plans to open her own school teaching English. I don't see why she doesn't help me understand Spanish grammar rules. [Christison, research data 3/25/2004]

Task: Reflect

1 Why do you think the Spanish tutor refuses to give the graduate student the grammar rules when she asks for them?
2 Do you think the Spanish learner in the vignette is justified in thinking she is a poor language learner? Why or why not?

Introduction

The term *grammar* refers to all of the rules that govern a language. You already know that there are rules for the English sound system and the system of words (see Chapters 6 and 7), but there are also rules (i.e., a grammar) for the system that governs the formation of sentences. In this chapter we will focus on the rules that govern how words combine to form units within sentences and how units within sentences combine with one another to form sentences.

Rules that govern the grammar of a language can be either *prescriptive* or *descriptive*. Within any community of language users, there are always established ideas about what constitutes "correct" and "incorrect" language. These ideas are called prescriptive rules, and in our experience they are the ones that make teachers the most nervous. English sentences like *She don't like that song* or *I ain't going* are judged to be incorrect by standards of Modern English according to prescriptive rules. A common prescriptive rule in English is: Don't use double negatives in English sentences (e.g., *I didn't take none.*). However, the use of double negatives is a common occurrence according to the descriptive rules of English because adult speakers of English in certain dialects use double negatives in everyday interactions. In addition, double negatives used to be standard in most varieties of English (Curzan & Adams, 2006)—as they are in other languages, such as Spanish and French. Prescriptive rules appear in grammar books and style guides, but descriptive rules do not. Descriptive rules are based on how language is actually used by speakers of a language and are concerned with the rules that govern its use.

When English language teachers think of the word *grammar* they often think of prescriptive grammar rules. Although knowledge of prescriptive grammar rules is useful, we believe that there are additional key concepts that are essential for teachers who work with English learners, such as how words behave grammatically in sentences, the systematic ways in which words combine to create well-formed phrases, clauses, and sentences, and the systematic ways in which clauses and sentences are combined to create more complex sentences.

It has also been our experience that most teachers feel uncomfortable when answering technical questions about English grammar and often lose their confidence, especially if they have to answer grammar questions in front of their peers. Many English language teachers who are native speakers of English believe that they should know the prescriptive rules of English grammar even if they have not studied English grammar formally. In fact, the teachers who often know the most about English grammar and feel comfortable answering questions about sentence structure for their students are often nonnative English-speaking teachers (NNESTs) (see Chapter 2) because NNESTs have consciously learned the rules that govern English and NS teachers often have not. In the vignette above, the graduate student was frustrated with her native Spanish-speaking tutor because she could not explain Spanish grammar rules to her. She assumed that because her tutor was educated and spoke "beautiful Spanish," she also had a conscious knowledge of Spanish grammar rules. The purpose of this chapter, whether you are a native English-speaking teacher (NEST) or a NNEST, is to help you develop both your conscious knowledge of English grammar and your confidence level in explaining English sentence structure to your English learners.

In this chapter, we will introduce some basic components of *syntax*—the level of grammar that refers to "the arrangement of words and morphemes in the construction of sentences" (Rowe & Levine, 2006). Because the chapter is meant to be a brief introduction to the subject, we have selected what we believe are the most essential components needed to understand the system of English syntax and not to overwhelm you with too much detail.

Subconscious Knowledge

The notion that syntax can be viewed as the study of how we use our subconscious or tacit knowledge to construct a sentence originated in the 1950s with Chomsky (1957, 1965). He broke with the dominant approach to linguistics study (see Bloomfield, 1933) that emphasized performance—describing what the speaker actually says (also known as *surface structure*). In Chomsky's view, language learning is motivated by an internal capacity to acquire language, a subconscious or *deep structure* knowledge about one's native language. He characterizes this subconscious knowledge as *competence* because it is based on what one knows subconsciously without any attempt to acquire the information consciously.

Subconscious knowledge can be characterized in the following ways.

Completeness

Adult first language (L1) speakers have a subconscious knowledge about the completeness of sentences. A *sentence* is a string of words that is judged to be complete by competent speakers of the language. For example, consider the following examples:

> *Bill is angry.*
>
> **His office crowded.*

When given these potential sentences in English, adult L1 speakers are able to tell you with complete accuracy that *Bill is angry* is a complete sentence in English and that **His office crowded* is not a complete sentence; however, they may not be able to recite the rule that the second set of words violates.

Ambiguity

Adult speakers can also recognize when a sentence is ambiguous. For example, *Mary owns large cars and houses.* This sentence is ambiguous because it can mean that Mary owns large cars and houses of any size or that Mary owns large cars and large houses.

There are two types of ambiguity. When the constituents of a sentence can be organized in multiple ways, we call this *structural ambiguity*, as in the example above. When words have more than one meaning, we call this *lexical ambiguity*. For example, *You lost me* can have at least three interpretations: (a) a request to repeat information because you are confused, (b) a sarcastic remark to someone who said something obvious, and (c) a description of a past event in which you were literally lost (Curzan & Adams, 2006). Because lexical ambiguity is a semantic problem rather than a syntactic one, we will not deal with it in this chapter.

Word Order

L1 speakers also have a subconscious knowledge of linear word order. *Linear word order* is the sequence that different types of words follow in a sentence. For example, consider the string of words *Bill supermarket the took to car corner his.* All L1 speakers know that this string of words does not form a sentence because the word order does not sound correct to native speakers; it is not consistent with English sentence structure rules. L1 speakers would also find assembling the string of words into a complete sentence an easy task (e.g., *Bill took his car to the corner supermarket* or *Bill took the car to his corner supermarket*), but they may not be able to give you the precise rules that come into play in creating a well-formed sentence using the random words. Linear word order is language-specific. In English and other analytic languages (see Chapter 7 for an explanation about analytic languages), word order is fairly inflexible because linear word order alone often dictates the grammatical function of a word.

The relationship that nouns, pronouns, and adjectives have with verbs and other words in the sentence is known as *case*. For example, in the sentence *Cats catch mice* the word *Cats* is the subject of the sentence because it is placed before the verb. If the sentence were *Mice catch cats*, then it would mean that the mice would be doing the catching. The position of *cats* and *mice* in the sentence relative to the verb determines their case. Other languages mark case with inflectional morphemes (see Chapter 7 for an explanation about inflectional morphemes); consequently, word order in languages with numerous inflectional morphemes is not as important as it is in English.

Adult L1 speakers also have a detailed subconscious knowledge of word order within phrases—meaningful combinations of words within a sentence. When given the sentence *The man went home* and asked to insert the following words—*tall, twenty-eight-year-old, Swedish,* and *blond*—in the correct order to describe or modify *man*, most native speakers will say *The tall, blond, twenty-eight-year-old Swedish man* without any noticeable hesitation. Adult L1 speakers may not be able to articulate the rules that govern the ordering of these words; nevertheless, they have subconscious knowledge of word order.

Sentence Classification and Construction

As we illustrated above, sentence construction is not just a series of randomly combined morphemes but is based on the application of rules that govern how units are combined. In order for a sentence to be considered complete, it must have two *constituents*. Constituents are grammatical units that are combined to create sentences. There are two obligatory units in a sentence—a *subject* (or the topic of a sentence) and a *predicate* (or the assertion made about the topic). In the sentence *The customer looked at the new car, the customer* is the subject and *looked at the new car* is the predicate. (See also phrase structure rules for verb phrases [VPs] in this chapter.)

Sentences can be classified in a number of different ways, but in this chapter we will focus on three ways: (a) the number of constituents, (b) the purpose of sentences, and (d) voice.

Number of Constituents

Sentences can be classified on the basis of how many subjects and verbs they contain.

Simple sentences. A *simple sentence* contains a subject and a verb. An example of a simple sentence is *Mary slept*, where *Mary* is the subject and *slept* is the verb. Simple sentences may also have more than one subject, such as in the sentence *Ken and Kevin slept*. *Ken* and *Kevin* are both subjects of the sentence and *slept* is the verb. Simple sentences may also have more than one verb, such as in the sentence *Ken slept and then left*. *Ken* is the subject and *slept* and *left* are both verbs. Any of these combinations of verbs and subjects make simple sentences.

Compound sentences. A *compound sentence* contains at least two simple sentences, which are combined with a *coordinating conjunction* (e.g., *and, or, but*) (see Parts of Speech or Lexical Categories in this chapter). An example of a compound sentence is the following: *Mary walked home, and Sam took the bus*. Here, *Mary walked home* is the first sentence and *Sam took the bus* is the second sentence. The word *and* is the coordinating conjunction.

Complex sentences. A *complex sentence* contains at least two simple sentences combined with a *subordinating conjunction* (e.g., *although, when, because*). (See Parts of Speech or Lexical Categories in this chapter.) An example of a complex sentence is the following: *John left when his sister arrived*. Here, *John left* is the first sentence, and *his sister arrived* is the second sentence. The word *when* is the subordinating conjunction.

Clauses. Before we talk about the last type of sentence, we need to introduce the notion of clauses. A *clause* is a group of words that contains a subject and a verb, so a clause might also be a sentence. We use the term to reference sentences within sentences, such as in the example compound and complex sentences above. We will introduce two types of clauses here. The first type is an *independent clause*. Within a compound sentence, an independent clause is a subject and a predicate followed or preceded by a coordinating conjunction, such as in the compound sentence above—*Mary walked home, and Sam took the bus*. *Mary walked home* and *Sam took the bus* are both independent clauses. A compound sentence is made up of two independent clauses. The other type of clause is called a *dependent clause*. A dependent clause is preceded by a subordinating conjunction.

For example, in the complex sentence *John left when his sister arrived*, the clause *when his sister arrived* is a dependent clause because it is preceded by the word *when*, which is a subordinating conjunction. Dependent clauses are not complete sentences in English; they cannot stand alone as a complete sentence. For example, *When his sister arrived* is not a complete sentence. Dependent clauses must be attached to independent clauses in order to form a complete sentence. In the complex sentence above, *John left* is the independent clause. Dependent clauses are also referred to as *subordinate clauses* or *adverbial clauses*.

Compound-complex sentences. The last type of sentence is the *compound-complex sentence*. It has at least one dependent clause and at least two independent clauses. An example compound-complex sentence is *She missed the announcement because she was absent from class, but she heard it on the radio later in the morning*. Here, *because she was absent from class* is the dependent clause. The independent clauses are *she missed the announcement* and *she heard it on the radio later in the morning*.

Task: Explore

Work with a partner. Generate four different types of sentences in English—one of each type. Circle the required constituents (i.e., subjects and verbs) and label the clauses. Check your work with another partnership or write selected sentences on the board for a large group discussion with your instructor.

The Purpose of Sentences

Another way that sentences can be categorized is on the basis of their purpose. There are four common ways in which sentences can be categorized according to their purpose—declarative, interrogative, imperative, and exclamatory.

Declarative sentences. The purpose of *declarative sentences* is to make statements, such as the following: *We took the car home. She can pay the bill. Her car is not red*. Statements can be of different types. *We took the car home* is a simple affirmative statement. *She CAN pay the bill*, with an emphasis on the word *can*, is an emphatic statement. *Her car is not red* is a negative statement. Negative statements express denial, refusal, or the opposite of something that is positive (e.g., *John is here / John is not here*).

Interrogative sentences. *Interrogative sentences* ask questions, as in the following sentences: *Who took the car home? Is this her car? What did she do with the car? She's going, isn't she?* There are basically three different types of questions in English—wh- questions, yes/no questions, and tag questions. *Who took the car home?* and *What did she do with the car?* are examples of *wh- questions*. *Wh- questions* begin with one of the wh- words—*who, what, when, where, why,* and *how. Is this her car?* is an example of a yes/no question because it can be answered with the words *yes* or *no. Tag questions* are statements followed by reduced yes/no questions that are syntactically related to the declarative statement, such as *She's going, isn't she?*

Imperative sentences. The purpose of *imperative sentences* is to give commands, as in the sentences *Shut the door. Give me the car keys. Take his car.* The subject in imperative sentences is understood to be *you* and is not written.

Exclamatory sentences. *Exclamatory sentences* show strong or sudden feelings, such as in the sentences *Oh, if I had only known!* I can't believe it! You cannot take my car!

Voice

English sentences are either in the *active* or *passive* voice. *Voice* is a reference to the relationship a verb has with its subject and object. All verbs can have an active voice, but only those verbs in English that take an object (see Lexical Categories in this chapter) can have a passive voice. In sentences with an active voice, such as *Bill ate the pie*, the grammatical subject of the verb (e.g., *Bill*) carries out an activity or purpose. In a sentence with a passive voice, the grammatical object (e.g., *the pie*) is moved to the place of the grammatical subject (*Bill*) and the verb undergoes a change to a passive construction to become *The pie was eaten by Bill*. The passive voice is often used to hide who is doing what to whom and who is responsible for what or when you may not know who is responsible; consequently, it is common to hear passive sentences without the *by* phrase, as in *The pie was eaten*.

Lexical Categories

In descriptive grammar we distinguish between the *grammatical form* of a word and its *function* in a phrase, clause, or sentence. Grammatical form refers to the lexical category of a word (e.g., whether it is a verb, noun, pronoun).

Traditionally, words can be categorized into eight *lexical categories* or *parts of speech*. Some of these parts of speech or lexical categories are referred to as open class categories and some of them are closed class categories. Open and closed classes are also referred to by some scholars as content (i.e., open) and functional (i.e., closed) categories. The *open class categories* are nouns, adjectives, verbs, and adverbs. We call them open class words because it is common for new words to be added to these categories. *Closed class categories*—auxiliary verbs, complementizers, conjunctions, determiners, intensifiers, prepositions, pronouns, and quantifiers—seldom admit new members to their ranks.

Nouns

A *noun* is defined as a person, place, thing, idea, quality, or condition. Nouns function in sentences as subjects, objects of verbs (i.e., they receive the action of the verb), and objects of prepositions as in the sentence *Mary* took the *cats* to the *hospital*. The underlined words are all nouns. The word *Mary* functions as the subject of the sentence, *cats* as the object of the verb, and *hospital* as the object of the preposition.

Nouns can also be defined on the basis of the place in specific environments in which they occur—for example, after articles (*a, an,* and *the*). The word *hospital* can be defined as a noun because it occurs after the article *the*. Nouns can also be defined on the basis of their occurrence after adjectives, and articles are technically adjectives. In addition, regular nouns can be defined on the basis of the addition of the inflectional morpheme -*s* (plural), which creates three allomorphs in spoken English—/ s /, / z /, or / ɪz /, as in the words *cats, dogs*, and *watches*.

There are different ways to classify nouns. *Proper nouns* reference specific people and places, such as *California Avenue, Café Madrid*, or *Jane Smith*. *Common nouns* are not specific, such as *avenue, café, man, door*, or *chair*. *Mass nouns* reference concepts, such as *beef, butter*, and *water*. We also differentiate between concrete and abstract nouns. *Concrete nouns* refer to tangible things, such as *tables, cars, dogs*, and *plants*. *Abstract nouns* reference intangible things, such as *faith, love*, and *kindness*.

English also characterizes some nouns as *countable* and others as *uncountable*. The concept of whether a noun can be counted is a grammatical one for English and has little to do with the physical notion of counting items. There is no logical reason why *milk, peanut butter, coffee*, and *water* should be classified as uncountable nouns; nevertheless, uncountable nouns cannot be made plural in the same way as regular nouns. In order to make uncountable nouns plural, we add specific quantifier phrases to the noun, such as *two cartons of milk, three jars of peanut butter, four cups of coffee*, or *five liters of water*. Of course, as we discussed in Chapter 6, languages are constantly changing and there are always exceptions being created, such as in the phrase we recently recorded, *Can you grab a couple of waters, please?* and *We'll just have two coffees.*

Pronouns

A *pronoun* substitutes for a noun or a noun phrase. Like nouns, pronouns can be placed in different categories. *Personal pronouns* take the place of specific persons or things. In sentences, they take the place of subjects (e.g., *she, he, you*) or objects (e.g., *her, him, them*). Personal pronouns are inflected for number, gender, and case, and they can also be *possessive*—showing ownership (e.g., *mine, hers, theirs*). Table 8.1 illustrates the pronouns in English, including those pronouns that function as adjectives.

There are four other types of pronouns. *Demonstrative* pronouns point out what is being referred to in the sentence (i.e., *this, that, these*, and *those*). In the sentence *This is my book*, the word *this* functions as a demonstrative pronoun. *Interrogative* pronouns are used to ask questions (e.g., *who, what, whoever*), as in *Who is going to call her? Relative* pronouns (e.g., *that, who, whom*) are used to relate or connect one phrase or clause to another phrase or clause (see the discussion of phrases in this chapter). In the sentence *I took the keys that were on the table*, the word *that* replaces the word *keys* and is used to link two clauses *I took the keys* and *The keys were on the table. Reflexive* pronouns are formed from personal pronouns and can be inflected for person and number, as shown in Table 8.2 below.

Table 8.1 Pronouns in English

Number	Person	Gender	Subject	Object	Possessive Adjective	Possessive Pronoun
Singular	First person	—	I	me	my	mine
	Second person	—	you	you	your	yours
	Third person	masculine	he	him	his	his
		feminine	she	her	her	hers
		neuter	it	it	its	—
		generic	one/you	one/you	one's/your	—
Plural	First person	—	we	us	our	ours
	Second person	—	you	you	your	yours
	Third person	—	they	them	their	theirs

Table 8.2 Reflexive pronouns

Reflexive Pronouns	Gender	Singular	Plural
First person	—	myself	ourselves
Second person	—	yourself	yourselves
Third person	masculine	himself	themselves
	feminine	herself	-
	neuter	itself	-

Adjectives

In general, *adjectives* give more information about nouns or pronouns. We call this concept of providing more information *modification*. For example, in the sentence *John is happy*, the word *happy* is an adjective because it gives us more information about John's state of mind. *Happy* is said to modify *John*. In the sentence *She lives in the white house*, the word *white* is an adjective because it gives us more information about *house*. The word *white* is said to modify *house*. *Article*s (i.e., *a, an,* and *the*) are also adjectives in this particular categorization; however, because they function differently from other adjectives and the system is quite complicated, a thorough discussion of the article system is beyond the scope of this chapter.

Adjectives also can show degrees and relationships, such as in the sentences *She is taller than I am (comparative)* or *He is the tallest person I know (superlative)*. The comparative and superlative forms are created by adding either an inflectional suffix *-er* or *-est* or the modifiers *more* and *the most* or *less* and *the least*. English follows the general rule that one-syllable adjectives take inflectional endings (e.g., *shorter/shortest*), three or more syllables take the modifiers (*more beautiful/the most beautiful*), and two-syllable adjectives can often do either (e.g., *prettier/the prettiest/* or *more pretty/the most pretty*). Of course, as with any rule in English, there are always exceptions. We wouldn't say *purpler*, and both of us think that *funner* and *funnest* sound strange.

Adjectives can appear in attributive or predicative positions. In general, the *attributive position* refers to the position before the noun, such as *smart students*. The *predicative position* refers to the position after the verb, such as *The soup smells tasty*.

Verbs

Verbs express actions, conditions, or states of being. They typically have five forms: the bare infinitive form, third person present tense singular, all past tense forms, progressive constructions, and the past participle. Table 8.3 lists the forms of verbs, with example sentences.

Table 8.3 Forms of verbs

Verb Form	Examples
Infinitive or base form	I *eat* lunch.
	She has gone *to eat* lunch.
	We *must eat*.
	We *don't eat*.
	Eat!
	I suggest that *she eat*.
Third person singular present tense	He *eats* lunch there every Saturday.
Past tense form (regular *-ed* and irregular forms)	She walk*ed* to the restaurant
	I *ate* lunch there yesterday.
Present participle (*-ing*)	We *are eating* lunch now.
	They *were eating* lunch there yesterday.
Past participle (-ed plus irregular forms)	She has eaten.
	They have written.
	The letter was mailed.
	The bread was cut.

Verbs can be *transitive* (taking a direct object), *intransitive* (not requiring an object), or *ditransitive* (taking both direct and indirect objects, such as in the sentence *He gave Lisa the book*—where *Lisa* is the indirect object and *book* is the direct object). Some verbs can also be both transitive and intransitive depending on the meaning of the verb. Some verbs are called *linking* or *copula* verbs. For example, in the sentence *John is happy* above, the verb *is* links the subject *John* and the adjective *happy*. These verbs do not show action but link the subject of a sentence to the adjective. Another category of verbs is called *auxiliary* verbs. These verbs are used to assist other verbs in forming tenses (i.e., past, present, and future). *To be* and *to have* are the main auxiliary verbs; however, *modals*, such as *may, might, should*, and *have to* are also considered in this categorization. Verbs can be recognized by their affixes, for example, -ate, -ify, ize, -en, and en-, such as in the words designate, exemplify, itemize, lighten, and enroll.

Main verbs occur after *auxiliary* or *modal* verbs (e.g., *You should study*). They also occur alone in imperative sentences (e.g., *Leave!*). They can appear alone after a subject (e.g., *We left*), and between a subject and an object (e.g., *We took her things*).

English has three tenses—past, present, and future. Each of these tenses can be combined with the *perfect aspect* (*have* plus *past participle*, such as *eaten, gone, taken, walked, put*, and *mailed*) or the *progressive aspect* (a form of the verb *to be* plus *-ing*) (Clark, 2003). Table 8.4 provides examples of how the tenses

Table 8.4 Examples of tense and aspect interaction in English

Tense	Aspect	Example Sentences
Present	—	She eats lunch.
	Progressive	She is eating lunch.
	Perfect	She has eaten lunch.
	Perfect progressive	She has been eating.
Past	—	She ate lunch.
	Progressive	She was eating lunch.
	Perfect	She had eaten lunch.
	Perfect progressive	She had been eating lunch.
Future	—	She will eat lunch.
	Progressive	She will be eating lunch.
	Perfect	She will have eaten lunch.
	Perfect progressive	She will have been eating lunch.

Note: This table is not intended to be an exhaustive list of tenses in English.

interact with the different aspects. In Table 8.4 below, *will* appears as the traditional future construction, although it is not the only way to reference the future in English. The *will* construction is the same as other modal verbs, such as *should, could, can, would, might.*

Adverbs

Like adjectives, *adverbs* can modify, and they modify verbs, adjectives, other adverbs, and even sentences. In the sentence *He quickly washed the dishes*, the adverb *quickly* modifies (or gives more information about) the verb *washed*. In the sentence *It was an extremely difficult exam*, the adverb *extremely* modifies or gives more information about the adjective *difficult*. In the sentence, *She performed exceedingly well on the last exam*, the adverb *exceedingly* modifies another adverb, *well*. Finally, in the sentence *Frankly, you should buy a new car*, the adverb *frankly* modifies the entire sentence. Sentence adverbs are also called *discourse* adverbs. Adverbs can also show degree, such as in the sentence above, *It was an extremely difficult exam*. Adverbs of degree tell us about the intensity of something. The words *too, enough, extremely*, and *very* are some examples of adverbs of degree.

Adverbs have different functions. There are adverbs of *manner* (e.g., *happily*). Manner adverbs describe how an action or state occurs. *Temporal* adverbs describe when an action or state occurs (e.g., *tomorrow, yesterday, soon*). *Place* adverbs describe where an action or state occurs (*e.g., somewhere*). There are also *frequency* (e.g., *never* and *occasionally*) and *direction* (e.g., *toward*) adverbs.

Adverbs can occur in different positions in a sentence, occurring at the beginning or end of a clause and directly before or after a main verb. All of the positions in the sentences below are grammatically correct:

> *Slowly* I read through the letter.
> I *slowly* read through the letter.
> I read *slowly* through the letter.
> I read through the letter *slowly*.

Even though there is considerable flexibility in adverb placement, adverbs cannot appear between an adjective and the noun it modifies, as in **a long absurdly lecture*.

Prepositions

Prepositions are difficult to define. Most often they are indicators of location or position (e.g., *up, down, in, on, into, by, off*). Prepositions can also be used to indicate direction, time, duration, manner, and other relationships. In English, prepositions introduce or come before nouns or noun phrases, such as *in the room* or *on the desk*.

Conjunctions

Conjunctions connect words or group of words. *Coordinating conjunctions* connect equal units, such as independent clauses (e.g., *John went home, but Mary didn't go with him*). There are five coordinating conjunctions—*and, or, nor, but,* and *so.* There are also *correlative conjunctions.* They also connect equal units, but the conjunctions occur in pairs (*either ... or, neither ... nor, not only ... but also*), such as in the sentence *She not only cooked the dinner but also did the dishes. Subordinating conjunctions* (e.g., *when, after, before, because, as soon as, while*) connect unequal units (e.g., dependent and independent clauses), such as in the sentence *As soon as she finished the dishes, she left.*

Interjections

An *interjection* is not a critical part of a sentence, grammatically speaking. It can be deleted from the sentence without destroying the grammatical structure of the sentence. However, interjections are important in writing and in spoken language because they are most often used to express emotions or feelings (e.g., *Oh*, *you can't mean that! Well, you don't really know what the truth is.*).

Determiners

Determiners introduce noun phrases, such as *the tall, blond, Swedish man.* They come before adjectives that modify nouns. In addition to the articles *a, an,* and *the,* determiners indicate quantity (e.g., *some, many, all*), number (e.g., *three, four, second, third*), and specification (e.g., *this* and *that*). All determiners except articles *a, an,* and *the* can also occur as pronouns, such as in the sentence *All of the boats have left.* They are considered pronouns when they stand alone and determiners when they modify.

Task: Explore

Determine the parts of speech of each word in the following sentences, including the subtypes of the part of speech. Discuss your results with a partner.

Some students never finish.

Some of the students failed the test.

She tested the food before she served it.

I have never been here before.

The boys became restless and left before they came home.

Phrases

The syntax of a language depends on how words work together as syntactic units or constituents. These syntactic units are arranged hierarchically:

sentence

↓

clause

↓

phrase

↓

word

Phrases are combinations of words that create syntactic units. There are five types of phrases in English—noun phrases (NP), verb phrases (VP), adjective phrases (ADJP), adverb phrases (ADVP), and prepositional phrases (PP). *Phrase structure rules* outline the rules that govern membership in these phrases and indicate how the phrases are embedded in clauses and sentences. In other words, they represent the hierarchical structure of constituents. Below is a summary of one relatively basic set of phrase structure rules for the major types of constituent phrases. The units in parentheses indicate that the constituent is optional.

NP→   (DET) (ADJ) N (PP)

ADJP → (ADV) ADJ

VP→   (ADVP) V (NP/S) (PP) (ADVP)

ADVP   → (ADV) ADV

PP→   P NP

The phrase structure rule for a noun phrase (NP) states that at the very least a noun phrase must have a noun since it is the only syntactic unit not in parentheses. Optional features of an NP are a determiner (DET), an adjective (ADJ), or a prepositional phrase (PP). Adjective phrases (ADJP) must have at least an adjective, with an adverb (ADV) being optional. A verb phrase (VP) must have at least a verb (V), but it can also have an ADVP, NP/S (noun phrase/sentence), a PP, and an ADVP. An ADVP must have at least an ADV, but it can also have a modifying ADV. A prepositional phrase (PP) must have both a P and an NP; there are no optional members in a PP.

   A phrase can function as a *nominal* (in other words, a constituent that functions as a noun), an adjective, or an adverb. Table 8.5 outlines the types of phrases and example sentences that represent the type.

   Phrase structure rules can be very helpful to you in understanding the overall structure of English sentences, and they seem to account for all of the various kinds of sentences we can create. However, in reality, these rules do not account for all surface structures.

Table 8.5 Types of phrases

Function	Types of Phrase	Example Sentences
Nominal	NP	I left *this hurried note.*
	PP	I left this hurried note *on the counter.*
	Infinitive phrase	I want *to know what the note said.*
	Gerund phrase	*Knowing what the note said* is important.
Adjectival	ADJP	I have an *incredibly cute* dog.
	PP	My dog eats the lids *from the cereal box.*
	Relative clause	I took the lids *that the dog had chewed.*
	Infinitive phrase	I want the dog *to stop chewing the lids.*
	Participial phrase	My dog is enamored *with chewing cereal box lids.*
Adverbial	ADVP	She uses the desk *ridiculously often.*
	PP	She uses the desk *with the new computer.*
	NP	He planned to use the desk *yesterday.*
	Infinitive phrase	She moved the desk *to get better light.*
	Participial phrase	She stayed up all night *typing the report.*

Types of Clauses

Relative Clauses

Relative clauses are clauses that are introduced by relative pronouns (*who, whom, whose, which, that*), such as in the sentences *The book that was on the table is missing* or *I know the man who is wearing the blue shirt*. Relative clauses function as adjectives and can modify either subjects or objects. In the sentence *The book that was on the table is missing*, the relative clause *that was on the table* gives more information about *the book*, which is the subject of the sentence. In the sentence *I know the man who is wearing the blue shirt*, the relative clause *who is wearing the blue shirt* gives more information about *the man*, which is the direct object in the sentence.

Relative clauses can be of two types—restrictive or nonrestrictive. *Restrictive relative clauses* limit information by specifying exactly what the noun is referring to—for example, *She needs to take the book that was written by her professor*. It is not just any book, but the book *that was written by her professor*. *Nonrestrictive relative clauses* provide additional information about the noun or noun phrases but do not restrict it, such as in the sentence *She needs to take the book, which she saw on the desk*.

Complementizer Clauses

Complementizer clauses are dependent clauses that function as NPs. They are typically introduced by *that* or other *wh-* words, such as *whether, why, what, where, who, whom*, or *how*. Complementizer clauses can serve as subjects in sentences. For example, in the sentence *That she lost the book surprised me*, the complementizer clause *that she lost the book*, functions as the subject of the sentence. In the sentence *We don't know whether she lost the book*, the clause *whether she lost the book* functions as the object of the verb *know*.

Conclusion

In this chapter we have introduced you to some basic concepts associated with English syntax (i.e., how morphemes and words are combined to form English sentences) that are designed to focus your attention on the big picture of sentence structure. Once you have a basic understanding of English syntax, you have the tools to help you build your confidence with English syntax and help you assist English language learners in classroom environments. We began our discussion with a brief overview of subconscious knowledge that adult speakers have of their L1. We then turned our attention to sentence classification and lexical categories. Rather than give you prescriptive rules for sentence structure, we have tried to describe how syntactic units combine to form sentences by introducing constituent hierarchy and basic phrase structure rules.

Task: Expand

If you are interested in learning more about English grammar, visit this popular site. It serves as an excellent tutorial and reference guide for both you and your students.

www.ccc.commnet.edu/grammar

Questions for Discussion

1   Consider the following sentences without referring to Table 8.4. Consider the sentences below. In each sentence, identify the type of phrase (e.g., NP, PP, ADJP) in italics and determine its function.

    a   I left *this hurried note*.
    b   My dog is enamored *with chewing cereal box lids*.
    c   I stayed up all night *typing the report*.
    d   I want *to know what the note said*.

e She uses the desk *ridiculously often.*

f He planned to use the desk *yesterday.*

2 This chapter focused on the kinds of sentences that adult L1 speakers accept as grammatical in their descriptive sense of grammaticality. What prescriptive rules can you think of in English that also deal with the issue of what constitutes a well-formed sentence in English? How might spoken English violate some of those rules?

References

Bloomfield, L. (1933). *Language.* New York, NY: Holt, Rinehart, and Winston.

Chomsky, N. (1957). *Syntactic structures.* The Hague, The Netherlands: Mouton.

Chomsky, N. (1965). *Aspects of the theory of syntax.* Cambridge, MA: MIT Press.

Clark, M. (2003). *The structure of English for readers, writers, and teachers.* Glen Allen, VA: College Publishing.

Curzan, A., & Adams, M. (2006). *How English works: A linguistic introduction.* New York, NY: Pearson Education.

Rowe, B. M., & Levine, D. P. (2006). *A concise introduction to linguistics.* New York, NY: Pearson Education.

9

BEYOND THE SENTENCE

Spoken and Written Language

VIGNETTE

This conversation took place between a teacher who is a native speaker of American English and an international student from Armenia in the (then) Soviet Union. The conversation took place before class. Pseudonyms are used to preserve anonymity.

Transcription conventions:

? = rising intonation

[= overlapping

. = slight pause

Clare:	*I have an "ian" maiden[1] name too so that's why I wondered about you what was the name of the place in Russia that you were from*
Katerina:	*Iskandar*
Clare:	*Iskandar?*
Katerina:	*Iskandar*
Clare:	*oh, Iskandar. That's the name of a place?*
Katerina:	*ian means from Iskandar*
	[
Clare:	*right uh so what part what's the province Iskandar is in?*
	[
Katerina:	*Caucasus I don't know*
	[
Clare:	*oh Caucusus Caucusus*
Katerina:	*because I don't know*

(continued)

157

(continued)

[

Clare: *Caucusus I'm sorry right Caucusus oh yea Caucusus mountains Caucusus mountains well there were a lot of Armenians in there well not necessarily in the Caucusus mountains was weren't there a lot of Armenian settlements? Not any more*

Katerina: *Yes I know*

[

Clare: *yes cause I used to study Soviet Russian language and culture and that sort of thing but how long ago did your family go to Iran?*

Katerina: *seventy years*

[

Clare: *seven years?*

Katerina: *Seventy years*

Clare: *Seventy years so your grandparents or great-grandparents*

[

Katerina: *grandparents*

Clare: *I guess they have quite a few nationalities there in Iran because of its location. They have quite a few minorities not minorities but different national groups*

Katerina: *yes people from*

[

Clare: *lots of different countries there Syrian and Turkish and you know originals back a few generations not right now*

[

Katerina: *uhm*

[Murray research data 7/20/1982]

Task: Reflect

1 Do you think this was a successful conversation?
2 What surprised you about this conversation?
3 In an ESL/EFL textbook, find a conversation where people are asking questions of each other to get to know each other. How different is the textbook conversation from the one above?
4 What strategies did Clare use to try to keep the floor—that is, to keep speaking?

Introduction

Most people when they see their first authentic transcript are surprised and even shocked because they thought that people spoke in sentences as they do when they write. On first glance, spoken conversation looks disorganized and even difficult to understand from a transcript. However, as we will explain in this chapter, spoken language is just as rule-governed as written language, even though it follows different rules. English language teachers need to understand the structures and features of both spoken and written language in order to be able to develop instruction that explicitly helps learners acquire the registers and genres they need for their specific purposes.

In Chapter 8 we provided you with tools for analyzing language at the sentence level. In this chapter, we go beyond the sentence to examine how spoken and written language are organized. Because each person's contribution in spoken conversation is not necessarily a complete sentence, as we saw in the vignette, each contribution is called an *utterance*. A number of disciplines study language beyond the sentence level so that terminology varies across the disciplines, and even within linguistics there is variation, depending on the school of linguistics. Van Dijk (1977) uses *text* for the abstract theoretical construct, with its linguistic realization being *discourse*, whereas for Halliday (1978) language is abstract and realized in *text* (either spoken or written). Some researchers use *text* for written language and *discourse* for spoken language (Cicourel, 1975) while others use *text* and *talk* (Tannen, 1982). Still there are other researchers who use *text, discourse,* and *conversation* almost interchangeably. *Ethnomethodologists* claim that conversation is the most basic of human language interactions and that all other types are variations on conversation (Schegloff, 1972). Conversation in lay terms seems to be something everyone recognizes even if they cannot identify its structure. However, even conversation has subsets, with casual conversation or *chat* the most difficult to describe.

We begin with a discussion of the differences between spoken and written language to show that the differences are less to do with whether the language is spoken or written, and more to do with who the interlocutors are (that is, the speakers), what their relationships are, and what they are talking about. We then discuss spoken language from a number of different perspectives. Finally, we describe the way written language is structured.

Differences and Similarities in Spoken and Written Language

It is important to begin with a discussion of how written and spoken language differ and are similar because the concept of literacy has been tied solely to the written language and associated with ways of thinking. This conceptualization of literacy has led to the practice of attributing different ways of thinking to literate and pre-literate cultures and to the development of large literacy programs around the world, not all of which have been beneficial to those who learn to become literate. *Orality* is often used to refer to spoken language, contrasting it with *literacy*. Although oral language preceded written language in human development, the written language has been much more extensively studied by linguists (and others), so there is a sense that, with some study, anyone can learn the rules of written language. Spoken language is also rule-governed, but native speakers of a language are not conscious of these rules. They are, however, aware when conventions have been breached.

Similarities in Spoken and Written Language

Whether spoken or written, language beyond the sentence has three characteristics. *Cohesion* refers to the linguistic features used to relate sentences or utterances to each other across sentence or utterance boundaries. *Coherence* refers to how the text makes sense. *Register* refers to varieties that result from characteristics of the use or function to which the language is put. *Genre* refers to the staged, culturally typical ways of engaging rhetorically with recurring situations (Ferguson, 1986; Martin, 1984). We will discuss each of these below.

Cohesion. Cohesion allows speakers and writers to indicate that passages of language of more than one sentence or utterance are a unified whole, rather than a collection of unrelated sentences. Proficient users of English would identify the following as not being a cohesive text:

> John walked into the living room. Therefore, she turned on the hose and dried the dishes.

However, they would also identify that the following short text is cohesive:

> After dinner, Jean brought the dirty dishes into the kitchen. He then filled the sink with hot soapy water and washed them. His sister Aimée dried them and put some in the cupboard. The rest she left on the counter, which she did every night. She hated washing the dishes. So, she always let her brother do that chore.

This short text illustrates a number of cohesive devices.

Lexical cohesion. *Lexical cohesion* refers to words in the same semantic field. So, in the text above, a number of nouns often occur in the same text because they are in the same semantic area. In this case, the semantic area is *meal in a house* and the nouns are *dinner, dishes, kitchen, sink, cupboard.* In addition, the use of the determiner *the* identifies that the writer is talking about a specific house. English, unlike some other languages, prefers synonyms to repetitions of the same word. So, in the above text, the writer uses the word *chore* as a synonym for *washing the dishes* because it has already been used twice in the passage (note we just used *text* and *passage* to avoid repetition). Choosing an appropriate synonym is often difficult for second language learners because they need to acquire a range of words with similar meanings. In speech, we often use the generic word *thing*, even though this is not considered appropriate in formal writing.

Reference. A number of parts of speech are used for *reference*, including determiners and personal, demonstrative, and comparative words. In Chapter 7, we discussed personal and demonstrative pronouns and adjectives, and comparative adjectives and adverbs. In the text above, the pronouns *he, his, she, her, that,* and *them* are all used to show the relationship across sentences. In spoken language, the physical context can usually explain references, such as *that book,* if the person is holding or pointing to the book. In written language, the writer needs to be more explicit and be certain that the reader knows what the reference word is referring to. The following is ambiguous:

> John and Howard went to the movies last night. It was a really scary movie, and he was frightened.

We don't know whether it was John or Howard who was frightened.

Grammatical cohesion. A variety of types of *grammatical cohesion* are illustrated in the text above. *Substitution* can be either nominal or clausal. *Some* and *the rest* both substitute for *dishes* in the text above. The verbal substitute in English is *do* and, in the above text, *did* substitutes for *left. Ellipsis* refers to omitting words, phrases, or clauses. In this same sentence, *the rest on the counter* is omitted. *Conjunctions* of various types (see Chapter 7) signify the relationship of ideas across sentences. In the above text, *then,* a temporal conjunctive, tells the reader that the washing of the dishes occurred after he brought them into the kitchen. *So* indicates that the reason she dried the dishes and put them away was because she hated washing dishes.

Coherence. Cohesion is a device for facilitating coherence of a text, but in and of itself it does not guarantee coherence. The following text, while employing a number of cohesive devices, is not coherent.

> We have lots of money. Money makes the world go round. The world is a sphere. A ball is also a sphere. However, a ball does not cost a lot.

This text utilizes cohesive devices of lexical cohesion, conjunction, and reference, but most readers would not consider it a coherent text because it does not entirely make sense. Yet the following example, which has little cohesion, is comprehensible.

> A: Have you got a light?

> B: Sorry, I don't smoke.

How do speakers know the second text makes sense? It is because it follows expected schemata about how texts function and because of the speakers' previous experiences with similar texts. *Schemata* are mental representations of information that are built up over time. As such, they are founded on background knowledge, textual knowledge, and cultural knowledge and frame how we interact. Over time, these become established in a speech community to become genres (see below).

Register. In Chapter 2, we discussed how language varies according to the characteristics of the user. Here, we show how language varies according to its use. Different linguistic traditions treat register differently, and here we will focus on those areas that these different traditions have in common. Linguistic features such as lexical cohesion and syntax are common across texts of the same register. For example, speakers of English would recognize a text with words such as *thunderstorm, isobars, humidity, wind velocity*, or *precipitation* as typical of a text about weather. These are all formal words, so the context must be formal; colloquial words would not be expected. If the speaker were talking with his friends after work, he might use more informal words such as *raining cats and dogs* (for heavy rain), *sticky* (for humid), *lousy* (for bad weather), or *blowing a gale* (for strong wind). Registers also have typical syntactic structures. For example, passive voice is often used in newspaper reports to avoid identifying the perpetrator. Future tense is used for weather forecasts while past is used for a weather report. Second language learners often find it difficult to choose the appropriate register for the particular context. They mix vocabulary and syntax from different registers—for example, using reduced forms in formal speech or a formal document.

Researchers have also identified a number of *simplified registers*. They are considered simplified because they do not follow the usual linguistic rules but instead use simplification such as abbreviations, acronyms, subject deletion, verb reduction, slow, exaggerated pronunciation and intonation, short sentences, special lexicons, and feedback devices that facilitate listener comprehension.

Simplified registers occur because of communication limitations. The speaker might perceive the listener to be not fully competent in the language and simplifies language to facilitate communication with the listener. Thus, we have *foreigner talk* (talking to a nonnative speaker [NNS]), *teacher talk* (teachers talking to students), and *caretaker talk* (adults talking to babies and young children). Other limitations may be because of time or space, and so we have newspaper headlines, advertising, and note-taking as simplified registers. More recently, we have seen the proliferation of simplified language in texting, which includes the different strategies mentioned above.

Genre. Different linguistic traditions also use the term *genre* differently. Here we will focus on common understandings of the term. Genres have specific schematic structures and use predictable language so that they have become conventions over time. Speakers of a language recognize and can differentiate among genres. They can recognize a wedding ceremony or a joke or a laboratory report. Table 9.1 shows the features of the genre *report*, while Table 9.2 shows the features for a *recount*. A recount is where a speaker or writer tells of an event she or he experienced.

These two genres are, therefore, distinguishable to competent speakers of English. However, young children often have difficulty moving from a recount of something that happened to them to the more objective, formal report structure, as in the following task.

Table 9.1 Structure of reports

Schematic Structure	Syntactic Features

• Opening statement of general classification
 • Series of descriptive paragraphs
   o Functions
   o Qualities
   o Behaviors
	• Generic (not specific) participants
	 • Simple present tense
	 • Verbs be and have
	 • Subject of sentences often the item being reported on

Table 9.2 Structure of recounts

Schematic Structure	Syntactic Features
• Orientation to the context • Records of events, usually series of paragraphs in temporal sequence • Reorientation with a closure of the events • Optional coda with a comment on the events	• Specific participants • Past tense • Verbs of action • Temporal connectives to indicate sequence of events • Time and place phrases

---

Task: Explore

The following text was written by a young child. She was asked to write a report. Identify the features of a report in her text. What features show that she has not yet acquired all the features of a report?

Things that float

Things float because they are light. Some things float and some things fly. I saw a boat floating on a big river. I saw a helicopter flying in the air. (Hammond, 1986, p. 84)

Register and genre intersect. Genres use specific registers. So, for example, a chemistry lab report includes the register of formal chemistry, as well as the schematic structure and syntactic features of the genre of report.

Differences in Spoken and Written Language

As well as having features in common, spoken and written language are different in how they are learned. Most people acquire spoken language naturally through interactions with other people. Writing, on the other hand, needs to be consciously taught. As well as being learned differently, speaking and writing have different conventions of use. Table 9.3 shows the differences between the two modes of interaction.

Although speaking and writing differ in many ways, there is no dichotomy between the two modes. Rather, variation is the result of who speaks to whom for what purposes. Therefore, a spoken formal speech has more attributes of

Table 9.3 Characteristics of spoken and written language

Spoken Language	Written Language
spontaneous	planned
interactive	edited
immediate style	reported style
situated context	abstract context
focus on involvement	focus on content
prosodic and paralinguistic features	punctuation/lexical items
a world of happenings	a world of things
more than one participant	single writer
fragmentary	integrative
inexplicit	explicit
meaning is what speaker meant	meaning is what speaker said

written language than does an informal written email because of the context of the situation—who is speaking to whom, about what, and for what purposes. We now move on to describing spoken language and written language.

Spoken Language

A number of different traditions and perspectives have been used to analyze spoken language. Researchers from a wide range of disciplines have studied spoken language: anthropology, education, sociology, linguistics, and philosophy. Some analysts have looked at the language only, especially at how the speakers organize their interaction; others have examined the language as it relates to the context; yet others have looked at what speakers are using language for; still others have looked at errors in spoken language.

Conversation Analysis

Conversational analysis (CA) approaches to spoken language seek to uncover order in what seems to be chaotic, and are mostly associated with a group in the United States called *ethnomethodologists*. To determine this order, they separate language from its context, adopting a bottom-up approach, beginning at the most local level. Further, they work on conversation as it unfolds, not even waiting until the conversation is over to begin their analysis. They take this approach because they maintain that a researcher must be at the same point of an utterance as the participants in order to understand why they do

165

what they do, how they do it, and how they make sense of it. This process may seem at odds with what we discussed in Part I about the importance of context; however, CA has described many phenomena not previously identified by other methods (e.g., turn-taking, adjacency pairs, and openings, which we discuss in detail below). The transcript is the sole data source for CA; therefore, transcripts include all pauses (including their lengths), often intonation patterns, and all vocalizations, even if they are not words. The unit of analysis is not the sentence. As we showed in the vignette, spoken language is not a series of sentences. Hence, a different unit of analysis had to be used—namely, an utterance, which refers to the content of a turn.

Discourse Analysis

In contrast to CA, *discourse analysis (DA)* considers both the transcript and the context, and in some linguistic approaches includes written language. As well as describing the context, many DA researchers also video-record the interaction and play it back to each participant, asking them what they were doing and questioning why they said or did what they did.

We will summarize the findings from both these approaches to studying spoken language and examine how conversations start and end, how people take turns in conversations, and what functions language carries out for its speakers. Finally, in the section on spoken language, we will briefly explore some of the differences between these rules for spoken interaction in different speech communities.

Openings and Closings

CA has shown that in English openings and closings are well-choreographed dances, with some obligatory and some optional elements. *Openings* in English usually begin with a greeting such as *hi* or *hello*; however, between friends, the greeting may be dispensed with, replaced by another opening, such as *Guess what?* When opening a conversation with a stranger, the usual form is *Excuse me.* *Closings* are carefully negotiated so that each speaker knows that the other has said all she or he wanted to say. Thus, closings begin with some indication of concluding the topic of conversation, such as *OK* followed by a comment. This concluding is usually followed by some indication of a future meeting. Or, there may be reference to the purposes of the conversation, such as *I just wanted to see how you were.* Only after these *preclosings* does the final farewell occur, with each speaker saying something like *bye* or *see you later.*

Task: Explore

Listen to several openings and closings of conversations in English. Transcribe them and identify the different parts.

Turn-taking

In any interaction between one or more people, the participants do not all talk at once, nor do they explicitly tell another person to begin speaking. The latter is unlike forms of communication, such as citizen band (CB) radio or air traffic control, where speakers say *over* when they end their turns and hand the turn over to their interlocutor. We all recognize that people in fact take turns at speaking, but how are those turns organized? That question is one of the key ones that ethnomethodologists set out to study, and they found that turns are orderly, with a number of mechanisms available to interlocutors. We illustrate each turn-taking mechanism with a sample from the transcript in the vignette.

- *Latch* is when the beginning of the next speaker's turn and the end of the speaker's turn are seamless. This mechanism is the preferred one in Standard American English (SAE).

  Katerina: *Iskandar*
  Clare: *oh, Iskandar. That's the name of a place?*

- *Overlap* is when the next speaker begins before the first speaker has ended and both briefly speak at the same time. This is dispreferred in SAE.

  Katerina: *ian means from Iskandar*
              [
  Clare: *right uh so what part what's the province Iskandar is in?*

- *Pause* occurs when there is extended time between one speaker's turn and the next. There is no such pause in the transcript.
- *Turn allocation* can occur when the speaker uses specific strategies to allocate the turn to the next speaker. Strategies include adjacency pairs, naming the next speaker, and question tags.
- *Adjacency pair* is when the first speaker's utterance requires a particular response from the listener. For example, greeting is usually followed by greeting; apology is usually followed by acceptance of apology; offer by

acceptance or refusal; and question by answer. In the following, Clare asks Katerina a direct question.

Clare: *yes cause I used to study Soviet Russian language and culture and that sort of thing but how long ago did your family go to Iran?*
Katerina: *seventy years*

- Naming the next speaker does not occur in the vignette, but it is especially useful in a conversation with more than two speakers.
- Question tags, like adjacency pairs, require the interlocutor to respond, such as

We should go to the market today, shouldn't we?

Processing Errors

In ELT, an error usually refers to a nontarget utterance made by the learner. However, an analysis of the spoken language of fluent speakers shows a variety of utterance errors that are a result of the mental processing of spoken language. *False starts* are when the speaker starts to say a word or phrase, but then changes it. *Repetition* is when a speaker repeats a word or phrase. *Pauses* within a turn can be either filled or unfilled. *Fillers* include expressions, such as *uhm* or *ah*. *Repair* is when speakers repair their own language or that of others to reduce ambiguity and achieve better communication. The following excerpt from the vignette illustrates these processing errors. However, there are no examples of false starts, such as *Where's the sto..sto..study hall?*

Clare: *Caucasus I'm sorry right* (filled pause) *Caucasus oh yea Caucusus mountains Caucasus mountains* (repetition) *well there were a lot of Armenians in there well not necessarily in the Caucasus mountains was weren't* (repair) *there a lot of Armenian settlements? Not any more*

A further category is called *slips of the tongue*. They result from anticipating a word or phrase, preserving a word or phrase already spoken, exchanging one for another, substituting, or adding. In all cases the word or phrase class is preserved, so nouns cannot be exchanged for verbs, for example. Some examples of slips of the tongue include:

- ones where the speaker substitutes an incorrect word, usually close phonetically but not semantically, such as *She was late for the apartment* (meaning appointment),

- ones where the speaker exchanges initial sounds, such as *I was looking for the spoop soon* (meaning soup spoon), and
- ones where the speaker exchanges actual words, such as *Put the dish in the soap* (meaning soap in the dish).

Teachers need to be able to distinguish between processing errors, such as the ones described above, and acquisition errors that learners make when they hypothesize and test the structures of English.

Speech Act Theory

Speech act theory complements CA because it seeks to understand the purposes or functions of the utterances in a turn. While it is possible to understand the literal semantics and syntax of an utterance, it is also important for listeners to ascertain (correctly) the speaker's intended meaning, that is, the *pragmatic* meaning. Theories of pragmatics set out to explain speakers' intentions, and one such theory is speech act theory, which has identified a variety of speech act types:

- *Representatives*—speech acts that represent the state of affairs, e.g., *assertions, statements, descriptions*. Such acts can be either true or false.
- *Commissives*—speech acts that commit the speaker to an action, e.g., *promise, pledge, threat*.
- *Directives*—speech acts that seek to have the listener do something, e.g., *commands, invitations, requests*.
- *Declaratives*—speech acts that make the thing they name happen, e.g., *blessings, firings, arrests*.
- *Expressives*—speech acts that tell the speaker's state of mind or attitude, e.g., *greetings, apologies, congratulations*.
- *Verdictives*—speech acts that judge or assess, e.g., *appraising, rating, assessing*.

Speech acts consist of both the utterance and the speaker's intention. The utterance is called the *locution* and the speaker's intention is called an *illocution*. So, for example, in the utterance *Can you please close the door?* the locution is a yes/no question, which asks whether the listener has the ability to (i.e., *can*) close the door. However, through conventional use, such a question has the illocutionary force of a *request* for the listener to close the door. Similarly, an indicative sentence, such as *It's cold in here*, may not be a *representative* making a statement of fact, but rather be an *indirect request* for someone to close a door or window or provide a sweater. Learners may misunderstand both utterances. Similarly, they may make requests only by using imperatives, such as *Close the door*. There is, thus, no one-to-one correspondence between a syntactic structure and a speech act. The question, then is, how do we know what speech act is being used? Some speech acts seem to be straightforward, especially the class of declaratives. The utterance *I now pronounce you man and wife* would seem to automatically make the couple married. But, what if the person saying it was not vested with the right to perform marriage? Many people have questioned speech act theory on this very point. However, two particular taxonomies were developed to form conditions on speech acts—those of Grice (1975) and Habermas (1979). These taxonomies were designed to explain how listeners interpret utterances.

Grice's maxims. A philosopher, Grice (1975), developed what he called his maxims of cooperative conversation, based on the notion that speakers will try to say what they want to say in a way that is appropriate for the listener and that conversation is principled. His maxims are therefore:

1 *Quality*—say only what you know to be true.
2 *Quantity*—say only as much as you need to for your listener to understand; that is, don't tell the listener what they already know.
3 *Relevance*—say only what is relevant to the purposes of the current conversation.
4 *Manner*—speak clearly and unambiguously.

Habermas's validity conditions. Another taxonomy was developed by Habermas (1979), who collapsed Grice's relevance and manner under comprehensibility and added another dimension, namely, appropriateness of the interpersonal relations of the interlocutors. Therefore, Habermas's four validity conditions that operate to ground speech acts are:

1 *Comprehensibility*—the speech act must be comprehensible so both speaker and listener can understand each other.
2 *Truth*—speak a propositionally true utterance so the listener can share the speaker's understandings.
3 *Sincerity*—speak sincerely so the listener will trust the speaker.
4 *Rightness*—speak in a way that is appropriate for the interpersonal relations between the speaker and the listener.

Habermas's rightness condition is evident in the following transcript:

B has just come home from work. His wife, D, is cooking. He starts going through the mail.
B: *I wonder if they paid up?*
D: *Yea.*
B: *We got $37 for your radiology tests.*
D: *Oh?*
B: *Well, that's 80 percent.*

This conversation would not be transparent to most people. The fact that B could just say *I wonder if they paid up* and D would both understand and not find this breaking Grice's maxims or Habermas's validity claims is because of the marital relationship between them and their shared knowledge. In this case, this is their shared knowledge that they were waiting to hear from their medical insurance company to see whether the company had paid for radiology tests. Habermas's rightness condition is, therefore, a very useful addition to Grice's maxims.

Cultural Variation in Spoken Language

Languages and dialects vary considerably in their conventions of spoken language. Because these conventions are largely subconscious, when learning another language people often apply the conventions from their first language, which may differ from those of the target language they are learning. For example, in opening a telephone conversation in the United States, speakers begin by identifying themselves. In French and some other languages, they also need to apologize for disturbing the recipient of the call. The lack of an apology can lead to miscommunications, and listeners may consider the speaker to be rude. Even in English, conventions vary according to the speech community. In some ethnic communities in the United States, overlapping, rather than latching, is the primary turn-taking device. Thus, when people whose community considers overlapping to be interrupting—and, hence, rude—encounter someone from a community that considers overlaps to be acceptable, they attribute the person's overlapping to rudeness and not to differences in turn-taking. In some Native American communities, neither latching nor overlapping is appropriate (Phillips, 1983). Rather, speakers leave a lengthy silence between turns. SAE speakers often feel the need to jump in because silence is dispreferred in the SAE speech community. When these children exercise lengthy silence between turns in class, SAE teachers move on to another child in the class, assuming incorrectly that the silence indicated that the child did not know the answer.

Written Language

We have already shown that written language uses cohesive devices to develop relationships across sentences, that there are written genres and registers, and that texts are expected to be coherent. The conventions for the schematic structure and syntactic features of genres are language- and culture-specific. Consequently, second language learners will bring with them conventions from their first language and may use them inappropriately in English. For that reason, it is important for learners to understand the structures of different genres in English, so they don't violate the conventions. Some of the most common genres in English are *recount, report, description*, and *argument*.

For centuries, literacy has been equated with written language, and various attributes have been associated with literacy, with some researchers claiming that literacy changes cognition, permitting logical thought (Havelock, 1982). Other research has shown that some of the ways of thinking attributed to literacy were, in fact, the result of schooling (Heath, 1983; Scribner & Cole, 1981). More recent work has viewed literacy as a sociocultural practice that is ideological. Literacy is more than decoding and encoding text. As Freebody and Luke (1990) note, literacy requires mastering a number of different roles:

1   *Code breaker*—ability to decode and encode.
2   *Text participant*—what does this mean?
3   *Text user*—what do I do with this?
4   *Text analyst*—what does this do to me?

Much of education has focused on the role of code breaker. This ability is essential for mastering the written word. For learners of English, this mastery can be complex if they already write in a language with an orthographic system that is different from English (i.e., non-alphabetic). There are many different ways for sounds to be represented by symbols. India alone has 25 different writing systems. Chinese uses a *logographic* system, in which a written symbol (a character) represents meaning. Arabic uses a *syllabic* system, where each symbol represents a consonant. Long vowels are represented by diacritics, but short vowels are not; the reader determines the short vowel from context. Even learners literate in languages that use an alphabetic system may have difficulties decoding. For example, Spanish has a consistent one-to-one correspondence between sound and letter, unlike English, which has an *opaque* system, where sounds can be represented by more than one letter (see Chapter 6).

Going beyond decoding, as suggested by Freebody and Luke (1990), as well as others, is referred to as a *critical approach* to literacy and "through schooling . . .

literacy practices provide the textual means by which dominant values and identities (e.g., avid consumers, obedient workers, patriotic citizens) are normalized and, at times, resisted" (Morgan & Ramanathan, 2005, pp. 151–152). Therefore, it is important for teachers to understand all the roles critical literacy requires and to question texts by asking the questions in the following task. Further, this view of literacy as a sociocultural practice has demonstrated that, in fact, it is not a practice, but multiple practices. Therefore, we need to talk about literacies—that is, the different practices one engages in when negotiating different texts in different contexts for different purposes.

Task: Explore

Find an advertisement in a newspaper or magazine. Answer the following questions (based on Baynham, 1995) about the text.

1   Why does this text exist?
2   What is its purpose?
3   Whose interests does it serve?
4   Whose interests does it undermine?
5   How does it achieve its purpose?

Task: Reflect

Think about what you had to know to be able to answer these questions. Would your students be able to answer as easily as you did? Would their answers have been the same? Why? What skills other than language skills did you need to answer these questions?

To be able to answer these questions requires understanding of genres and their purposes and of *intertextuality*. Intertextuality refers to understanding how one text is similar to or different from all the other texts you have encountered, which requires commonsense, linguistic, and cultural knowledge. The last question in the task above (non-linguistic skills) is one that is increasingly important as *multimodal literacy* has become as important as language skills in both the print and online worlds. Multimodal literacy goes beyond digital literacy, which often

173

conjures only the notion of being able to use computer technology. One perspective on multimodal literacy that is useful for language teachers is that of Anstey and Bull (2011), for whom

> [a] text may be defined as multimodal when it combines two or more semiotic systems. There are five semiotic systems in total, which are conceptualized as follows:
>
> 1   Linguistic: comprising aspects, such as vocabulary, generic structure, and the grammar of oral and written language;
> 2   Visual: comprising aspects, such as colour, vectors, and viewpoint in still and moving images;
> 3   Audio: comprising aspects, such as volume, pitch, and rhythm of music and sound effects;
> 4   Gestural: comprising aspects, such as movement, speed, and stillness in facial expression and body language; and
> 5   Spatial: comprising aspects, such as proximity, direction, position of layout and organisation of objects in space.
>
> (2001, n.p.)

Multimodal literacy has its roots in *multiliteracies*, a term developed by the New London Group (Cope & Kalantzis, 2000), which was designed to encapsulate the changing nature of literacy in a world that has culturally diverse literacy practices and whose technology is changing literacy communities. For example, email, Twitter, and Facebook have all provided us with new literacies. Multimodality will be discussed again in detail in Chapter 15. Despite many claims to the contrary, (multimodal) literacy is vital for English learners to be able to negotiate their way in the 21st century. Both multiliteracy and multimodal literacy approaches to the teaching of language and literacy are examples of the critical approach, which was introduced and discussed previously in this chapter (see also Rajendram, 2015, for a literature review).

Conclusion

In this chapter we have introduced you to some of the features of spoken and written language. These features are all ones that learners need to acquire in order to become proficient in English. Because the conventions of texts, written or spoken, are not in the conscious minds of language users, they are not aware of the conventions of their own language and when they might be applying conventions from their first language to English texts. Additionally, texts are one way in which power is distributed in society. By applying questions from a critical perspective, English language teachers can become aware of how texts position them and their learners.

Task: Expand

Heath, S. B. (1983). *Ways with words: Language, life and work in communities and class-rooms.* Cambridge, England: Cambridge University Press.
This is a seminal work on the roles of orality and literacy in three different communities in the US. It is the report of a multi-year ethnography, highly readable, and an essential resource for language educators.

Kern, R. (2000). *Literacy and language teaching.* Oxford, England: Oxford University Press.
Kern's volume is a thorough discussion of literacy and the teaching of reading and writing in language education. He includes technology as an integral aspect of literacy.

UNESCO Education Sector (2004). *The plurality of literacy and its implications for policies and programmes.* Retrieved from http://unesdoc.unesco.org/images/0013/001362/136246e.pdf
UNESCO has a multi-decade history of promoting literacy development around the world. This position paper provides an excellent overview of how their understandings about policies for literacy education have evolved based on research.

Note

1 A maiden name is the name a woman had before she changed her name on marrying. Clare's name before she married ended in *ian*, which is a common ending for Armenian family names.

References

Anstey, M., & Bull, G. (2011). Helping teachers to explore multimodal texts. *Curriculum and Leadership Journal, 8*(16). Retrieved from www.curriculum.edu.au/leader/helping_teachers_to_explore_multimodal_texts,31522.html?issueID=12141

Baynham, M. (1995). *Literacy practices.* Harlow, Essex, England: Longman.

Cicourel, A. V. (1975). Discourse and text: Cognitive and linguistic processes in studies of social structure. *Versus, 12,* 33–84.

Cope, B., & Kalantzis, M. (Eds.,) (2000). *Multiliteracies: Literacy learning and the design of social futures.* London, England: Routledge.

Ferguson, C. A. (1986). The study of religious discourse. In D. Tannen & J. E. Alatis (Eds.), *Georgetown University Roundtable on Language and Linguistics 1985* (pp. 205–213). Washington, DC: Georgetown University Press.

Freebody, P., & Luke, A. (1990). Literacies programs: Debates and demands in cultural context. *Prospect, 5*(7), 7–16.

Grice, H. P. (1975). Logic and conversation. In P. Cole & J. Morgan (Eds.), *Syntax and semantics 3: Speech acts* (pp. 41–58). New York, NY: Academic Press.

Habermas, J. (1979). *Communication and the evolution of society.* Boston, MA: Beacon.

Halliday, M. A. K. (1978). *Language as social semiotic.* London, England: Edward Arnold.

Hammond, J. (1986). The effect of modelling reports and narratives on the writing of year two children from a non-English speaking background. *Australian Review of Applied Linguistics, 9*(2), 75–93.

Havelock, E. (1982). *The literate revolution in Greece and its cultural consequences.* Princeton, NJ: Princeton University Press.

Heath, S. B. (1983). *Ways with words: Language, life and work in communities and classrooms.* Cambridge, England: Cambridge University Press.

Kern, R. (2000). *Literacy and language teaching.* Oxford, England: Oxford University Press.

Martin, J. R. (1984). Language, register and genre. In F. Christie (Ed.), *Children writing: Reader* (pp. 21–30). Geelong, Australia: Deakin University Press.

Morgan, B., & Ramanathan, V. (2005). Critical literacies and language education. *Annual Review of Applied Linguistics, 25,* 151–169.

Phillips, S. U. (1983). *The invisible culture.* New York, NY: Longman.

Rajendram, S. (2015). Potentials of the multiliteracies pedagogy for teaching English language learners (ELLs): A review of the literature. *Critical Intersections in Educational, 3,* 1–18. Retrieved from www.researchgate.net/publication/315857819_Potentials_of_the_Multiliteracies_Pedagogy_for_Teaching_English_Language_Learners_ELLs_A_Review_of_the_Literature

Schegloff, E. A. (1972). Notes on conversational practice: Formulating place. In P. P. Giglioli (Ed.), *Language and social context* (pp. 95–135). Hammondsworth, England: Penguin.

Scribner, S., & Cole, M. (1981). *The psychology of literacy.* Cambridge, MA: Harvard University Press.

Tannen, D. (Ed.). (1982). *Spoken and written language: Exploring orality and literacy.* Norwood, NJ: Ablex.

Van Dijk, T. A. (1977). *Text and context: Explorations in the semantics and pragmatics of discourse.* London, England: Longman.

UNESCO Education Sector (2004). *The plurality of literacy and its implications for policies and programmes.* Retrieved from http://unesdoc.unesco.org/images/0013/001362/136246e.pdf

Part III

LEARNING

Part III provides a general introduction to both first and second language acquisition and to general learning theory. Chapter 10 introduces the readers to basic concepts related to the role of theory construction and theories in language learning and covers selected concepts that are derived from learning theory in educational psychology and language learning. Concepts, such as skill development and the development of strategies for learning, instructional discourse, feedback, and scaffolding are also discussed as they relate to what we know about learning and, more specifically, language learning.

Chapter 11 is an introduction to the field of second language acquisition (SLA) and provides an overview of some important concepts that have moved the field to the level of maturity it enjoys today. We will cover briefly each of the following concepts, with an emphasis on their pedagogical implications and contributions: contrastive analysis, language transfer, error analysis, morpheme studies, first language acquisition, and Universal Grammar.

In Chapter 12 we will continue to explore SLA by looking specifically at some research studies in SLA that have definite pedagogical applications, such as research focused on input, interaction, teacher talk, output, and nonlanguage influences on SLA, such as attitude and motivation. In addition, the chapter presents specific commentary on the role of SLA researchers in furthering our understanding of SLA and how the role of research intersects with the role of classroom teachers.

Chapter 13 looks at four of the most popular concepts for promoting learning in classroom settings: (a) preferred ways of perceiving and processing information, also known as learning styles, (b) learning strategies, (c) language learning and intelligence, and (d) cooperative learning.

10

THEORIES OF LEARNING

VIGNETTE

I am participating in an eight-hour in-service training with a group of middle school teachers. We have been working together for about 14 months on a U.S. federal grant focused on improving reading instruction with adolescent learners, in particular English language learners and other learners at risk. We are using a conceptual model that we have created especially for the grant in which teacher indicators associated with concept oriented reading instruction (CORI) have been identified from the research. At the lunch break, I sit down informally with five teachers, all from the same middle school but with differing skills as teachers. The topic of the in-service training for the day is formative assessment, so I ask them if they would talk to me about how they know their students are learning. I'm surprised at the different answers they give me:

> *"If they do well on the unit test . . ."*

> *"The way they talk about the concepts when I ask questions in class and the questions they ask me . . ."*

> *"Whether they have achieved the lesson's objectives . . ."*

> *"If they pay attention and if they complete their worksheets . . ."*

> *"They do KWL[1] charts."*

> [Christison, personal research notes, 2009]

Task: Reflect

What is your definition of learning? Based on the responses above, how do you think each teacher would define learning? Which teacher's view is most similar to your own view? Why? Which teacher's view is the most different from your own view? Why? How do you know when your own students are learning or have learned a concept? Share your answers with a partner if possible.

Introduction

Most of us take the process of learning for granted. Because learning is something that we have been doing all of our lives, we never stop to think about what it really means when we say, "My students are learning." The teachers in the vignette that introduced this chapter expressed different ideas about what constitutes learning and about what happens when learning takes place. Some teachers make the assumption that, because they have taught something, it means their students have also learned. Other teachers set benchmarks in order to recognize certain behaviors so that when these behaviors are identified, learning has occurred—the assumption being that learner behaviors are indicators of learning. That teachers have different ideas about learning is not uncommon. In fact, if you were able to compare your answers to the reflection task with a partner, it is likely that your views about learning might be different from your partner's. It is not unusual for teachers to construct their notions about learning differently.

Explanations about what happens when learning takes place are known as *theories of learning*, and these theories provide us with conceptual frameworks for interpreting examples of learning that we observe in real-life situations. There are numerous theories of learning in the literature, such as: *connectionism*, with its focus on behavioral psychology (Thorndike, 1932); *constructivism* or *social constructivism* (Piaget, 1955), in which the learner actively constructs or builds new ideas or concepts based on current knowledge or experience; *connectivism* (Siemens, 2005), which focuses on available technologies in order to make connections in learning; and *discovery learning*, in which learners "learn by doing" (Lee & Anderson, 2013; Tuovinen & Sweller, 1999).

Rather than focus this chapter on a series of brief overviews of specific theories of learning, we have chosen to focus our attention more broadly on two basic distinctions that underpin theories of learning, that is, whether learning is conceptualized as conditioned or cognitive. In addition, we will look at these two distinctions and how they might inform second language (L2) pedagogy and research. For the purposes of this chapter, *learning* will be defined broadly as a process that brings together cognitive, emotional, and environmental influences for the purpose of making changes in one's knowledge, skills, values, and worldviews (adapted from Illeris, 2000). Learning also refers to a relatively permanent change in behavior as a result of practice or experience.

Although the study of learning and theories of learning have been at the core of the fields of psychology and education for almost a century, the theories and the possible implications and applications of these theories have received little serious attention from L2 teachers and teacher educators.[2] This observation is supported by the fact that general theories of learning have not been routinely included as topics in introductory L2 methodology textbooks for English language teachers (Harmer, 2007; Peregoy & Boyle, 2008; Richards & Rodgers, 2014), nor do they appear frequently on the conference programs in applied linguistics or English language teaching (for example, see TESOL programs from 1990 to 2012) or in professional journals devoted to both L2 teaching and research (see *TESOL Quarterly* and *Applied Linguistics* from 2000 to 2017. The reason for this oversight is, in part, rooted in historical developments in the field of L2 pedagogy, but also in the limitations of the theories themselves.

Learning theorists, such as Watson (1913), Pavlov, (1927), and Skinner (1978, 1988), were known as *behaviorists*. They believed that learning involved a patterning of overt responses. In other words, learning a new behavior happens as a result of conditioning—either *classical conditioning*, where the behavior becomes a reflex response, as in the case of Pavlov's experiments with dogs or *operant conditioning*, where behavior is reinforced by a reward or punishment, as in Skinner's experiments. *Operant* refers to the way in which the behavior operates in the environment. In this view of learning, knowledge resides in physical responses not cerebral exercise (Sprinthall, Sprinthall, & Oja, 1994). For certain kinds of learning, this point of view makes perfect sense. For example, it is almost impossible to teach someone how to tie a necktie using words alone; you have to practice with the necktie over and over again. A person who can tie a necktie on himself, often cannot tie one on another person because learning the task is tied to one's own physical movements and is physical rather than cognitive.

Other learning theorists, such as Bode (1929), Bruner (1990), and Wertheimer (1982, 1985), believed that the behaviorist view did not account for all types of learning. These theorists incorporate a Gestalt view of learning. This view of learning includes looking at patterns in human behavior rather than at isolated events, conceptualizing the memory system as an active processor of information, and considering prior knowledge as an important component in a theory of learning. In general, these theorists see learning as cognitive in nature, believing that learning requires thinking and insight and that learning occurs when we discover solutions for ourselves.

After decades of heated debates on the relative merits of these two theories, most psychologists today have reached the conclusion that we have at least two separate modes for learning and memory, one called *declarative* and the other *procedural*. Declarative learning and memory are associated with factual information—dates, names, past events, etc.—while procedural learning and memory are dependent on motoric patterning and conditioning. Two main schools of thought emerged from the theoretical debates, association and cognitive learning. Association theorists see learning as the result of connections or associations between sense impressions and responses and, as such, they share similarities with the behaviorist view of learning. On the other hand, cognitive theorists view learning as the ability to perceive new relationships, solve new problems, and gain a basic understanding of a subject area. Although each position makes a tenable case for its points of view, there are shortcomings with both theories as they pertain to language.

Since Noam Chomsky wrote his review of B. F. Skinner's *Verbal Behavior* (Chomsky, 1959), it has become widely accepted that the ability to learn one's first language includes one's genetic predisposition. Chomsky proposed a "system of principles, conditions, and rules that are elements or properties of all human languages" (1975, p. 29). As a result of Chomsky's work, most L2 scholars agree that neither the behaviorist nor the cognitive view of learning is a perfect fit for second language acquisition (SLA) and that the "behaviorist position with regard to language learning (whether first or second) [is] untenable" (Gass & Selinker, 2001, p. 104). In addition, the cognitive view does not adequately consider that children learn their first language (L1) swiftly, efficiently, and largely without instruction or practice of any sort (Daniels, 2008). Although many second language researchers (for example, see Krashen, 1982; White, 2003) support Chomsky's view that there is a genetic component associated with language acquisition, an equal number of scholars believe that learning requires thinking and insight and view the learner as an active participant in the process; consequently, cognitive theories of second language acquisition have also garnered considerable support among second language researchers and scholars.

There is perhaps an additional reason why English language teachers have not been seriously considering general theories of learning in L2 teaching. Until recently English language teachers thought of themselves as teaching only language and viewed the process of language learning as different from general learning in content areas. As discussed in Part I, Language and Identity (Chapters 1–5), the profile of English learners in many contexts has changed rather dramatically in recent years. For example, the changing demographics and the increase in English learners in K-12 schools in English-speaking countries have changed the role of the content teacher. Content area teachers must not only develop expertise in specific content areas but also expertise in teaching language. (See Volumes II and III for more information on teaching content.) If content teachers are to be successful in helping English learners gain content area mastery at the same time they are learning English (Stoller, 2004), they must develop language awareness. In response to learner needs, teachers in EFL contexts are also experimenting with the integration of content and language because language learning can no longer be as compartmentalized as it was in the mid-20th century. This shift away from traditional language teaching, with its focus almost exclusively on language structure, has resulted in a cadre of language teachers who have begun to explore cognitive learning theories as they apply to concept and content learning with L2 learners; nevertheless, the historical significance of the linguistic view of SLA cannot be overlooked.

Because we believe that general learning theory has often been short changed in the field of L2 learning and because our own experiences as both language learners and teachers have benefited from a number of key concepts that underpin these prominent learning theories, we want to introduce you to a selected number of ideas that spring from both psychology and general education. These ideas include the following: (a) transfer of learning, (b) modeling, (c) chunking, and (d) principles of learning.

Transfer of Learning

In this chapter, we will make a distinction between transfer of learning and language transfer. Although language transfer remains an important concept in SLA, particularly historically, many cognitive theorists in SLA have tried to dismiss the importance of language transfer because the concept has been traditionally associated with behaviorist thought. As Gass and Selinker (2008) point out, "a way of arguing that second language learning was not a behaviorist-based activity was to argue that transfer was not a major, or even an important factor in attempts to account for second language learning" (p. 104). The concept of language transfer and its history in the development of the field of second language acquisition (SLA) will be dealt with in Chapter 12. In this chapter, we will focus on transfer of learning, which we believe is a different process.

One of the goals of education is to take what we learn in the classroom and transfer that knowledge to future situations outside of the classroom. Basic math skills, such as learning to add, subtract, multiply, or divide, and being able to spell words correctly, are skills that result in success in the classroom. However, they are also skills, and if they are mastered to a certain level of competency they have a compelling advantage for individuals in real life situations. Transfer of learning takes place when one learning task influences another one. Transfer can be positive when one task facilitates the learning of another task, or it can be negative when one task inhibits the learning of another task. For example, learning to ride a motorcycle is easier if you can already ride a bike. If you know how to add a list of numbers correctly on a classroom exam, you will be more accurate in adding the costs of grocery items when you are shopping and trying to determine if you have enough money. Transfer may also be interpreted as negative. If you learn how to hit a baseball with your elbows out, you will have a more difficult time learning to hit a golf ball with your elbows in (Sprinthall et al., 1994). Because modern language teachers are concerned with learning disciplinary content and language, transfer of learning becomes a critical factor to explore, because the ability to adapt skills to new contexts is increasingly valued in the workplace. For example, in recent years, there has been a shift away from highly specific vocational training toward the development of transferable knowledge and skills, such as problem-solving and teamwork (see Volume II). This perspective is being realized in the classroom as teachers focus students on specific learning strategies. Practices such as these reflect current theories of transferability of learning from one context to another, as well as the integration of knowledge and skills.

In this chapter, we have selected four subcomponents associated with transfer of learning for you to consider: (a) the learning curve, (b) learning to learn, (c) the spacing effect, and (d) learning from the whole to parts.

The Learning Curve

The acquisition of new information or of a new skill proceeds in a predictable way. For example, we generally start learning new information rather slowly, particularly if we have no background in the area and no topical knowledge on which to draw. After this slow start, we begin to pick up speed rather dramatically. A common experience in the learning curve is the so-called *a-ha phenomenon*—the moment when information comes to us suddenly and without effort (similar to *insight* in Gestalt psychology). Learners feel very positive about learning during this time. Eventually, the speed of learning slows down and begins to level off. When this leveling off occurs, learners reach a *plateau*. When students are learning new skills and concepts in a classroom, including another language, this process will likely occur over and over again, as learners encounter a series of plateaus. Knowing that these plateaus are a normal part of learning can be useful in dealing with discouragement, which is a common phenomenon for many English learners.

Learning to Learn

Harry Harlow coined the term *learning sets* to describe the phenomenon of learning how to learn. Harlow spent most of his professional career working at the primate lab at the University of Wisconsin and found that monkeys solved oddity problems by developing strategies or rules for learning rather than from "the restrictions of the slow, trial-and-error process" (Harlow, McGaugh, & Thompson, 1971, p. 301). Harlow's ideas carry over into human behavior as learners in classroom settings are taught how to learn new concepts and ideas (Fender, 2004; Olivier & Bowler, 1996). When instruction targets specific strategies, research has shown that learners demonstrate an increased ability to identify relationships that help them in the retention of concepts that are presented orally, as well as in written materials (Brown, Campione, & Day, 1981; Guthrie, 2008; Novak, 1980). Many adult immigrant and refugee English learners in the United States, Australia, and Canada come to the English as a second language (ESL) classroom with little formal education or experience with classroom learning. English language teachers who work with adult English learners must not only teach them English but must also teach them how to learn in a new context.

The Spacing Effect

The value of *spaced learning* (in other words, a series of short learning sessions carried out over a long period of time) over *massed learning* (a dose of learning in one long session) is called the *spacing effect*. There has been a long and solid record of careful documentation in educational psychology that supports the facilitative nature of the spacing effect (for a summary of studies, see Dempster, 1988). On the strength of this record, teachers should make an effort to consider the spacing effect in their planning and lesson delivery and in the development of curricula. The research evidence also suggests that teachers should encourage learners to space their study times and warn them against such practices as cramming for exams.

Learning from the Whole to Parts

The more meaningful material is to learners, the easier the material is to learn; consequently, when you break it up, you risk making the material less meaningful and, thereby, more difficult to learn. It is important to keep a subject internally coherent and meaningful when setting up efficient learning conditions (Covington, 2000). In addition, material that is learned in parts will eventually have to be put back together again, and this process can be extremely time-consuming. Having stated reasons in favor of learning from whole to parts, we recognize that how well one learns new information piece by piece or all at once (even though superficially) is also a matter of *learning style preference*—a preferred way of perceiving and processing information. (See Chapter 13 for a discussion of preferred ways of learning.)

Modeling

The concept of *modeling* as a subject of academic inquiry can be attributed to the work of Bandura (1977) and his social learning theory. Bandura's model of learning suggests that learning takes place when internal cognitive structures interact with the environment. We may in some ways be products of our environment, but we can also choose and shape our environments. In interactions with others, we modify our behavior based on how others respond to us. Although Bandura recognizes the importance of Skinner's work in that some learning takes place as a result of direct reinforcement of behavior, he also believes that we learn by imitating behaviors that are modeled by our primary reinforcers (e.g., parents, teachers, or peers).

In some cases, such as in a classroom environment, it is enough for learners to merely witness what a teacher does over time. We refer to this type of modeling as *vicarious learning* or *indirect modeling* because the learner's attention is not drawn to a specific behavior. It is important to note that a teacher's likes and dislikes may be transmitted vicariously to learners (e.g., *I love music, but I hate math*). A teacher's behavior (including attitude) toward minority-group learners can also have a significant effect on how learners perceive themselves and on how other learners perceive them. Teachers and other adults must constantly monitor their behaviors because indirect modeling on the part of the teacher can and does influence learners' behaviors. Many learners, particularly young children, have been known to model their teacher's behavior so closely that they can almost become the teacher (Sprinthall et al., 1994).

Teachers also use *direct modeling*, particularly in strategy instruction, as a way of teaching students how to learn. Strategy instruction focuses on "intentional, planned, goal-directed procedures that one evokes prior to, during, or after performing a task" (Alexander & Judy, 1988, p. 376). Direct modeling in strategy instruction is concerned with demonstrating how to use a strategy, when to use it, and why it is being used (Swan, 2003). Direct modeling is also effective in giving complex instructions in multistep activities or projects and is crucial in working with English learners because it provides another vehicle for making the L2 comprehensible. The teacher may model the desired behaviors by demonstrating the behaviors with some of the learners or modeling the behaviors himself/herself. Modeled behavior can be retained longer if the learner can describe the desired behavior in words, such as when the teacher implements a brief comprehension check after giving instructions. In classroom settings learners may also repeat desired behaviors based on visual imagery alone without verbal coding. For example, English language teachers who work with young learners or adults who have not yet acquired literacy skills often use pictures instead of text when giving sequenced instructions. Instead of checking comprehension verbally, comprehension is checked by pointing to the visual cues and having students respond. If students are not able to respond, teachers can model the behavior again.

Chunking

Most laypersons have heard something about George A. Miller's famous 1956 study entitled "The Magical Number Seven, Plus or Minus Two: Some Limits on our Capacity for Processing Information." Even if you do not know the details of the study, you are likely familiar with the magical number seven—the idea that short-term memory has the capacity for about "seven, plus or minus two" chunks of information. A *chunk* can be defined as a collection of elements having strong associations with one another but weak associations with elements within other chunks (Gobet et al., 2001; Gobet, de Voogt, & Retschitzki, 2004). For example, try recalling the following numbers 8015817367. This may seem difficult at first, but if we tell you the number is a mobile phone number in the United States, and you are familiar with phone numbers in the United States, you will most likely divide the number into three chunks, 801 581 7367. Instead of remembering 10 different and unrelated digits, which is beyond the magical "seven, plus or minus two," you need to remember only three groups, which is within the "seven, plus or minus two" constraint. In addition, you might also make other connections that will help you recall the numbers, such as the fact that 801 might be a familiar area code. New information is easier to remember if it can be presented in manageable chunks and if it can be connected to something you already know.

Look at the letters in the following sequence for five seconds and then try to recall them in their exact order:

ITCI AFB IIO UNB CCD

Unless you are unusual, you will most likely find it a bit challenging. However, if we place these same letters into different chunks that connect with something you already know, you will no doubt find the task much easier:

IT CIA FBI IOU NBC CD

Instead of recalling 16 letters, as in the first example, chunking allows you to recall only five.

Principles of Learning

Thorndike (1932) is perhaps best known for his principles of learning or laws of learning. Thorndike was a behaviorist, so he held a view of learning as a series of stimulus-response (SR) connections. Essentially, his principles of learning were originally meant to describe the ways in which the SR connections could be strengthened or weakened. Modern educational psychologists and educators have interpreted the principles more loosely and extended the principles beyond their original intent (see Sousa, 2005), as applying to learning environments more broadly, and we present them here in that manner. Thorndike's original principles were *readiness, effect*, and *exercise*. Since Thorndike first outlined these principles in the early part of the 20th century, three additional principles have been added—*primacy, recency*, and *intensity*.

Readiness

The principle of *readiness* is based on the premise that individuals learn best when they are ready to learn, including mental, emotional, and physical readiness (Bergen, 2002; Sessa & London, 2008). In addressing this principle, teachers must consider how to get learners ready to learn. In other words, this principle suggests that teachers play a pivotal role in creating conditions for learning in the classroom (Perry, Woolley, & Ifcher, 1995). When students are prepared for learning, they interact with new ideas and concepts in ways that allow them to make important connections that lead to expertise and continued learning. For example, teachers might identify the purpose of the lesson, project, or activity in order to prepare English learners for instructional tasks. English learners need to know *why* they are doing what they are doing and *how* it will benefit them in their lives.

Effect

The principle of *effect* states that learning is enhanced when it is accompanied by a pleasant or satisfying feeling, so most learners will be motivated to do what is necessary for the pleasant feelings to continue. It is generally the instructor who takes responsibility for setting up a learning situation in such a way that learners can see evidence of their progress and feel positive about the degree of success they are having. Learning experiences that produce frustration or confusion violate the principle of effect. For example, if an instructor teaches material that is too difficult for the learners, they will likely feel frustrated over time. However, positive reinforcement is an important component of this principle, and effective praise is an important tool in helping learners develop positive feelings about learning (see Brophy, 1981, and Volume II).

Exercise

The principle of *exercise* is based on the idea that we remember the things that are most often repeated. Research has shown that we retain information longer when the way the information is repeated or practiced is meaningful. Meaningful practice includes three basic components: (a) working with information or skills that learners perceive as interesting, (b) working with information or skills that learners perceive as valuable, and (c) receiving immediate and appropriate feedback. In addition, repetition of the task or the principle of multiple *responses* is also important in meaningful practice. For example, teachers who pay attention to recycling material and providing numerous opportunities for learners to work with concepts at different levels are addressing the principle of exercise through multiple responses. Learners should be given opportunities to offer many different responses until they achieve success. The process of trial and error allows learners to experiment with a variety of responses until they settle on the one that results in the outcome for which they are looking.

Task: Explore

Make a list of five suggestions teachers can use for helping learners to get ready to learn.

Primacy

The principle of *primacy* is about the effect of being first in a learning episode. We tend to remember best the information that comes first. What we hear or see first creates a strong impression in the mind, and these impressions are difficult to forget; consequently, the first part of a learning episode seems like an ideal time to present new information. The principle of primacy retains its effect even if the information we present first is not particularly important or interesting, such as correcting homework or taking roll. Teachers miss an excellent opportunity to promote learning when they fail to take the principle of primacy into consideration.

Recency

The principle of *recency* states that we remember best the things that we learned most recently. In a classroom setting, learners will have an easier time remembering information given to them at the end of the class. Teachers who provide reviews and summaries at the end of a class period help learners retain and remember information by capitalizing on the principle of recency. The further a learner is removed from the new fact or recently acquired understanding, the more difficulty the learner will have in recalling the information. Consequently, the closer the learning episode is to the actual need to apply the information or use the skill, the more likely the learner will be able to perform successfully.

The concept of primacy began with Ebbinghaus (1913) and his studies on long lists of nonsense syllables (e.g., *cav, rek, vum*). He coined the term *serial position effect* to refer to the finding that recall accuracy varies as a function of an item's position in a list. Dempster (1987) added considerable strength to Ebbinghaus's original ideas by providing one possible explanation for the primacy effect (i.e., that items at the beginning of the list were recalled more often than items in the middle or at the end). Initial items presented in a learning episode are most effectively stored in long-term memory (LTM) because more processing time has been devoted to them. Most individuals rehearse the first few items in the list several times as they work their way through the list. A possible reason for the recency effect (i.e., that items at the end of the list were recalled more often than items in the middle of the list) is that the items may still be present in working memory when recall is solicited. The middle items in a list do not benefit from either the primacy or the recency effect. When items in a list are presented quickly, the primacy effect is reduced. The speed with which items

Table 10.1 Average primetimes and downtimes in learning episodes of varying lengths

Total Learning Episode Time	Primetime Minutes (1)	Downtime Minutes	Primetime Minutes (2)
20 minutes	10	2	8
40 minutes	20	10	10
80 minutes	25	30	25

are presented does not have an effect on recency. On the other hand, recency is reduced when an interfering task is given during recall.

Sousa (2005) extended the ideas from the principles of primacy and recency to classroom management concepts by introducing the *primacy-recency effect* and the ratio of primetimes and downtimes in learning episodes of different lengths.

Primetimes in a learning episode occur at the beginning (primacy effect) and at the end (recency effect). Downtimes occur in the middle. In a 20-minute learning episode, learners are in primetime 90 percent of the time and in downtime only 10 percent of the time. As the learning episodes get longer, the amount of time learners spend in downtime increases. In a 40-minute learning episode, downtime increases from 10 percent in a 20-minute learning episode to 25 percent in a 40-minute learning episode, and to 40 percent in an 80-minute learning episode. The longer the learning episodes, the more time learners will spend in downtime. The question teachers must concern themselves with is how to structure learning episodes to take advantage of primetimes.

Intensity

The principle of *intensity* states that new concepts that are taught intensively are more likely to be retained. Although classrooms impose limitations on learning and the amount of realism one can bring into a classroom, we believe there is much that teachers can do to address this principle, such as using a wide variety of instructional aids, giving learners access to interesting texts, and providing opportunities for collaboration. Classroom tasks that involve learners in real-world interaction are by definition more involved (i.e., more cognitively complex) and more involving of the learners—engaging them physically, emotionally, socially, and cognitively—and are more intense. Therefore, an implication for the principle of intensity is that tasks that involve learners in real-world interaction (Guthrie, 2008; Swan, 2003) will result in increased learning. Demonstrations, role-playing, and projects are examples of classroom activities that increase intensity in learning.

Task: Explore

Work with a small group and plan a possible lesson for a specific context that demonstrates the application of the primacy-recency effect.

Conclusion

In this chapter we have tried to focus your attention on learning by getting you to think about what it is and how you know that learning has occurred in the classroom. In addition, we have introduced you to some general theories of learning and provided a brief discussion as to why these theories of learning are important considerations for teachers of ELs. In addition, we have discussed concepts related to theories of learning, such as transfer of learning and how it differs from language transfer. Included in our discussions were also the concepts of modeling and chunking. Finally, we turned our attention to six principles of learning—readiness, effect, exercise, primacy, recency, and intensity.

Task: Expand

www.learningtolearn.com
This is a student success program for higher education.

www.learningtolearn.group.shef.ac.uk
This is an online site for those who want to learn how to learn.

www.learntolearn.sa.edu.au
This is the homepage for schools and children's services on learning how to learn in South Australia.

Questions for Discussion

1   Discuss the strengths of both the behaviorist and cognitive views of learning for English language teaching.

2   What is transfer of learning? How do you think it is different from language transfer?

3   Do you think that traditional ways of organizing and managing classroom instruction are conducive to the primacy-recency effect? Why? Why not? Provide examples.

4   Provide three concrete examples of the main concepts associated with transfer of learning.

Notes

1   A KWL chart is a three-column chart with the column headings *KWL*, representing what learners know, want to know, and have learned. The KWL chart is used to find out what students know before they begin studying a topic, what they want to know about the topic, and, after the lesson, to find out what they have learned.

2   An exception is certainly Part I of Earl Stevick's *Memory, Meaning, and Method: Some Psychological Perspectives on Language Learning* (1976), in which he examines some of the research that has been done on memory and discusses the biological bases for memory, verbal memory, and memory and the whole person. In fact, Stevick's book is devoted to exploring the teaching and learning of second languages in terms of the total human experience.

References

Alexander, P. A., & Judy, J. A. (1988). The interaction of domain-specific and strategic knowledge in academic performance. *Review of Educational Research*, *58*, 375–404.

Bandura, A. (1977). *Social learning theory*. Englewood Cliffs, NJ: Prentice Hall.

Bergen, D. (2002). The role of pretend play in children's cognitive development. *Early Childhood Research & Practice*, *4*(1). Retrieved from http://ecrp.uiuc.edu/v4n1/bergen.html

Bode, B. H. (1929). *Conflicting psychologies of learning*. Boston, MA: D. C. Heath & Company.

Brophy, J. (1981). Teacher praise: A functional analysis. *Review of Educational Research*, *51*, 26.

Brown, A. L., Campione, J. C., & Day, J. D. (1981). Learning to learn: On training students to learn from texts. *Educational Researcher*, *10*, 14–21.

Bruner, J. S. (1990). *Acts of meaning*. Boston, MA: Harvard University Press.

Chomsky, N. (1959). Review of B. F. Skinner, *Verbal Behavior*. *Language*, *35*, 26–58.

Chomsky, N. (1975). *Reflections on language*. New York, NY: Random House Publishers.

Covington, M. V. (2000). Goal theory, motivation, and school achievement: An integrative view. *Annual Review of Psychology*, *51*, 171–200.

Daniels, H. A. (2008). Nine ideas about language. In V. P. Clark, P. A. Eschholz, A. F. Rosa, & B. L. Simon (Eds.), *Language*, 6th ed. (pp. 3–20). New York, NY: St Martin's Press.

Dempster, F. N. (1987). Effects of variable encoding and spaced presentation on vocabulary learning. *Journal of Educational Psychology*, *22*, 1–21.

Dempster, F. N. (1988). The spacing effect: A case study in the failure to apply the results of psychological research. *American Psychologist, 43*, 627–634.

Ebbinghaus, H. (1913). *Memory: A contribution to experimental psychology* (H. A. Rogers & C. E. Bussenius, Trans.). New York, NY: Teachers College. (Original work published in 1895.)

Fender, G. (2004). *Learning to learn: Strengthening study skills and brain power.* Nashville, TN: Incentive Publications.

Gass, S. M., & Selinker, L. (2008). *Second language acquisition.* Mahwah, NJ: Lawrence Erlbaum Associates.

Gobet, F., Lane, P. C. R., Croker, S., Cheng, P. C. H., Jones, G., Oliver, I. . . . J. M. (2001) Chunking mechanisms in human learning. *Trends in Cognitive Sciences, 5*, 236–243.

Gobet, F., Voogt, A. J., & Retschitzki, J. (2004). *Moves in mind: The psychology of board games.* Hove, England: Psychology Press.

Guthrie, J. (2008) (Ed.). *Engaging adolescents in reading.* Thousand Oaks, CA: Corwin Press.

Harlow, H. F., McGaugh, J. L., & Thompson, R. F. (1971). *Psychology.* San Francisco, CA: Albion.

Harmer, J. (2007). *The practice of English language teaching.* White Plains, NY: Longman.

Illeris, K. (2000). *Learning theory and adult education.* Paper presented at the AERC Conference in Vancouver, Canada. Retrieved from http://newprairiepress.org/cgi/viewcontent.cgi?article=2260&context=aerc

Krashen, S. (1982). *Principles and practice in second language acquisition.* Oxford, England: Pergamon Press, Inc.

Lee, H. S., & Anderson, J. R. (2013). Student learning: What has instruction go to do with it? *The Annual Review of Psychology, 64*, 445–469. doi:10.1146/annurev-psych-112011-143833

Miller, G. A. (1956). The magical number seven, plus or minus two: Some limits on our capacity for processing information. *Psychological Review, 63*, 81–97.

Novak, J. (1980). *Handbook for learning how to learn program.* Ithaca, NY: New York State College of Agriculture and Life Sciences.

Olivier, C., & Bowler, R. E. (1996). *Learning to learn.* New York, NY: Fireside/Simon & Schuster.

Pavlov, I. P. (1927). *Conditioned reflexes.* London, England: Oxford University Press.

Peregoy, S. F., & Boyle, O. F. (2008). *Reading, writing, and learning in ESL: A resource book for K12 teachers,* 5th ed. New York, NY: Pearson/Allyn & Bacon.

Perry, M., Woolley, J., & Ifcher, J. (1995). Adult abilities to detect children's readiness to learn. *International Journal of Behavioral Development, 18*(2), 365–381.

Piaget, J. (1955). *The child's construction of reality.* London, England: Routledge & Kegan Paul.

Richards, J. C., & Rodgers, T. S. (2014). *Approaches and methods in language teaching.* 3rd ed. Cambridge, England: Cambridge University Press.

Sessa, V. I., & London, M. (2008). Intervention to stimulate group learning in organizations. *Journal of Management, 27*(6), 554–573.

Siemens, G. (2005). Connectivism: A learning theory for the digital age. *International Journal of Instructional Technology and Distance Learning*, *2*(1). Retrieved from http://itdl.org/Journal/Jan_05/article01.htm

Skinner, B. F. (1978). Why don't we use the behavioral sciences? *Human Nature*, *1*(1), 32.

Skinner, B. F. (1988). What ever happened to psychology as the science of behavior? *Counseling Psychology Quarterly*, *1*, 111–122.

Sousa, D. A. (2005). *How the brain learns*, 3rd ed. Thousand Oaks, CA: Corwin Press/Sage Publications.

Sprinthall, N. A., Sprinthall, R. C., & Oja, S. N. (1994). *Educational psychology: A developmental approach*, 6th ed. New York, NY: McGraw Hill Inc.

Stevick, E. J. (1976). *Memory, meaning, and method: Some psychological perspectives on language learning*. Rowley, MA: Newbury House Publishers.

Stoller, F. L. (2004). Concept-based instruction: Perspectives on curriculum planning. *Annual Review of Applied Linguistics*, *24*(1), 261–283.

Swan, E. A. (2003). *Concept-oriented reading instruction*. New York, NY: Guilford Press.

Thorndike, E. (1932). *The fundamentals of learning*. New York, NY: Teachers College Press.

Tuovinen, J. E., & Sweller, J. (1999). A comparison of cognitive load associated with discovery learning and worked examples. *Journal of Educational Psychology*, *91*(2), 334–341.

Watson, J. B. (1913). Psychology as the behaviorist views it. *Psychological Review*, *20*, 158–177.

Wertheimer, M. (1982). *Productive thinking*. Enlarged edition, Phoenix edition. Chicago, IL: University of Chicago Press.

Wertheimer, M. (1985). A gestalt perspective on computer simulations of cognitive processes. *Computers in Human Behavior*, *1*(1), 19–33.

White, L. (2003). *Second language acquisition and universal grammar*. Cambridge, England: Cambridge University Press.

11

AN INTRODUCTION TO SECOND
LANGUAGE ACQUISITION

VIGNETTE

We have been practicing numbers from 1 to 100 for the past couple of days. My students are now working in dictation pairs with number flash cards. One student has the flash cards and dictates the number; the other student writes. I watch them thoughtfully as they try to communicate with each other. Their communication is a bit rocky, but I stop myself from getting up to help them out. Ali, my 50-year-old student from Iran, comes to the number 33 on the flash cards. He dictates to Miguel, who is from Mexico. "Durdi Dri," says Ali. Miguel looks puzzled and writes nothing. Ali repeats the number. "Durdi Dri," he says. Still Miguel looks puzzled. "Wha'dyou say?" he says. This time in a louder voice, Ali says again, "Durdi, Dri." Ali's loud voice catches the attention of Fong, my 40-year-old Chinese student. Fong leaves his own partner and comes over to take a look. Fong looks at the number 33 written on Ali's flash card and says, "Ah . . . Furti Fli, Miguel. Furti Fli." Miguel looks at Ali and Fong in total confusion. He looks like he's thinking that his two classmates must be some type of aliens. "Espeak Inglés," he says. Ali shrugs and turns the flash card around for Miguel to see. Miguel smiles. "Ah . . .," he says. (Recognition dawning on him at last.) "Thirti Tri!" I smile. [Personal notes, Sharron Bassano, 1982]

Task: Reflect

Why do you think each of the students in the above vignette pronounces the number 33 in a different way?

Introduction

In terms of its beginnings, the field of *second language acquisition (SLA)* was closely connected to interests related to second language (L2) pedagogy. Although many SLA scholars have research interests that are closely tied to L2 pedagogy, the field of SLA has grown and expanded since its inception to include researchers and scholars from many diverse disciplines who are not principally concerned with language teaching. These scholars come from such diverse fields as linguistics (e.g., sociolinguistics, pragmatics, psycholinguistics), communication, psychology, and cognitive science. For example, theoretical linguists study how languages are learned in order to investigate "the distinctive qualities of the mind that are, so far as we know, unique to humans" (Chomsky, 1968, p. 100). In addition, researchers interested in intercultural communication might study patterns of interaction in order to separate patterns of nonnative speech from characteristics of individual personality. Despite these non-pedagogical leanings that characterize the field of SLA today, the field still has much to offer L2 teachers in terms of providing information to teachers, especially in terms of developing an appreciation for the complexities involved in the process of SLA and an increased understanding of the nature of language itself.

In this chapter, we will introduce you to the field of SLA by looking at some significant historical developments, both pedagogical and non-pedagogical, that have helped define the field. We believe that it is important for all language teaching professionals to become familiar with the basic research in SLA that underpins what we know about how languages are learned.

Several key questions frame much of the research in SLA. The question of *what* is being learned in the acquisition of a second or foreign language is foremost among questions that researchers ask. In order to answer this question, researchers investigate what sounds and sound combinations are possible in a language under investigation (see Chapter 6 for more information on phonology), and what sounds and sound combinations are not possible. In addition,

SLA researchers study word formation (see Chapter 7), the rules that govern how words fit together to form sentences (see Chapter 8), the construction of meaning, and language in different contexts (e.g., see Chapter 3). SLA can refer to any language we acquire after our mother tongue. This additional language can be a second, third, fourth, etc., language acquired. Researchers in the field of SLA also investigate the acquisition of more than one mother tongue (i.e., bi- and multilingualism).

The question of how languages are learned also involves several concepts related to the use of the term *acquisition*. An L2 can be learned consciously, such as in a formal classroom setting, subconsciously through interaction and daily use of the language in real-life contexts, or a combination of both (Krashen, 1982). The word *acquisition* can also refer to *when* different features are acquired. Do we say that a feature has been acquired when it first appears in second language speech or writing, when it appears correctly in more instances than it appears incorrectly, or when it has been fully acquired and the learners make few (if any) errors in their speech or writing? Researchers in the field of SLA construct theories and conceptual models to answer these and other questions.

The basic assumption that SLA researchers and scholars make is that L2 learners create a language system. Selinker (1972) coined the term *interlanguage* to refer to this system, which is composed of features of both the native language (NL) and the target language (TL); it is the term most commonly used today to represent learner language, and it is this interlanguage system that researchers investigate.

In a short introductory chapter on SLA, it is impossible to cover every major contribution to the field. As authors, we have selected some basic concepts in the development of the field that we believe will assist you in gaining a more sophisticated understanding of the nature of language and an appreciation for the contributions the field of SLA has made to English language teaching. In no way are we suggesting that the concepts we present in Chapters 11 and 12 are the only ones of major importance or that we are doing more than providing you with an introduction to the field. We will cover briefly each of the following concepts with an emphasis, where possible, on their pedagogical implications and contributions: contrastive analysis, language transfer, error analysis, morpheme studies (orders of acquisition and developmental sequences), first language acquisition, and Universal Grammar. Because we can only *introduce* these concepts to you, we urge you to consult the references and familiarize yourself with additional research by reading the original works cited in this chapter.

Before you begin working your way through this chapter, take a few moments to reflect on what you already know about how languages are learned, by answering the following true/false questions.

198

Task: Reflect

Decide whether the following statements are true or false. Record your answers on a separate piece of paper. Discuss your answers with a colleague. Then, read the chapter. Return to these statements after you have completed the chapter and see if your answers and points of view have changed.

1 Learning a second or foreign language is like learning your first language.
2 Second and foreign language learner errors are the result of interference from the native language.
3 Second language learners must develop a new set of habits through practice drills and repetition.
4 Language teachers should correct and eradicate learner errors as quickly as they can.
5 Children are better language learners than adults.
6 Children acquire second languages in a natural order that is unaffected by classroom instruction.

Key Historical Developments in SLA

Contrastive Analysis

The field of SLA has its roots in Robert Lado's seminal work entitled *Linguistics Across Cultures* (1957) and in the idea that, in the process of acquiring an L2, learners rely extensively on their native language (NL). Lado states that "individuals tend to transfer the forms and meanings and the distribution of forms and meanings of their native language and culture to the foreign language and culture" (p. 2). It was precisely the phenomena outlined in the classroom vignette above that motivated contrastive analysis (CA). Why are learners performing differently? Does NL play a part? The principal motivation behind Lado's work was the need to create pedagogical materials. In order to produce these materials, he wanted to conduct a CA. In other words, he believed that what he needed to do was make comparisons between the native language and the target language in question. By understanding the similarities and differences between the two languages, he theorized that he could determine the focus needed for language teaching. The basic principle governing CA was that features of the target language that are similar to the native language are easier for learners to acquire and features that are dissimilar are more difficult to acquire and need more focus and attention in the classroom. For example, CA would predict that Spanish-speaking students learning English would have difficulty making alveolar stops /t/ and /d/ in English because Spanish has dental stops rather than alveolar ones. The reverse would also be true for English speakers learning Spanish. English speakers would have difficulty with Spanish dental stops. In fact, CA would be correct in its predictions in such cases. Lado believed that L2 teachers would want classroom materials to help learners produce the sounds correctly and create grammatical sentences and that students would benefit from these activities.

Although the principle governing CA seems intuitively attractive, it does not explain learners' errors in all instances. There are errors that L2 learners make that cannot be predicted. In fact, some errors that are predicted to occur do not and some errors that are not predicted to occur actually do. CA is based on a theory of language transfer that claims that language is the result of habit formation and that learning a second or foreign language is the result of establishing a new set of habits. Therefore, the pedagogical application that resulted from the CA hypothesis was focused on the development of new habits in the TL. Classroom activity that supported this hypothesis was directed towards repetition and the use of drills to help learners form new habits in the TL. Even though CA cannot account for all second language errors, the concept that old knowledge/skills, such as those associated with language, are transferred to a new situation remains an important concept in SLA and does account for an important subset of errors and correct forms. The difficulty lies in determining which errors can be attributed to NL and which errors cannot.

Language Transfer

Closely associated with contrastive analysis is the concept of language transfer. Language transfer has its roots in psychology and in the theory of behaviorism, which states that "transfer of training from old to new situations is part and parcel of most, if not all, learning" (Postman, 1971, p. 109). Gass and Selinker (2008, p. 67) offer examples of language transfer from Italian speakers learning Spanish:

Mangia bene il bambino. *[correct Italian]*
Eats well the baby. *[direct English translation]*
Come bien el niño. *[Spanish produced by Italian speakers]*

The hypothesis is that Italian speakers learning Spanish transfer Italian word order to Spanish. Because Spanish and Italian word order are the same, Italian speakers learning Spanish produce the correct sentence. Although some researchers use the terms *positive* and *negative transfer* and refer to negative transfer as *interference*, Gass and Selinker (2001, pp. 67–68) suggest that the process is simply language transfer and that it is native speaker perceptions of the process that determine whether the transfer is *positive* or *negative*.

There are two well-accepted positions that have developed relative to language transfer in SLA—the *a priori*, which is the predictive or strong position, and the *a posteriori*, which is the explanatory or the weak position. The strong position would support the creation of language teaching materials based on language transfer targeting areas for instruction in which learners would have the most difficulty. The weak position focuses on identifying and explaining interlanguage errors.

When researchers began to look at the actual errors that learners made, it became clear that these errors went beyond the simple explanation provided by language transfer or NL interference. For example, French learners of English never prepose the object pronoun but follow correct English word order, thereby producing a violation of French word order:

Je les lis. *[French word order]*
I read them. *[produced by French L2 learners of English]*
I them read. *[not produced by French L2 learners of English]*.

For English speakers learning French, the reverse is true. English speakers learning French follow English language word order.

I read them. *[English word order]*
Je lis les. *[produced by English L2 learners of French]*
Je les lis. *[French word order not produced]*

If language transfer is the sole driving force behind SLA, then why is there a difference between French speakers learning English and English speakers learning French? The sole explanation cannot be language transfer. The answer to the question of what drives second language acquisition is far more complex.

Task: Explore

Think of a language that you have studied other than English or one with which you are familiar. Can you think of at least two second language errors either in oral or written form that you have made or ones that you have heard someone else make that you believe were a result of language transfer? Write down your examples and share them with a friend, teacher, or colleague.

Errors and Error Analysis

In his seminal article entitled "The Significance of Learner Errors," Corder (1967) stated that the answer to what drives second language acquisition could be found by studying learners themselves and the errors they make. He believed that learner errors were important and should be collected and analyzed. The process of analyzing learner errors came to be known as error analysis (EA) and, for a time, EA was a major movement in the early development of the field of SLA.

EA had an obvious pedagogical motivation, and a great deal of research that supported EA was carried out in language classrooms. The steps (Corder, 1981) typically followed by EA researchers and classroom teachers were the following: (1) collect data, (2) identify errors, (3) classify errors, (4) quantify the errors, (5) analyze source of errors, and (6) offer remediation. Although this approach seems fairly straightforward, there were problems associated with these steps.

One of the principal problems with both CA and EA was situated in the difficulty of identifying the source of learner errors—in other words, which errors are associated with native language interference and which errors are developmental and not associated with language interference. Researchers proposed different ways of categorizing and talking about different types of errors, such as interlingual vs. intralingual. Interlingual errors involve cross-linguistic comparisons (e.g., interference from L1), while intralingual errors are developmental in nature. Dulay and Burt (1974) were among the first researchers who recognized the difficulty in determining whether the source of an error is of one type or another. It is important for SLA researchers to sort out error types to develop an understanding of what drives SLA (Schumann, 1979).

Researchers such as Schachter (1974) found additional problems with EA. Schachter's research recognized the inadequacies of error analysis and helped us understand more about the specific features of learner *interlanguage*. By look-ing at the relative clause errors that speakers from five different native language backgrounds made in English, she demonstrated that by focusing only on errors we do not get a true picture of *interlanguage*. For example, in Schachter's study, the results obtained through error analysis alone present a skewed picture of the learner interlanguage. In Schachter's data, Persian and Arabic L1 speakers had the largest number of relative clause production errors in English; yet, they have relative clause structure more similar to English (i.e., the relative clause is placed after the noun it modifies). Chinese and Japanese L1 speakers have relative clause structure that is less similar to English (i.e., the relative clause is placed before the noun it modifies); yet, these subjects had fewer relative clause production errors. This result seems counterintuitive because one would sup-pose that the L2 learners who have NL structures more similar to TL structures to acquire the TL structure more easily than L2 learners who have NL structures more dissimilar to the TL. By analyzing not only learner errors, but by also looking at the total number of instances of use and the total correct uses of the form, we get a more complete understanding of L2 learner behavior relative to this structure. Because Persian and Arabic relative clause structure is similar to English relative clause structure, Persian and Arabic L1 speakers feel more comfortable using the structure and use it more often; consequently, they make more mistakes than L1 speakers of Japanese or Chinese who use the structure less often and avoid its use when they can. When they do use it, they pay con-siderably more attention to the structure than their Persian or Arabic peers, thereby resulting in fewer instances of use and with fewer overall errors. This information would not have come to light through error analysis only. The anal-ysis of non-errors gives us important information about the developing system of L2 learners.

Kleinmann's (1977) study with Arabic speakers vs. Spanish and Portuguese speakers with the use of passives, present progressive, infinitive complements, and direct object pronouns clearly demonstrated the concept of avoidance with these subjects. The difficulty level of four structures being investigated was pre-dicted to vary based on native language. Unlike Schachter's study, Kleinmann determined that the subjects knew the rules for the structures in question so that the differences in performance between the two groups could not be attributed to differences in knowledge of the structures. An analysis of learner language, including learner errors, showed that the two groups performed dif-ferentially. Although the source of avoidance is in dispute (i.e., Is the source the NL, TL, or the inherent difficulty of the structure in question?), the two groups performed differently relative to the structures in question.

Morpheme Order Studies

Based on the original research done in first language acquisition by Brown (1973), Dulay and Burt (1974, 1975) conducted research using the "Bilingual Syntax Measure" (BSM) with elementary school children learning English as a second language. Although their research relied on methodology from Brown's L1 research, it suggested a different theoretical orientation. The early morpheme study research suggested that native language was less of a factor in second language acquisition than mental processes and innate propensity for language common to all humans. In addition to the studies done with L2 children, Bailey, Madden, and Krashen (1974) conducted research with adults and found similar results. By looking at a set of morphemes in English (e.g., pronoun case, article, singular form of *to be* [copula], *-ing*, singular auxiliary, possessive, plural, third person singular, past regular tense, and irregular past tense), Dulay and Burt found that similar patterns of development were present in L2 speakers learning English regardless of native language background. In other words, L2 speakers of English acquired features of these inflectional morphemes in roughly the same order even though the acquisition of the morphemes did not occur at precisely the same age. Their research acknowledged that variance in order of acquisition could be a result of several factors, such as salience (e.g., whether features are stressed or not, such as *-ing* vs. *-ed*) and lack of exception (e.g., possessive *-'s* is used without exception but past tense *-ed* is not). Their research emphasized a view of second language acquisition that was not behaviorist in origin (i.e., not a result of imitation and practice) but rather mentalist in nature (i.e., acknowledging an innate mechanism).

While morpheme order studies made a significant contribution to the field of SLA, the studies were not without their problems. Porter (1977) used the BSM with English-speaking children ages two and four and the same scoring procedure as the one found in Dulay and Burt (1973), but she arrived at an order for her subjects that was closer to the L2 order than the predicted L1 order. This result led researchers to wonder if the orders in the original study conducted by Dulay and Burt were a manifestation of the BSM rather than of actual acquisition orders. However, an interpretation of the results remains unclear because other L2 studies (Krashen, Butler, Birnbaum, & Robertson, 1978; Krashen et al, 1977; and Larsen-Freeman, 1975) not using the BSM found results similar to those of the BSM. Differences in orders of acquisition could be accounted for in other ways. Larsen-Freeman (1978), in analyzing her 1975 study, stated that "the results of this study showed individual variability and native language background to exert some influence on the way morphemes were ordered by language groups within a task" (p. 372), thereby recognizing the influence of NL on orders of acquisition.

In addition to these problems, one of the most serious concerns was with the methodology itself. Wagner-Gough and Hatch (1975) noted that just because the morpheme was present in learner data did not mean that the form had been acquired. In other words, the methodology allowed the presence of the morpheme in learner data to be counted in all instances—both in appropriate and inappropriate contexts. Therefore, given the fact that morphemes in inappropriate contexts were counted in acquisition order data, it is hard to make a case for an order of acquisition. The method of counting morphemes may have been flawed and may not reflect accuracy; yet, accuracy is certainly a necessary component in determining an order of acquisition.

Despite the problems with morpheme studies, it is important to recognize that these studies have been influential because SLA researchers and L2 teachers recognize both orders of acquisition (i.e., the acquisition of inflectional morphemes relative to one another, such as the fact that third person singular is acquired much later than the plural markers -s) and developmental sequences (i.e., stages in the development of a specific structure, such as negation or question formation) in L2 learner language. There are a number of questions from the morpheme studies that remain unanswered, such as the fact that this area of research does not give us an explanation for the order.

As a result of the morpheme study research, the concept of language transfer emerged once again as a plausible explanation for orders of acquisition (Larsen-Freeman, 1978). However, language transfer *revisited* emerged as a concept that was not competing for wholesale acceptance as an explanation for learner errors but, rather, as a concept that could be applied judiciously to help researchers understand *how* and *when* second language learners rely on their native languages.

The revisited version of language transfer included a broadened concept of language transfer (Kellerman and Sharwood Smith, 1986) that included not only language transfer in the more traditional sense, but also such concepts as avoidance, language loss, and rate of learning. Language transfer revisited also placed the learner in the center of the determination of transfer, recognizing that transfer is regulated by such factors as knowledge of the target language, as well as one's perceived distance from it (Schumann, 1978). Therefore, it may be very difficult to predict exactly how one's NL influences SLA.

Task: Explore

Think of a language that you have been studying. Which language structures were easy for you to acquire? What language structures were more difficult? If you are teaching English to speakers of other languages, what English structures are your students having difficulty acquiring? Are these structures a part of the order investigated by SLA researchers?

First Language Acquisition

It may seem like an unusual departure to include a section on first language acquisition (FLA) in a chapter on second language acquisition (SLA); however, there have traditionally been close research ties between the two fields, and the morpheme order studies have their roots in FLA research (Brown, 1973) and in the idea that there is a predictable order of acquisition of certain inflectional morphemes in English.

We believe that when most people begin studying about SLA, they do so by comparing SLA with what they believe the process of FLA to be. This is true even though few people have actually studied FLA formally, and most laypersons do not have a sophisticated view of the process. It is important for teachers, scholars, and researchers who are new to the field of SLA to develop an informed understanding of both FLA and SLA acquisition processes in order to understand how FLA is different from SLA and how the two processes intersect. For example, age of acquisition is not an issue in FLA because everyone with normal intellectual development and in normal circumstances learns a first language (L1); yet, it is an issue in SLA. Early and late bilingualism (i.e., whether exposure to the second or foreign language occurs before or after puberty) is known to be a factor affecting outcomes in SLA. These are important issues for teachers who are working with both young and adult language learners.

There are also similarities between FLA and SLA. Both FLA and SLA proceed in stages, although the stages are different.[1] The first stage in FLA begins before children can actually speak and is characterized by the ways in which very young children attempt to communicate their needs, such as by crying, smiling, and cooing. When the sounds are interpreted as "words" by parents or other caregivers, such as *dadda* and *mama*, children have moved to the babbling stage (about six months). Meaning is often attached to babbling through the use of stress and intonation, so children are definitely communicating their needs and wants through their developing language system.

As babbling progresses, it eventually turns into the use of words, although the change from babbling to words is not immediate, nor is it linear (Vihman, 1996). There also seems to be a point in FLA when children recognize that words refer to things in their environment. This is the point when the use of words increases and babbling decreases. For most children, this happens between 14 and 16 months.

During the word stage, the use of words in FLA fulfills a number of different functions. Words can refer to specific objects (e.g., ball, truck, bottle), individuals (e.g., mom, dad), or actions that individuals take in the environment (e.g., walk, eat, talk), as well as both grammatical (e.g., giving a command) and social (e.g., saying goodbye) functions. In terms of function, adult language does not always correspond to child language. Children both under- and overextend language use. One of our grandchildren (MaryAnn's) uses the word *ball* to represent most toys—a clear example of overextension. At the same time, he perceives the word *flower* to refer only to *roses*, a clear underextension.

Child pronunciation differs from adult pronunciation in terms of perception and production. To begin with, children can perceive a difference in pronunciation even if they themselves are not able to make the difference in their own speech. A child asking her mother for a *wet rag* asked for a *wet rug*, a request that was clearly a mystery for the mother. In responding to the child's request, the mother queried, *A wet rug?* The frustrated child said, *No, a wet rug, a wet rug* back to the mother. Clearly the child perceived the difference between *rug* and *rag* in adult speech but was not able to make the distinction in her own speech. In addition to differences in perception, child pronunciation also differs in production, specifically the ability to delete and substitute sounds. Ingram (1986) gave us an example of *dedo* for *potato* (deletion). One of us (MaryAnn) recorded other deletions and substitutions—for example, *teat* for *treat* and *cash* for *crash*. Foster-Cohen (1999) also discussed examples from Smith (1973), whose child made regular substitutions with /d/, /g/, and /z/. In this case, the child had the ability to make the appropriate sounds but could not put the sounds in the appropriate environments.

At the same time that a child's pronunciation is changing and developing, so is their control of syntax. Children eventually move from the one-word stage and begin to combine words. When children begin combining words, they usually begin with content words, such as *mommy help* or *daddy up*. Function words, such as articles and grammatical endings, are missing from child language at this stage. Eventually a child's language evolves from two words into *telegraphic* speech. *Telegraphic* speech is characterized as *the minimum language needed to communicate the message*, much like the language adults use when sending a telegram. As children develop language skills, their utterances become longer. L1 researchers pay attention to the length of utterances, which is referred to as mean length of utterance (MLU), as evidence of FLA (i.e., the longer the utterance, the more developed the L1 system is thought to be).

In addition to MLUs, L1 researchers have also looked at the developmental sequences of specific grammatical features, such as negation, question formation, and relative clauses. For example, children in the early developmental stages of question formation use intonation to form questions while children in later developmental stages are capable of using inversion with wh- questions (i.e., inverting subject/verb word order for questions (e.g., *Where can I find them?* vs. **Where I can find them?*).

Universal Grammar

As L2 researchers and teachers moved away from behaviorist notions of language acquisition, they moved towards emerging mentalist views. These views led researchers in SLA to consider the research in linguistics on language universals; namely, *typological universals* (i.e., what types of languages are possible).[2] Typological universals have been important in SLA because they inform our thinking about what constitutes a definition of a natural language. Greenberg (1963) proposed that it was possible to generalize across geographically nonadjacent languages regarding the possibilities for the types of structures that could occur. For example, in relative clause formation, the basic principle is that one can predict the types of relative clauses a given language will have based on a hierarchy (Keenan & Comrie, 1977).[3] Subject relative clauses are lowest in the hierarchy, with direct object relative clauses ranking higher. The claim is that languages that have indirect object relative clauses will also have direct relative clauses. Those that have direct object relative clauses will also have subject relative clauses, and so forth. The questions that this hierarchy poses are interesting from both a pedagogical and non-pedagogical standpoint. From a pedagogical standpoint, the hierarchy is interesting because it tells us something about the nature of abstract knowledge in the mind and access to the language faculty. If a hierarchy exists in SLA, then this hierarchy has implications for L2 pedagogy. For example, teaching lower-ordered hierarchical features before higher-ordered hierarchical features might make the structures more available for L2 learners.

Language transfer is essentially data-driven and descriptive rather than theory-driven. Universal Grammar (UG) is theory-driven and has its roots in typological universals. Chomsky (1975) defines UG as "the system of principles, conditions, and rules that are elements or properties of all human language (p. 2)." As such, UG "is taken to be a characterization of the child's pre-linguistic state" (Chomsky, 1981, p. 7). The basic premise behind UG is that it is the driving force in FLA and represents the "relevant component of the language faculty" (Chomsky, 1968, p. 167). "If properties of human language are part of the mental representation of language, it stands to reason that they do not cease being properties in just those instances in which a nonnative language system is being employed" (Gass & Selinker, 2001, p. 169). If these concepts are true, then it must also be true that impossible phenomena in world language systems are also impossible in interlanguages. Even when interlanguage forms violate target language norms, they do not violate language universals because the interlanguage forms may be present in some world language. "Whatever is true for primary languages must also be true for interlanguages" (Eckman, Moravcsik, & Wirth, 1989, p. 195).

The main question relative to UG for SLA—and ultimately, by extension, for L2 pedagogy—is the extent to which the constraints that govern natural languages also govern interlanguage systems. The theory of UG makes the assumption that language is comprised of a set of abstract principles that "characterize core grammars of all natural languages" (Gass & Selinker, 2001, p. 169). Along with these invariable principles, there are also parameters. The concept of parameters refers to the restrictions or the finite set of options (Ellis, 1994) on the variation of the principles, and they also determine the extent to which languages can vary (Cook, 1997). One of the problems with language transfer, particularly with CA, is that there is no way to show how related structures are linked in the minds of second language users (Gass & Selinker, 2001). UG links structures through its principles and parameters. Based on this notion, the main issue for SLA—and, ultimately, for L2 pedagogy—is whether parameters can be reset and, if so, how best to reset them.

One of the most interesting aspects related to the concept of parameters is that parameters often involve clustering. An example of clustering is known as pro-drop. *Pro-drop* is short for languages that allow for the omission of the subject pronoun, such as Spanish and Italian (e.g., *Tengo el libro* vs. *Yo tengo el libro*). There are a number of properties associated with this parameter, such as the omission of the subject pronoun itself and the inversion of subjects and verbs in declarative vs. interrogative sentences. Languages will either have all of the properties associated with the pro-drop parameter (such as Italian and Spanish do) or none of them (such as English and French). White (1985) and Lakshmanan (1986) have both presented data to support this hypothesis. Being able to determine the specific principles and parameters for an interlanguage could help L2 pedagogues in constructing more effective and efficient classroom learning activities.

Children learning their first languages are able to learn complex sets of language abstractions with considerable speed and ease without having been exposed to the language abstractions extensively through input. This concept is known as the *Poverty of Stimulus*. UG postulates that humans are equipped with an innate mechanism (i.e., a language faculty) that limits or constrains the possibilities for grammar. The *Subset Principle* in UG is a learning principle that predicts the following: when there are choices to be made, learners will choose the smaller grammar. In other words, they will choose the grammar that is a subset of another. There is empirical evidence to suggest that this is the case (Trahey & White, 1993; White, 1989, 1991). Gass and Selinker (2008) provide a non-language example of the Subset Principle in order to help clarify the principle.

> To think of this in non-language terms, consider two cultures that use different counting systems: The first counts by 1s so that the following are all possible: 1, 2, 3, 4, 5, 6, 7, 8, 9, 10; the second counts by even numbers only, so that the following are possible: 2, 4, 6, 8, 10. Clearly, the second system is a subset of the first, allowing only a portion of the first system. Now assume that you are a member of the first culture, but you have recently moved to a country where the second system is the norm. Obviously, you will not hear any use of 1, 3, 5, 7, 9, and you might make the reasonable assumption that not hearing those numbers is nothing more than an accidental occurrence. That being the case, you would use your superset system until or unless someone specifically provided you with some feedback (correction). There is nothing from the input that will inform you that odd numbers are not possible. Now take the opposite situation: You are a member of the second culture and have moved to a place where culture one's system is the norm. You will immediately notice from the input that there is new information to learn (1, 3, 5, 7, 9) and can therefore modify your system on the basis of listening (or reading). Thus, moving from a subset system to a superset system requires only that the information be available from the input, whereas moving from a superset system to a subset system requires additional information (e.g., correction or some prior knowledge about language counting possibilities).
>
> (p. 172)

The above example provides non-language support for the two kinds of evidence that learners use to hypothesize about the correctness of language forms.

These two types of evidence are positive evidence (i.e., what speakers get from the input) and negative evidence (i.e., what speakers get from feedback on the correctness of the L2 language they generate).

In the field of SLA, the question surrounding UG for researchers has focused on access. Is the innate language faculty that children have access to in constructing their L1 grammars available in SLA? White (2000) suggests that there are five positions concerning the availability of UG in SLA. These positions focus on two variables—language transfer and access to UG. Four of the five positions support access to UG in some form or other (Eubank, 1994; Schwartz, 1998; Schwartz & Sprouse, 1994; Vainikka & Young-Scholten, 1996). Language transfer can either be full, partial, or no transfer. UG access can either be full, partial, or no transfer. For example, in the full transfer/no access version (White, 2000), the initial state of learning in the L2 is the L1 final state. L2 learners have access to UG only through the L1. This is quite different from the second position, in which there is no transfer/full access view (Epstein, Flynn, & Martohardjono, 1996, 1998). In this position the starting point for SLA is UG itself. L1 and L2 acquisition proceed in the same way and end up at the same point. The UG perspective in SLA is tied to the concept of learnability and the issue of positive evidence because the hypothesis is that it is through positive evidence in the input and the super-set/subset relationships that learners are able to reset a parameter and move towards the TL norm.

Conclusion

In this chapter on SLA, we have introduced you to key concepts that have been influential in the development of SLA—contrastive analysis, language transfer, error analysis, and morpheme order studies. In addition, we have covered other important concepts, such as language universals and universal grammar, and provided you with some general information on FLA. The information presented in this chapter is by no means meant to be exhaustive. There are certainly other concepts important for L2 pedagogy. Of course, we have not included them in this introduction because of space issues; we have had to be selective. In Chapter 12, we will take another look at the field of second language acquisition by looking at some additional research in SLA that has definite and specific pedagogical applications, such as input, interaction, teacher talk, output, and non-language influences on SLA, such as attitude and motivation.

Task: Expand

If this chapter has piqued your interest in the research in second language acquisition, you may want to explore the following books in order to deepen your understanding.

Ellis, R. (1994). *The study of second language acquisition.* London, England: Oxford University Press.

This book serves as a comprehensive and accessible introduction to second language acquisition research and as a reference book in general for the field of study. The first section provides a general framework for the study of second language acquisition. Other sections in the book deal with learner language, the linguistic environment and external factors, learner internal mechanisms, and individual differences among language learners. There is also a section that deals specifically with classroom second language acquisition.

Gass, S. M., Behney, J., & Plonsky, L. (2013). *Second language acquisition: An introductory course,* 4th ed. New York, NY: Routledge.

This introductory text is in its fourth edition and has been very popular for students studying second language acquisition. There are 16 chapters that provide an excellent overview of the field, including chapters on working with second language data and data analysis.

Questions for Discussion

1 Why did contrastive analysis (CA) fall out of favor with SLA researchers?
2 What were the specific problems associated with error analysis (EA)? Provide specific examples of the problems.
3 Define the behaviorist and mentalist views of SLA and discuss their differences.
4 Explain why principles and parameters are important in UG.
5 Explain the morpheme order studies and their importance in SLA.

Notes

1 See Chapter 12 for a discussion of stages in SLA.
2 Also known as implicational universals, in which language elements are predicted by implication through the existence of other language elements.

3 The hierarchy is the following: subject relative clause, direct object relative clause, indirect object relative clause, oblique or object of preposition relative clause, genitive relative clause, object of comparative clause.

References

Bailey, N., Madden, C., & Krashen, S. (1974). Is there a "natural sequence" in adult second language learning? *Language Learning, 24*, 235–243.

Brown, R. (1973). *A first language*. Cambridge, MA: Harvard University Press.

Chomsky, N. (1968). *Language and mind*. New York, NY: Harcourt Brace Jovanovich.

Chomsky, N. (1975). *Reflections on language*. New York, NY: Pantheon.

Chomsky, N. (1981). *Lectures on government and binding*. Dordrecht, The Netherlands: Foris.

Cook, V. (1997). *Inside language*. London, England: Edward Arnold.

Corder, S. P. (1967). The significance of learners' errors. *International Review of Applied Linguistics, 5*, 161–170.

Corder, S. P. (1981). *Error analysis in interlanguage*. Oxford, England: Oxford University Press.

Dulay, H., & Burt, M. (1973). Should we teach children syntax? *Language Learning, 23*, 245–258.

Dulay, H., & Burt, M. (1974). You can't learn without goofing. In J. Richards (Ed.). *Error analysis: Perspectives on second language acquisition* (pp. 95–123). London, England: Longman.

Dulay, H., & Burt, M. (1975). Creative construction in second language learning and teaching. In M. Burt & H. Dulay (Eds.), *On TESOL '75: New directions in second language learning, teaching, and bilingual education* (pp. 21–32). Washington, DC: Teachers of English to Speakers of Other Languages.

Eckman, F., Moravcsik, E., & Wirth, J. (1989). Implicational universals and interrogative structures in the interlanguage of ESL learners. *Language Learning, 39*, 173–205.

Ellis, R. (1994). *The study of second language acquisition*. London, England: Oxford University Press.

Epstein, S., Flynn, S., & Martohardjono, G. (1996). Second language acquisition: Theoretical and experimental issues in contemporary research. *Brain and Behavioral Sciences, 19*, 677–714.

Epstein, S., Flynn, S., & Martohardjono, G., (1998). The strong continuity hypothesis in adult L2 acquisition of functional categories. In S. Flynn, G. Martohardjono, & W. O'Neil (Eds.), *The generative study of second language acquisition* (pp. 61–77). Mahwah, NJ: Lawrence Erlbaum.

Eubank, L. (1994). Optionality and the initial state in L2 development. In T. Hoekstra & B. Schwartz (Eds.), *Language acquisition studies in generative grammar* (pp. 369–388). Amsterdam, The Netherlands: John Benjamins.

Foster-Cohen, S. (1999). *An introduction to child language development*. London, England: Longman.

Gass, S. M., Behney, J., & Plonsky, L. (2013). *Second language acquisition: An introductory course*, 4th ed. New York, NY: Routledge.

Gass, S. M., & Selinker, L. (2008) *Second language acquisition. An introductory course*, 2nd ed. Mahwah, NJ: Lawrence Erlbaum.

Greenberg, J. H., (1963). Some universals of grammar with particular reference to the order of meaningful elements. In J. H. Greenberg (Ed.), *Universals of language* (pp. 73–113). Cambridge, MA: MIT Press.

Ingram, D. (1986). Phonological development: Production. In P. Fletcher & P. Garman (Eds.). *Language acquisition*, 2nd ed. (pp. 223–239). Cambridge, England: Cambridge University Press.

Kellerman, E., & Sharwood-Smith, M., (Eds.). (1986). *Cross-linguistic influence in second language acquisition*. Elmsford, NY: Pergamon.

Keenan, E. & Comrie, B., (1977). Noun phrase accessibility and Universal Grammar. *Linguistic Inquiry, 8*, 63–69.

Kleinmann, H. (1977). Avoidance behavior in adult second language acquisition. *Language Learning, 27*, 93–107.

Krashen, S. (1982). Principles and practice in second language acquisition. London, England: Pergamon.

Krashen, S., Butler, J., Birnbaum, R., & Robertson, J. (1978). Two studies in language acquisition and language learning. *International Review of Applied Linguistics, 39*(1), 73–92.

Krashen, S., Houck, N., Giunchi, P., Bode, S., Birnbaum, R., & Strei, G., (1977). Difficulty order for grammatical morphemes for adult second language performers using free speech. *TESOL Quarterly, 11*, 338–341.

Lado, R. (1957). *Linguistics across cultures*. Ann Arbor: University of Michigan Press.

Lakshmanan, U. (1986). The role of parametric variation in adult second language acquisition: A study of the "pro-drop" parameter. *Papers in Applied Linguistics—Michigan (PALM), 2*, 97–118.

Larsen-Freeman, D. (1975). The acquisition of grammatical morphemes by adult ESL students. *TESOL Quarterly, 9*, 409–430.

Larsen-Freeman, D. (1978). An explanation for the morpheme acquisition order of second language learners. *Language Learning, 26*, 125–134.

Porter, J. (1977). A cross-sectional study of morpheme acquisition in first language learners. *Language Learning, 27*, 47–62.

Postman, L. (1971). Transfer, interference and forgetting. In J. W. Kling & L. A. Riggs (Eds.), *Woodworth and Schlosberg's experimental psychology* (pp. 1019–1132). New York, NY: Holt, Rinehart & Winston.

Schachter, J. (1974). An error in error analysis. *Language Learning, 24*, 205–214.

Schumann, J. (1978). The pidginization process: A model for second language acquisition. Rowley, MA: Newbury House.

Schumann, J. (1979). The acquisition of English negation by speakers of Spanish: A review of the literature. In R. Andersen (Ed.), *The acquisition and use of Spanish and English as first and second languages* (pp. 3–32). Washington, DC: Teachers of English to Speakers of Other Languages.

Schwartz, B. (1998). On two hypotheses of "transfer" in L2A: Minimal trees and absolute influence. In S. Flynn, G. Martohardjono, & W. O'Neil (Eds.), *The generative study of second language acquisition* (pp. 35 59). Mahwah, NJ: Lawrence Erlbaum.

Schwartz, B., & Sprouse, R. (1994). Word order and nominative case in nonnative language acquisition: A longitudinal study of (L1 Turkish) German interlanguage. In T. Hoekstra & B. Schwartz (Eds.), *Language acquisition studies in generative grammar: Papers in honor of Kenneth Wexler from the 1991 GLOW Workshops* (pp. 317 368). Amsterdam, The Netherlands: John Benjamins.

Selinker, L. (1972). Interlanguage. *International Review of Applied Linguistics, 10,* 209 231.

Smith, N. (1973). *The acquisition of phonology: A case study.* Cambridge, England: Cambridge University Press.

Trahey, M., & White, L. (1993). Positive evidence and preemption in the second language classroom. *Studies in Second Language Acquisition, 15,* 181 204.

Vainikka, M. & Young-Scholten, M. (1996). The early stages of adult L2 syntax: Additional evidence from Romance speakers. *Second Language Research, 12,* 140 176.

Vihman, M. (1996). Phonological development: The origins of language in the child. Oxford, England: Basil Blackwell.

Wagner-Gough, K., & Hatch, E., (1975). The importance of input in second language acquisition studies. *Language Learning, 25,* 297 308.

White, L. (1985). The "pro-drop" parameter in adult second language acquisition. *Language Learning, 35,* 47 62.

White, L. (1989). *Universal Grammar and second language acquisition.* Amsterdam, The Netherlands: John Benjamins.

White, L. (1991). Adverb placement in second language acquisition: Some effects of positive and negative evidence in the classroom. *Second Language Research, 7,* 133 161.

White, L. (2000). Second language acquisition: From initial to final state. In J. Archibald (Ed.), *Second language acquisition and linguistic theory* (pp. 219 234). Amsterdam, The Netherlands: John Benjamins.

12

SECOND LANGUAGE ACQUISITION
AND SECOND LANGUAGE PEDAGOGY

VIGNETTE

I have been working in Brazil for about two weeks, conducting teacher education workshops, visiting English language teaching programs, and observing classrooms and teachers. This morning, I visited one of the largest centers in Brasilia and observed four different teachers in action. There was one native speaker (NS) teacher and three non-native English-speaking teachers (NNESTs). All of them were experienced and well-prepared teachers working with adolescents and young adult learners. The teachers followed similar routines in their classes. They introduced the grammatical structures on which they were going to work and explained the rules, mostly in English. Then, they set up practice sessions and activities in pairs and groups. At the end of their classes, they conducted reviews of the key grammatical points. Students actively participated in the interactive practice sessions and review work and, based on what I observed, I'd say that most of the students learned what was being taught. After each class, some students approached me with questions, wanting opportunities for interaction. It struck me as curious that on more than one occasion I heard the students make mistakes in using the structures they had just worked on during the lesson and had used correctly in the review. [Excerpt from Research notes/Christison]

Task: Reflect

Think about your experiences as either a language learner or a language teacher in the classroom. Do you think language learners acquire the structures they are taught in the classroom? Talk about the experiences you have had that support your point of view.

Introduction

In Chapter 11, we learned that the early work in second language acquisition (SLA) research was motivated by the pedagogical interests of the researchers because many of these researchers had been teachers or were still practicing teachers. As teachers, these researchers were interested in how effective different teaching methodologies—for example, grammar translation, audiolingualism, the Silent Way (Gattegno, 1972, 1976), the Natural Approach (Terrell, 1977, 1982), and community language learning (see Richards & Rodgers, 2014—were in terms of what learners could and could not do with the target language. The studies that focused on method comparisons were largely inconclusive, failing to support one methodology over another. For example, Smith (1970) and Scherer and Wertheimer (1964) compared grammar translation with audiolingual methodology and found no significant differences between the two in terms of learning outcomes. The failure of the early studies on the effectiveness of different methodologies led researchers to consider questions that were not directed towards a specific methodology but were directed to how learners acquire a second language (L2). These early researchers used case studies to help them learn about the process of SLA. Although most of the early case study research dealt with individual learners and was situated in natural settings outside of the classroom, the researchers identified constructs that teachers could easily understand and relate to, such as the nature of learners' errors and the order in which certain features of the second language (L2) were acquired (Dulay & Burt, 1973).

In an introductory chapter on SLA and L2 pedagogy, it is impossible to cover all of the research that is germane and important to L2 teachers. Consequently, we have made some decisions about what to include that are based on our own experiences as English language teachers and L2 teacher educators. We begin the chapter with a brief introduction to the methods that have been used for researching language learning in classroom contexts. We have selected the following subfields of SLA for review: the role of input and interaction in SLA and the study of form focused instruction. Finally, we turn our attention to two non-linguistic factors that influence SLA: attitude and motivation.

Methods of Researching Language Learning in Classrooms

There are a number of different research traditions that have been used in L2 classroom contexts. Following the work of Chaudron (1988) we will consider four research traditions: (1) psychometric, (2) interaction analysis, (3) discourse analysis, and (4) ethnographic. The *psychometric tradition* can be defined in terms of experimental and quasi-experimental research methodologies with control and experimental groups and/or pre- and post-testing. This type of research design was used in the comparative methods studies mentioned earlier (see Scherer & Wertheimer, 1964; Smith, 1970). However, with the exception of Asher (1977), who reviewed a study designed to compare *Total Physical Response (TPR)*[1] with other methodologies (Asher, Kusudo, & de la Torre, 1974), comparative methods studies did not produce evidence of the superiority of one method over another, although there were differences in outcomes (Spada, 1986, 1987). Of course, there could be several reasons for the lack of method superiority. Perhaps, as Clark (1969) and Lightbown (1990) suggest, the differences between the methods being compared were not sufficiently clear because there were similarities among the methodologies being researched. Another reason might be that learners benefit differentially from different methods (a point we will return to in Chapter 13). However, in a study that was designed to compare differences between communicative language teaching (CLT) and non-CLT classrooms, Allen, Swain, Harley, and Cummins (1990) found that learners achieved similar outcomes in each context. Based on outcomes from the method comparison research, researchers came to the conclusion that this type of research design was likely not the most appropriate design for investigating the effect that language teaching has on L2 learning (Ellis, 2004, 2012).

Another type of research methodology that has been used for investigating language classroom is called *interaction analysis*. It involves using a system for coding specific classroom behaviors. According to Long (1980), there are three different systems for coding: (1) *category coding*, in which each event is coded each time it occurs; (2) *sign coding*, in which each event is coded only once within a specified time span; and (3) *rating coding*, in which an estimate of the frequency of the event is determined after the event has occurred. In order to conduct this type of research, specific behaviors must be isolated and coded on a form each time the behavior occurs (Long, 1980). The relative importance of the behaviors being observed is generally determined by the researchers' (and/or teachers') assumptions, which are based on classroom experience, rather than a specific theoretical model. It is difficult to make comparisons across studies because researchers focus on different behaviors. Without a theoretical model to guide interaction analysis, there is the risk of producing simple lists of disconnected behaviors with no basis for determining what behaviors to consider in combination.

Discourse analysis is used to describe interactions that occur in the classroom and draws on the work of Sinclair and Coulthard (1975). Researchers in discourse analysis try to understand the function of individual utterances and how these utterances work together to form larger discoursal units (see Chapter 9 for additional information). Researchers in SLA have used discourse analysis to develop an in-depth understanding of specific areas of discourse, such as teacher feedback and teacher questioning (Long & Sato, 1984).

Ethnography is the study of individuals in their own environment, such as teachers and learners in classrooms. Ethnographic research stresses the importance of using multiple data sources, such as observations, question-naires, and face-to-face interviews, to explore multiple perspectives. (see Chapter 5 for further information). Ethnographers in L2 research have used several different approaches to data collection (Long, 1980). Mehan (1979) used an approach to ethnography that focused on soliciting responses from participants to repeated viewings of videotapes, and Wong-Fillmore (1985) conducted her research using *microethnography*, which restricts the research focus to those activities that are considered real for the participants, such as studying how learners form groups, how they stay on task, or what teachers do during group work.

Areas of Investigation in Pedagogical Research

Both teachers and researchers are interested in looking at factors that might influence language learning, such as input, interaction, and form-focused instruction. Both researchers and language teachers concluded several decades ago that classrooms differ on more than just a single variable, such as method (Gaies, 1983). Language classrooms are socially constructed events (Lantolf, 1994; Vygotsky, 1978; Woods, 2003), and the focus of classroom research is to understand these events, to dissect them into their component parts, and to determine how these events affect second language learning.

Input

As a variable in the process of second and foreign language learning, and as an area of investigation, the concept of input has had an interesting and varied history. In the behaviorist view of learning, input was the primary external mechanism (Gass & Selinker, 2008) but was not a causal variable itself. When behaviorism fell out of favor and researchers became more interested in the internal mechanisms that govern second language acquisition, the role of input changed. In a cognitive view of SLA, input is seen as the trigger that sets off the internal mechanism (Krashen, 1981, 1985; Long, 1983b). It is accepted common knowledge that we make gains in a second or foreign language when we understand what people say to us and what we read. Although researchers agree on the importance of input in the process of SLA, they disagree on the strength of its importance. In other words, is it the primary causal variable or is it one of a number of variables responsible for SLA, such as motivation, opportunities for output, individual differences, and negative affect? In addition, we know little about the effects of intensity and duration of input relative to the acquisition of a second language. For many researchers, input and its role in SLA remain complicated issues within the field. However, if you accept the premise that comprehensible input is important for making gains in a second or foreign language, then the role of input in the classroom must be a principal concern for language teachers.

Relative to input, language classrooms are most useful at the beginning levels when learners are unable to access comprehensible target language in the real world. An experienced professional language teacher can modify target language input so that beginning language learners can understand almost all of the input they hear for the duration of the class. Beginning language students would be unable to comprehend this much language during the same time frame in the real world. In the case of foreign language learning, the classroom may be the only source of reliable input in the target language for learners at all levels.

Most language teachers are concerned with providing optimal input in the classroom. In order to make language comprehensible, teachers need to slow down the input and articulate words more carefully. Selecting vocabulary that students will understand, repeating and rephrasing, avoiding slang words, and simplifying syntax all make input easier to understand. Selecting content that is interesting and/or relevant is also important because it encourages the listener to focus on the meaning of the message and on communication. Both content and language features of input must be constantly recycled and reintroduced in the classroom. Most language teachers seriously underestimate how much comprehensible input is required for learners to both understand the language being used and to recognize it in environments outside of the classroom. It takes a skilled teacher to be able to adjust target language input to the level of their students because a language learner is always a moving target. Input that is a bit beyond the proficiency level of most students is considered ideal (Krashen, 1981) because it encourages students to continue to stretch their language learning skills, while still providing them with enough comprehensible input that they will also be motivated to interact and use the target language.

One of the shortcomings of classroom input is that it can be quite limited. This limitation is particularly problematic in traditional classrooms because most of the activity is oriented towards instructional tasks that are quite dissimilar to tasks in the real world. In order to increase opportunities for varied input, teachers have to exercise considerable creativity to expand task types by using realia, role plays, problem-solving tasks, and varied texts. English language teachers should also think about the ways in which the language is used in the real world and concentrate on designing classroom activities so that they are as similar to real-world activities as is possible.

Task: Expand

Work with a partner. Think of three common language learning activities for the classroom. Discuss the role of input in each activity. Who gives the input? How would you characterize the input? What is the relationship between input and output?

Interaction

Historical developments. Most researchers who are interested in SLA and language pedagogy recognize that interaction in the classroom is both a linguistic and a social phenomenon (Lantolf & Appel, 1994) and that the role of interaction is central to the study of second language acquisition. The focus on classroom interaction has placed an emphasis on the study of learner discourse and social interaction and the ways in which learners manipulate their interlanguage resources to make their messages understandable to others. To date, a large number of studies have been done in SLA that deal with input and interaction, and these studies have provided us with a wealth of information about the nature of L2 development and the internalization of L2 knowledge (see, for example, Ellis, 2014; Gass & Mackey, 2013; Gass, Behney, & Plonsky, 2013; Ortega, 2008).

The focus on interaction has changed dramatically since the early 1970s, when interest in classroom interaction among SLA researchers and scholars was in its infancy. Interaction was seen as a vehicle for the reinforcement of grammatical features and specific structures that had been introduced and taught during the lesson. In the vignette that serves as an introduction to this chapter, the teachers were using interaction for this purpose—to reinforce the grammatical features being taught. The research done by Hatch and Wagner-Gough (1976) was the first of a number of studies that went beyond the reinforcement view of interaction and focused on how learner participation in classroom interaction provided opportunities for language to develop separately from the intended practice.

Long (1983a) and Gass and Varonis (1985) investigated talk directed towards L2 learners by native speakers (NS) and the interactions in which they participated. Their research demonstrated that NNS/NNS interactions differed from NS/NNS interactions in terms of their conversational structure. Although the structures of NNS/NNS interactions were not unique, certain structures were more abundant. Long proposed that these interactions could serve as the optimal input needed for L2 learning. Even though the early research into NNS/NNS interactions was promising, it did not resolve all issues. Sato (1986) argued that the role of interaction in language learning was much more complex than researchers thought and that input and interaction were not sufficient to trigger second language acquisition. Swain (1985) argued for *comprehensible output* (in contrast to comprehensible input) and suggested that speaking requires learners to think about the syntactic structure of their utterances and that the act of comprehending does not require that we draw on our knowledge of L2 syntax in the same way as when we are providing output in response to input.

Long (1983b) and Holliday (1995) demonstrated that it is *negotiation of meaning* that has a positive effect on the quality of learners' immediate production. In addition, Pica (1994, 1996) outlined the ways in which interaction can serve as an important source of linguistic data. Mackey (1995) found that certain types of interaction have a positive effect on L2 development—for example, the short-term development of question formation.

Current research. The research on input and interaction has continued for the past three decades with different foci, such as studies on L2 output and reformulations (Adams, 2007; Gass, 2003; Gass & Mackey, 2006),[2] learners' interpretations of *recasts* (Carpenter, Jeon, MacGregor, & Mackey (2006),[3] the relationship between implicit and explicit learning (DeKeyser, 2003), negotiated interaction (Eckerth, 2009; Mackey, 2007), *noticing* and *consciousness raising* (Adams, 2003; Eckerth, 2008; Schmidt, 1990),[4] and instructed SLA (Doughty, 2003, 2004).

Formal Instruction

The research in SLA on formal instruction has attempted to answer the following question: under what conditions do language learners acquire the structures that they are taught? The answer to this question is not a direct one. In the vignette at the beginning of this chapter, the writer observed that in informal conversations the learners were not able to accurately use the structures they had been taught during formal instruction. Both language learners and teachers have reported on this phenomenon.

The research in SLA has focused on two different approaches to teaching language structures in the classroom. The first approach is known as *focus on forms*. In this approach, linguistic forms are isolated and taught individually, followed by interactive practice activities. This is the approach used by the teacher in the vignette at the beginning of this chapter. The other approach is known as *focus on form*. In this approach, the teacher pays attention to both the form and its meaning, and classroom activity revolves around working with the form as it is embedded in a specific text or using the form interactively to complete certain tasks. In focus on form instruction, teachers must decide how to draw students' attention to the specific form on focus and how to provide corrective feedback so that learners notice the form (Schmidt, 1990) and develop a conscious awareness about its use (Eckerth, 2009; Schmidt & Frota, 1986). The focus on form approach is popular among teachers because it allows for the integration of both fluency and accuracy. However, Norris and Ortega (2000), in their meta-analysis on the effectiveness of L2 instruction, found that explicit treatments had a slight advantage over implicit treatments, thereby giving the focus on forms approach an advantage. Nevertheless, it is important to point out that the challenge for the focus on form approach is to determine how to make the form(s) explicit without moving learners away from the focus on larger chunks of text and on participation in tasks. Norris and Ortega also found that treatments combining both an explicit and an implicit focus have the potential to yield the best results. This would suggest an advantage for the focus on form approach, because teachers have an opportunity to expose students to structures implicitly in the form on both texts and tasks.

Task: Expand

Work with a colleague to describe a focus on forms and focus on form lesson. What role does input and interaction play in each of these classrooms?

Learner Attitudes

Learners have attitudes about a number of different things—the target language, the community of L2 speakers, the target culture, their teachers, and classroom learning, to name a few. Most teachers would agree that learners' attitudes affect language learning in the classroom. When learners have positive attitudes about the target language, the culture, and the speakers, these attitudes are thought to have a positive influence on learning outcomes. Similarly, negative attitudes are thought to adversely affect learning and, ultimately, L2 proficiency.

In a discussion of attitudes, Baker (1988) outlines some important considerations for language teachers that we have found most helpful.

1 Attitudes can be modified by experience. This factor is important for English language teachers to remember because classroom experiences can change learners' (and teachers') attitudes from positive to negative, or vice versa.

2 Even though attitudes can be modified by experience, it is also important to remember that, once attitudes have been set, they tend to persist and are somewhat difficult to change. For example, if your learners have positive attitudes, they will not need major and persistent interventions for these attitudes to continue. However, it can also mean that changing attitudes from negative to positive may require more than one positive experience.

3 Attitudes are not inherited; they are learned through experiences and interactions with others. Although it may take more than one positive learning experience in a classroom to develop positive attitudes toward language learning, it is important to remember that it is possible to change attitudes. Creating positive classroom experiences with learners is one way to bring about that change.

4 While it may be true that we are predisposed to act in certain ways based on our experiences and the way in which our experiences have been influential in forming attitudes, it is also important to remember that the connection between actions and attitudes is not a strong one.

5   Attitudes are both cognitive and affective. Language learners can think about their attitudes, so they are cognitive. In addition, they have feelings attached to their attitudes, so they are also affective.

6   We find it useful to think of attitudes on a continuum, so they vary in degree and strength. It may take only a slight change in attitude to move it from negative to positive, or vice versa. For this reason, English language teachers must always be cognizant of the fragile nature of attitudes and carefully monitor classroom events.

In SLA research, there are two different approaches to investigating learner attitudes. The first approach is through self-reporting measures, such as questionnaires. Gardner and Lambert (1972) used this direct approach in their seminal research investigating learners' attitudes towards learning French. Although some researchers have questioned the efficacy of this approach, other researchers have stated that the efficacy of questionnaire research is related to the design of the questionnaire rather than the method itself. Carefully designed questionnaires can improve reliability and construct validity and make it possible to achieve desired results. The second approach to investigating learner attitudes has been an indirect one, asking learners to make judgments. For example, bilingual speakers are asked to read the same passages in two different languages. Learners hear both passages and are asked to make judgments about the readers.

Learner Motivation

SLA researchers consider motivation an important factor in second language acquisition even though there have been differing opinions on the way in which motivation is conceptualized (Crookes & Schmidt, 1989). Skehan (1989) suggested four hypotheses for motivation. First, motivation can come from an inherent interest in a specific task; in other words, participating in the task is something we like to do. Second, motivation can come from the skills we have for participating in the task. The hypothesis is that when we have the requisite skills for participating in a task, we are motivated to do so. Csikszentmihalyi (1990) captures this idea in his theory of flow. *Flow* occurs when the task in which we are involved matches the skill level we have. Most of us can resonate with the experience of becoming so involved in a task that we lose track of time. According to Csiksentmihalyi, this type of experience is called flow. The third hypothesis for motivation is that humans are naturally curious; consequently, we bring a natural curiosity to our participation in all tasks. This natural curiosity is called *intrinsic motivation*. The challenge for language teachers is to understand what factors learners naturally bring to the task of learning and make use of these factors. The final hypothesis for motivation suggests that making use of external incentives, such as extra credit or rewards like candy bars and treats, can be motivating in the short term. This concept is known as *extrinsic motivation*. Extrinsic motivators can be very effective in producing behavior or changes in behavior, particularly if teachers want an immediate response and are not likely to get it in any other way. Nevertheless, it is important to remember that the behavior change is often short-lived and can result in lower-quality performance over time, such as in diminished complex and creative thinking and failure to complete multistep problem-solving tasks.

Motivation is a central component of Gardner's socio-educational model (1985). In his research he worked with two different types of motivation—integrative and instrumental. *Integrative motivation* derives from a personal interest in speakers and the culture of the target language, such as the motivation a young woman might have to learn the language of her spouse's family. *Instrumental motivation* derives from the practical benefits of learning, such as getting a job, a degree, or a promotion. In English as a foreign language context, an instrumental reason for learning the target language may be the most important one. Of course, it is possible for learners to have both integrative and instrumental motivation (Muchnick & Wolfe, 1982). Gardner (1980, 1985) found a positive correlation between integrative motivation and L2 achievement, but other researchers (Oller, Baca, & Vigil, 1977) did not, suggesting that the constructs associated with motivation are not as easy to operationalize as we once assumed.

Gardner's research has sometimes been criticized because it used self-report questionnaires, which do not provide any indication of *effort*, a construct that is often associated with motivation (see Vroom, 1964 and his theory of expectancy). Gliksman (1976) identified behaviors associated with learner effort, such as receiving directed teacher questions, volunteering answers, and receiving positive feedback and reinforcement from the teacher. The higher the integrative motivation (as indicated on the self-report questionnaires), the more these behaviors associated with effort were present.

Gardner's research also distinguished between instrumental orientation and instrumental motivation. *Instrumental orientation* is measured through the self-report questionnaires and depicts one's mindset towards certain features identified in the questionnaire. Instrumental motivation could be measured by rewarding behaviors, such as giving learners extra points on their grade for performing a task successfully. Much of Gardner's research focused on instrumental orientation, and there have been few studies done that investigate the direct effect of instrumental motivation on second and foreign language learning, although some recent studies have focused on learners' perceptions in dual language immersion contexts (see Knell & Chi, 2012; Lindholm-Leary, 2011, 2016).

Conclusion

We began this chapter by reviewing some methods that have been used for conducting SLA research with pedagogical applications, such as experimental and ethnographic methods, and then turned our attention to specific areas for research investigation to include input, interaction, and form-focused instruction. The chapter also concluded with a brief overview of two non-language factors in SLA, attitude and motivation.

Task: Expand

Ellis, R. (2012). *Language teaching research and language pedagogy*. Hoboken, NJ: Wiley Blackwell.

This book examines current research that is centered on second language classrooms. It investigates the implications of the research in SLA for the teaching and learning of foreign languages, including English. It offers insights into the inherent complexities associated with instructed SLA in classroom contexts.

Ellis, R., & Shintani, N. (2013). *Exploring language pedagogy through second language acquisition research*. New York, NY: Routledge.

This book is part of the Routledge Introduction to Applied Linguistics series, in which applied linguistics is a core topic. The book is a resource for teachers who are interested in SLA and may lack the background and experience necessary to read research articles. The purpose of the book is to distill complex and sometimes conflicting findings and help the reader conceptualize the relationship between SLA theory and research and L2 pedagogy.

Questions for Discussion

1 Name two reasons why comparative methods studies were unsuccessful in providing evidence for the superiority of one method over another?

2 Do you believe that language classrooms are socially constructed events? Why? Why not?

3 Discuss the possible roles of interaction in language classrooms.
4 Can students have both instrumental and integrative motivation? How do you know? Should teachers address motivation differently in the classroom for students who are motivated in different ways?
5 Which of the hypotheses about attitude that were covered in this chapter do you find most interesting? Why?

Notes

1 Total Physical Response (Asher, 1977) is an input method for teaching second and foreign languages that has been principally used with beginners. In its simplest form, teachers give commands to students, such as *touch your head, open your mouth, turn off the lights, sit down,* and students respond with the physical movement. Sequences are often contextualized and some individuals have experimented with TPR for intermediate and advanced language learners (Ray & Seely, 1998; Seely & Romijn, 1995).
2 Reformulations can include restatements, summaries, and linguistic paraphrases.
3 Semantic derivations (i.e., meaning is preserved but the lexico-syntactic structures change).
4 According to Schmidt (1990), the relationship between subconscious and conscious knowledge and how this knowledge is internalized revolves around the question of consciousness. The first level of consciousness is awareness or noticing, followed by three other levels of consciousness. Schmidt believes that the role of subconsciousness in language learning has been exaggerated.

References

Adams, R. (2003). L2 output, noticing, and reformulation: Implications for IL development. *Language Teaching Research, 7*(3), 347–376.

Adams, R. (2007). Do second language learners benefit from interacting with each other? In A. Mackey (Ed.), *Conversational interaction in second language acquisition.* (pp. 29–51). Oxford, England: Oxford University Press.

Allen, P., Swain, M., Harley, B., & Cummins, J. (1990). Aspects of classroom treatment: toward a more comprehensive view of second language education. In B. Harley, P. Allen, J. Cummins, & M. Swain (Eds.) (1990), *The development of second language proficiency* (pp. 57–81). New York, NY: Cambridge University Press.

Asher, J. (1977). *Learning another language through actions: The complete teacher's guidebook,* 5th ed. Los Gatos, CA: Sky Oaks Publishing.

Asher, J., Kusudo, J., & de la Torre, R. (1974). Learning a second language through commands: The second field test. *Modern Language Journal, 58,* 24–32.

Baker, C. (1988). *Key issues in bilingualism and bilingual education.* Bristol, England: Multilingual Matters.

Carpenter, H., Jeon, K., MacGregor, D., & Mackey, A. (2006). Learners' interpretation of recasts. *Studies in Second Language Acquisition, 28,* 209–236.

Chaudron, C. (1988). *Second language classrooms*. Cambridge, England: Cambridge University Press.

Clark, J. (1969). The Pennsylvania project and the "audio-lingual vs. traditional" question. *Modern Language Journal*, *53*, 388 396.

Crookes, G., & Schmidt, R. (1989). Motivation: Reopening the research agenda. *University of Hawaii Working Papers in ESL*, *8*, 217 256.

Csikszentmihalyi, M. (1990). *The psychology of optimal experience*. New York, NY: Harper Perennial.

DeKeyser, R. (2003). Implicit and explicit learning. In C. J. Doughty & M. L. Long (Eds.), *A handbook in second language acquisition* (pp. 313 348). Oxford, England: Blackwell Publishers.

Doughty, C. (2003). Instructed SLA: Conditions, compensation and enhancement. In C. J. Doughty & M. L. Long (Eds.), *The handbook of second language acquisition* (pp. 256 310). Oxford, England: Blackwell Publishers.

Doughty, C. (2004). Effects of instruction on learning a second language: A critique of instructed SLA research. In B. VanPatten, J. Wiliams, S. Rott, & M. Oerstreet (Eds.), *Form-meaning connections in second language acquisition* (pp. 181 202). Mahwah, NJ: Lawrence Erlbaum.

Dulay, H. & Burt, M. (1973). Should we teach children syntax? *Language Learning*, *23*, 245 258.

Eckerth, J. (2008). Investigating consciousness-raising tasks: Pedagogically-targeted and non-targeted learning gains. *International Journal of Applied Linguistics*, *18*(2), 119 145.

Eckerth, J. (2009). Negotiated interaction in the L2 classroom. *Language Teaching*, *42*(1), 109 130.

Ellis, R. (2004). *SLA research and language teaching*. Oxford, England: Oxford University Press.

Ellis, R. (2012). *Language teaching research and language pedagogy*. Hoboken, NJ: Wiley Blackwell.

Ellis, R. (2014). *Understanding second language acquisition*. Oxford, England: Oxford University Press.

Ellis, R., & Shintani, N. (2013). *Exploring language pedagogy through second language research*. New York, NY: Routledge.

Gaies, S. (1983). The investigation of language classroom processes. *TESOL Quarterly*, *17*, 205 18.

Gardner, R. (1980). On the validity of affective variables in second language acquisition: Conceptual, contextual, and statistical considerations. *Language Learning*, *30*, 255 270.

Gardner, R. (1985). *Social psychology and second language learning: The role of attitude and motivation*. London, England: Edward Arnold.

Gardner, R., & Lambert, W. (1972). *Attitudes and motivation in second language learning*. Rowley, MA: Newbury House Publishers.

Gass, S. (2003). Input and interaction. In C. J. Doughty & M. L. Long (Eds.), *The handbook of second language acquisition* (pp. 224 255). Oxford, England: Blackwell Publishers.

Gass, S., & Mackey, A. (2006). Input, interaction, and output: An overview. *AILA Review 19*, 3–17.

Gass, S., & Mackey, A. (2007). Input, interaction, and output in second language acquisition. In B. VanPatten & J. Williams (Eds.), *Theories of second language acquisition* (pp. 175–199). Mahwah, NJ: Lawrence Erlbaum.

Gass, S., & Mackey, A. (2013). *The Routledge handbook of second language acquisition*. New York, NY: Routledge.

Gass, S., & Madden, C. (Eds.) (1985). *Input in second language acquisition*. Rowley, MA: Newbury House.

Gass, S. M., & Selinker, L. (2008). *Second language acquisition: An introductory course*. New York, NY: Routledge.

Gass, S., & Varonis, E. (1985). Variation in native speaker speech modification to non-native speakers. *Studies in Second Language Acquisition, 7*, 37–57.

Gass, S. M., Behney, J., & Plonsky, L. (2013). *Second language introduction*, 4th ed. New York, NY: Routledge.

Gass, S., Mackey, A., & Ross-Feldman, L. (2005). Task based interactions in classroom and laboratory settings. *Language Learning, 55*(4), 575–611.

Gattegno, C. (1972). *Teaching foreign languages in schools: The Silent Way*, 2nd ed. New York, NY: Educational Solutions.

Gattegno, C. (1976). *The common sense of teaching foreign languages*. New York, NY: Educational Solutions.

Gliksman, L. (1976). Second language acquisition: The effects of student attitudes on classroom behavior. Unpublished MA thesis, University of Western Ontario.

Hatch, E., & Wagner-Gough, J. (1976). Explaining sequence and variation in second language acquisition. *Language Learning*, Special Issue, *4*, 39–47.

Holliday, L. (1995). NS syntactic modifications in NS/NNS negotiations as input data for second language acquisition of syntax. Unpublished doctoral dissertation, University of Pennsylvania, Philadelphia.

Knell, E., & Chi, Y. (2012). The roles of motivation, affective attitudes, and willingness to communicate among Chinese students in early English immersion programs. *International Education, 41*(2), 66.

Krashen, S. (1981). *Second language acquisition and second language learning*. Oxford, England: Pergamon.

Krashen, S. (1985). *The input hypothesis: Issues and implications*. London, England: Longman.

Lantolf, J. P. (1994). Sociocultural theory and second language learning: Introduction to special issue. *Modern Language Journal, 78*(4), 418–420.

Lantolf, J., & Appel, G. (Eds). (1994). *Vygotskian approaches to second language research*. Norwood, NJ: Ablex.

Lightbown, P. (1990). Process-product research on second language learning in classrooms. In B. Harley, P. Allen, J. Cummins, & M. Swain (Eds.), *The development of second language proficiency* (pp. 82–109). New York, NY: Cambridge University Press.

Lindholm-Leary, K. J. (2011). Student outcomes in Chinese two-way immersion programs: Language proficiency, academic achievement and student attitudes. In D. J. Tedick, D. Christian, & T. W. Fortune (Eds.), *Immersion education: Practices, politics, possibilities* (pp. 81–103). Clevedon, England: Multilingual Matters.

Lindholm-Leary, K. J. (2016). Students' perceptions of bilingualism in Spanish and Mandarin dual language program. *International Multilingual Research Journal, 10*(1), 59–70.

Long, M. (1980). Inside the black box: Methodological issues in classroom research on language learning. *Language Learning, 30,* 1–42.

Long, M. (1983a). Does second language instruction make a difference? A review of the research. *TESOL Quarterly, 17,* 359–382.

Long, M. (1983b). Native speaker/non-native speaker conversation and the negotiation of comprehensible input. *Applied Linguistics, 4,* 126–141.

Long, M. H., & Sato, C. J. (1984). Methodological issues in interlanguage studies: An interactionist perspective. In A. Davies, C. Criper, & A. Howatt (Eds.), *Interlanguage* (pp. 253–279). Edinburgh, Scotland: Edinburgh University Press.

Mackey, A. (1995). Stepping up the pace: Input, interaction, and interlanguage development. An empirical study of questions in ESL. Unpublished doctoral dissertation, University of Sydney, Australia.

Mackey, A. (2007). Interaction as practice. In R. DeKeyser (Ed.), *Practice in a second language* (pp. 85–110). Cambridge, England: Cambridge University Press.

Mehan, H. (1979). *Learning lessons: Social organization in the classroom.* Cambridge, MA: Harvard University Press.

Muchnick, A., & Wolfe, D. (1982). Attitudes and motivations of American students of Spanish. *Canadian Modern Language Review, 38,* 262–281.

Norris, J. M., & Ortega, L. (2000). Effectiveness of L2 instruction: A research synthesis and quantitative meta-analysis. *Language Learning, 50,* 417–528.

Oller, J., Baca, L., & Vigil, A. (1977). Attitudes and attained proficiency in ESL: A sociolinguistic study of Mexican Americans in the southwest. *TESOL Quarterly, 11,* 173–183.

Ortega, L. (2008). *Understanding second language acquisition.* New York, NY: Routledge.

Pica, T. (1994). Research on negotiation: What does it reveal about second-language learning conditions, processes, and outcomes? *Language Learning, 44,* 493–527.

Pica, T. (1996). Second language learning through interaction: Multiple perspectives. *Working Papers in Educational Linguistics, 12,* 1–22.

Ray, B., & Seely, C. (1998). *Fluency through TPR storytelling,* 2nd ed. Berkeley, CA: Command Performance Language Institute.

Richards, J., & Rodgers, T. (2014). *Approaches and methods in language teaching,* 3rd ed. Cambridge, England: Cambridge University Press.

Sato, C. J. (1986). Conversation and interlanguage development: Rethinking the connection. In R. R. Day (Ed.), *Talking to learn: Conversation in second language acquisition* (pp. 5–22). Rowley, MA: Newbury House Publishers.

Scherer, A., & Wertheimer, M. (1964). *A psycholinguistic experiment in foreign language teaching*. New York, NY: McGraw Hill.

Schmidt, R. (1990). The role of consciousness in second language learning. *Applied Linguistics, 11*, 129–158.

Schmidt, R., & Frota, S. (1986). Developing basic conversational ability in a second language: A case-study of an adult learner. In R. R. Day (Ed.), *Talking to learn: Conversation in second language acquisition* (pp. 237–322). Rowley, MA: Newbury House Publishers.

Seely, C., & Romijn, E. (1995). *TPR is more than commands at all levels*. Berkeley, CA: Command Performance Language Institute.

Sinclair, J., & Coulthard, M. (1975). *Towards an analysis of classroom discourse*. Oxford, England: Oxford University Press.

Skehan, P. (1989). *Individual differences in second language learning*. London, England: Edward Arnold.

Smith, P. (1970). A comparison of the audiolingual and cognitive approaches to foreign language instruction: The Pennsylvania foreign language project. Philadelphia, PA: Center for Curriculum Development.

Spada, N. (1986). The interaction between type of contact and type of instruction: Some effects of the L2 proficiency of adult learners. *Studies in Second Language Acquisition, 8*, 181–199.

Spada, N. (1987). Relationships between instructional differences and learning outcomes: A process-product study of communicative language teaching. *Applied Linguistics, 8*, 187–155.

Swain, M. (1985). Communicative competence: Some roles of comprehensible input and comprehensible output in its development. In S. Gass & C. Madden (Eds.), *Input in second language acquisition* (pp. 235–255). Rowley, MA: Newbury House Publishers.

Terrell, T. D. (1977). A natural approach to second language acquisition and learning. *Modern Language Journal, 61*, 325–336.

Terrell, T. D. (1982). The natural approach to language teaching: An update. *Modern Language Journal, 66*, 121–132.

Vroom V. H. (1964). *Work and motivation*. New York, NY: Wiley.

Vygotsky, L. (1978). *Mind in society: The development of higher psychological processes*. Cambridge, MA: Harvard University Press. [Published originally in Russian in 1930.]

Wong-Fillmore, L. (1985). When does teacher talk work as input? In S. M. Gass & C. Madden (Eds.), *Input in second language acquisition* (pp. 17–50). Cambridge, MA: Newbury House Publishers.

Woods, D. (2003). The social construction of beliefs in the language classroom. In P. Kalaja & A. M. F. Barcelos (Eds.), *Beliefs about SLA: New research approaches* (pp. 201–230). New York, NY: Springer.

13

LEARNING THEORIES IN THE CLASSROOM

VIGNETTE

I work in an elementary[1] school and teach sixth grade. The school population is over eighty percent English language learners, and we have children from 18 different countries in six grades who speak 13 different home languages. The diversity of our student population and the number of English language learners we have in our classes, presents challenges for us as instructors. Many of us have decided to meet in content and grade level teams after school or at common lunch hours once a week in order to talk about how to improve our instruction. My sixth grade language arts team has decided to work on learning strategies for the next term. In our initial discussions on how to proceed, we realized that we have many different views about what constitutes a learning strategy. Some of my colleagues interpret learning strategies as school-related tasks, such as how to study, manage time, use resources, or take notes in class. Others define learning strategies in terms of text comprehension, such as finding the main idea, skimming, summarizing, and using graphic organizers. Still others thought about teaching students how to learn and how to evaluate their own learning. One teacher said that she wanted them to learn how to work effectively in groups and with each other. As a team, I think we are very confused about learning strategies. Before we can move ahead with our plans, we need to come to some sort of agreement. [Sixth grade language arts teacher/ Christison data, 2004]

Task: Reflect

The teachers on this team happen to be situated in a North American context; however, the difficulties the team is experiencing relative to meeting the instructional needs of their diverse group of learners could be true of English language teachers situated in almost any context. Are any of the views these teachers express consistent with your own views about learning strategies? Do you have a view that is not represented among these teachers? Do you think that some of the views expressed by the teachers in this scenario are incorrect? Share your ideas with your colleagues, if possible.

Introduction

All teachers are concerned about learning in the classroom and most teachers have a keen interest in experimenting with theories of learning, especially those that hold the promise of creating optimal learning opportunities for their students. In the past two decades in the field of L2 pedagogy, many theories of learning have been promoted and encouraged. L2 teachers have embraced some of these ideas quite strongly, and both the theories and the concepts associated with them have become part of what might be considered standard second language teaching. These concepts center on answering the following questions: Can you teach someone how to learn? Do preferences for learning have an impact on how and what we learn? Does learning affect our basic intelligence? Can working with others promote learning? In this chapter, we look at four of the most popular concepts for promoting learning in classroom settings—learning strategies, preferred ways of learning or learning styles, learning and intelligence, and cooperative learning. It is not possible within the scope of this chapter to provide a comprehensive review of the research and concepts in each of these areas; consequently, we have tried to select information that we believe is relevant to second language (L2) classrooms and have cited additional works that we hope you will explore on your own.

Learning Strategies

For the purposes of this chapter, we will distinguish between two different types of learning strategies: language learning strategies and skill learning strategies. According to Tarone (1980), a *language learning strategy* is "an attempt to develop linguistic and sociolinguistic competence in the target language" (p. 419) and examples of language learning strategies include memorizing new vocabulary, initiating conversations with native speakers, and making inferences. Other types of language learning strategies are explored by Oxford (1990), O'Malley and Chamot (1990), and Wenden and Rubin (1987). Skill learning strategies focus on the learners' attempts to become skilled communicators (Cohen, 1990; Ellis, 1994) and involve many different types of activities, such as strategies for reading, writing, studying, and remembering information, effectively interacting with others, studying for tests, and motivating oneself to learn. In the vignette above, the sixth grade language arts teacher expressed concern that her team had so many different ideas about learning strategies and that they were unable to provide a precise definition for a learning strategy; however, it seems that each of the ideas provided by the team (e.g., how to study and how to understand text) is represented in the literature on learning strategies. No single strategy can be a panacea; many different strategies are necessary for learner success, particularly in classroom settings. The most effective strategy instruction occurs when it is integrated into regular classroom instruction (Cohen, 1998; Oxford & Leaver, 1996).

One of the most useful frameworks for working with learning strategies in the classroom has been provided by Chamot and O'Malley (1994). We focus on their framework here as an example of how learning strategies might be organized. The framework allows teachers to select specific learning strategies and to implement them in the classroom based on what skills students need in order to be successful with language and with different types of content.

In this framework learning strategies are divided into three different categories—metacognitive, cognitive, and socio-affective. *Metacognitive strategies* are strategies for thinking about one's own learning, and they are further divided into planning, monitoring, and evaluating. Planning strategies include advance organization (such as previewing the text, getting the main ideas, and identifying the organizing principles), organizational planning (i.e., planning what tasks to do and in what order to do them), and self-management (i.e., selecting and arranging the conditions that help one learn). Monitoring strategies include monitoring comprehension (i.e., checking one's comprehension while listening and reading) and monitoring production (i.e., checking one's speaking and writing while it's taking place). Evaluating is the ability to self-assess, such as when learners keep a learning log or are able to reflect back on what they have learned.

Cognitive strategies focus on learning how to think. They include resourcing (i.e., the ability to use reference materials), grouping (i.e., the ability to classify information and construct graphic organizers), elaboration of prior knowledge (i.e., the ability to use what you know to further your learning), note-taking, deduction/induction (i.e., the ability to apply rules or figure them out), summarizing, imagery (i.e., using mental images to solve problems), auditory representation (i.e., mentally replaying words and information in one's mind), making inferences (i.e., using text information to guess meaning or to make predictions).

Socio-affective strategies focus on helping students develop skills for working with others and for creating a positive learning environment. They include questioning, cooperation (i.e., working with others to complete tasks and solve problems), and self-talk (i.e., private, internal speech directed towards positive thinking). See Chamot and O'Malley (1994) for a complete listing of strategies and a useful summary framework that can be used for lesson planning purposes.

The framework is not meant to be exhaustive (e.g., there are no word-identification strategies or sentence writing strategies), but it provides an excellent tool for teachers who wish to experiment with learning strategies in their classrooms. Anderson (2005) provides a comprehensive review and discussion of learning strategies.

Preferred Ways of Learning

Types of Learning Styles

That some individuals are more successful than others in learning a second language is perhaps the one statement in SLA on which all L2 scholars seem to agree. Individual differences (i.e., nonidiosyncratic differences) in learners, such as age, aptitude, motivation, attitude, and socio-psychological factors (e.g., preferred ways of perceiving and processing information) are suggested as the causal variables for differing L2 learning profiles (see Chapter 12 for a discussion of non-language factors). In addition to individual differences in language proficiency, there are also other differences. For example, not all learners achieve the same level of concept mastery in content area studies regardless of language background.

Preferred ways of perceiving and processing information are often referred to in educational circles as learning styles, and learning styles (in particular the perceptual learning styles—auditory, visual, kinesthetic, and tactile) have been at the forefront of L2 methodological concerns for almost two decades (Christison, 2003; Dörnyei, 2005; Reid, 1997) with most of the focus on how to address different learning styles in the classroom in order to create optimal learning environments for all students regardless of their individual preferred ways of learning.

Table 13.1 Learning styles taxonomy

Learning Styles Taxonomy for the L2 Classroom		
Cognitive Styles	*Sensory Styles*	*Personality Styles*
Field dependent/Field independent	Perceptual: visual, auditory, kinesthetic, tactile	Tolerance of ambiguity: global and language
Analytic/Global	Environmental: physical and sociological	Right and left hemisphere dominance
Reflective/Impulsive		

Although perceptual learning styles are the most familiar learning styles for teachers, they are in fact only one type of style. Table 13.1 below presents an extended list of styles for you to consider (see Christison, 2003, for more information).

Table 13.1 presents sample learning styles in three different categories—cognitive, sensory, and personality—with specific examples in each category. The list is not meant to be exhaustive but is meant to represent some of the most common styles mentioned in the literature. By reviewing these different styles, we hope to introduce you to the importance of considering individual differences in instructional design, as well as give you some basic tools for recognizing learner behaviors that are associated with certain styles or preferred ways of learning. In addition to the learning styles we introduce in this chapter, there are, of course, other taxonomies for learning styles, applications, and theories. For example, see Dunn and Dunn (1978, 1984, 1993), McCarthy (2000), and Sprenger (2008). Even though we cannot cover all learning styles in this short chapter, we believe that, through the introduction that we provide to some basic concepts about learning styles in classrooms, English language teachers can be better equipped to plan for instruction in ways that take learner differences into account.

Cognitive learning styles. We introduce you to three different types of cognitive learning styles—field dependent/independent, analytic/global, and reflective/impulsive. *Field independent learners* prefer to work with information in a step-by-step format and learn most effectively when information is presented sequentially. They prefer to work with details first and to construct the big picture from the details. As language learners, they are often more accurate than fluent learners because paying attention to details is their natural way of processing information. *Field dependent learners* prefer to work with information that is presented in context, such as when the main concepts are identified and details

237

are supplied at a later date. As language learners, they are often quite fluent; however, they may have difficulty in focusing on the details and developing accuracy.

Another distinctive feature of cognitive learning styles is characterized by the difference between analytic and global learners. *Analytic learners* prefer to work alone and also prefer to work at their own pace. These learners enjoy autonomous and self-directed learning opportunities, such as independent projects and self-directed language learning programs. Online learning courses, where the individual students rather than the teacher determine the rate at which learning proceeds, are popular with analytic learners. *Global learners* often work more effectively in groups and prefer classrooms where teachers use pair and group work to process new information.

Reflective learners like to have time to consider new information before responding. As language learners, they are not risk takers; consequently, they are often reluctant to make contributions in class. In selecting classroom activities, teachers must think about lowering the potential for risk-taking for these learners. Second language teachers who provide learners with advance organizers allow for group discussion, and provide ample wait time after asking questions, are demonstrating the use of instructional strategies that meet the needs of reflective learners in their classrooms. At the other end of the continuum are the impulsive learners. These students learn more effectively when they can respond to new information immediately. As learners, they are often the first to respond to questions and offer their opinions, and they are characterized as risk-takers. A quick-response brainstorming session is one type of activity that works well for learners with an impulsive learning style.

Sensory learning styles. There are two types of sensory learning styles— perceptual and environmental. *Perceptual learning* styles include visual, auditory, kinesthetic, and tactile. *Visual learners* prefer to work with written language or to receive visual reinforcement of concepts in the form of charts, pictures, graphs, etc. while auditory learners prefer to receive new information by listening and by speaking. For *auditory learners*, classroom activities that provide opportunities for interaction with the teacher and other learners in the classroom, as well as language learning activities that provide individual language learners with opportunities to listen and respond, are generally preferred. *Kinesthetic learners* appreciate classroom instructional tasks in which there is movement associated with learning, such as when learners retrieve materials from a central location, write on the board, change groups or partners, or reform groups. *Tactile learners* prefer to learn when there is an opportunity to use manipulative resources, such as handouts or flash cards, or realia, like old clothes, kitchen items, or other things from real-world contexts that are useful for the purposes of language learning.

The other type of sensory learning style is environmental, and it includes physical and sociological learners. *Physical learners* are sensitive to the physical characteristics of their environment, such as whether a classroom has artificial or natural light, whether the temperature is too hot or cold, and whether the desks or chairs are comfortable. It is an accepted fact that physical characteristics of the environment can affect learning, but physical learners are more sensitive to their environment in this way than most individuals. *Sociological learners* are affected by the individuals in their environment; consequently, they are sensitive to the configuration of space in a classroom, such as whether chairs or desks are in straight rows or small groups, because how we use space affects our interaction with others. Sociological learners are usually aware of who is present in class or who might be absent. They can usually tell you with whom they have interacted during any class period, as well as the interaction patterns of their classmates. Teachers who pay attention to grouping configurations and interaction patterns of their learners are demonstrating sensitivity to sociological learners.

Personality learning styles. *Tolerance of ambiguity* refers to how comfortable a learner is with uncertainty, with language and in general. Some students do well in situations where there are several possible answers; others prefer one correct answer. Teachers who provide learners with both options are addressing this learning style. *Right and left hemisphere dominance* may be another personality type of learning style. Left-brain dominant learners tend to be more visual, analytical, reflective, and self-reliant, while right-brain dominant learners tend to be more auditory, global, impulsive, and interactive. Teachers who vary classroom activities are more successful in reaching both types of learners.

Learning Style Models

In addition to considering learning styles individually, another way to think about learning styles is to consider them within a system or a conceptual model. We introduce two of the most popular learning style models—the Kolb Experiential Model and the Myers-Brigg Personality Type Indicator. These models are commonly used in both business and education.

Kolb experiential learning model. *The Kolb Experiential Learning Model* (Kolb, 1984) offers teachers a model or system for understanding individual learning styles. In addition, it provides a vehicle for explaining the cycle of experiential learning that is common for all of us in real-life contexts. In his model, Kolb presents two intersecting continua, each with two different learning styles at the opposite ends. The horizontal continuum represents the way in which we process information by doing, in other words, active experimentation (AE) on the left and watching (reflective observation—RO) on the right. This horizontal continuum intersects with a vertical one. The vertical continuum represents the ways in which we perceive information. At opposite ends of the vertical continuum are concrete experimentation (CE) at the top (i.e., perceiving through feelings) and abstract conceptualization (AC) at the bottom (i.e., perceiving through thinking). When the continua intersect, they create quadrants that represent four different learning styles—CE/RO (diverging), AC/RO (assimilating), AC/AE (converging), and CE/AE (accommodating). In addition to identifying the four styles, Kolb's model also presents the following cycle of learning: (1) our concrete experiences provide a basis for (2) observations and reflections. These observations and reflections are distilled into (3) abstract concepts and are used in (4) active experimentation. Kolb's model suggests that in the process of learning, we touch all bases—experiencing, reflecting, thinking, and acting. The challenge for classroom teachers in using the model is to determine how to provide learning opportunities that address each of the four styles, as well as the four-stage cycle of learning.

Task: Expand

Work with a partner or in a small group. Use the prose given above that describes the Kolb Experiential Learning Model and make a conceptual figure representing the concepts. Exchange your model with another partnership or group. Find a figure representing the model on the internet (e.g., www.businessballs.com/kolblearningstyles.htm). Is your representation of the model the same or different? If your model is different, how is it different?

Myers-Briggs Type Indicator. Another learning styles model that has been quite popular with English language teachers, especially in the workplace, is the Myers-Briggs Type Indicator (MBTI®)[2] (Myers & McCaulley, 1985; Myers & Myers, 1995). The model was created in 1943 and has been around for more than 75 years. There are 16 MBTI® types, which are derived from a combination of four different continua. These continua are described as follows.

Extraversion/Introversion focuses on your natural energy orientation. When you feel the need to restore your energy, do you need private time alone (*intro-version*—I) or do you interact with other people (*extraversion*—E). The second continuum focuses on the natural ways we have of understanding the world around us. *Sensing* (S) individuals understand best through experience. They like to think about life in the here and now and prefer working with concepts that are clear and well defined. *Intuitive* (N) individuals think about the future and get the most pleasure from thinking about abstract and theoretical concepts. The third continuum explores how we form judgments. *Thinking* (T) individuals need facts and prefer to reach conclusions through a logical process. They also respond best when there are tasks that need to be accomplished. *Feeling* (F) individuals use basic instinct to reach conclusions and prefer to make decisions through a process of general consensus. The final continuum represents one's orientation towards the outside world. *Judging* (J) individuals prefer to gather facts and details before taking action. They also like to keep ahead of deadlines and, consequently, are always making lists and schedules. *Perceiving* (P) individuals prefer variety in their lives and often take action before they have all of the details or even a clear plan. They are good at working on more than one task and frequently mix work and pleasure.

As indicated above, 16 personality types are possible within the model MBTI® (i.e., INTP, INTJ, INFP, INFJ, ISTP, ISTJ, ISFP, ISFJ, ENTP, ENTJ, ENFP, ENFJ, ESTP, ESTJ, ESFP, ESFJ).[3] Each personality type is defined by a combination of the position (or score) on each of the four continua and by the interaction of the four continua. Teachers may benefit greatly from becoming familiar with the basic descriptors for each continuum because these descriptors provide reasonable explanations for why learners (and other teachers) behave in certain ways in response to the external world.

Learning and Intelligence

The relationship between intelligence and learning is central to the concept of intelligence (i.e., how it is defined) and has been at the core of theoretical debates about intelligence in both education and psychology for decades. In the traditional view of intelligence, intelligence is seen as a genetic capacity; in other words, we are born with a certain intelligent quotient (IQ). In the genetic capacity view, intelligence is a static construct (i.e., there is a g factor), meaning that intelligence does not change over one's lifetime as a result of one's life experiences or education (i.e., as a result of learning new concepts and skills). The general public seems to have embraced this theory of intelligence believing that intelligence is synonymous with one's score on the intelligence (IQ) test (Kail & Pellegrino, 1985). The IQ test was first designed by Alfred Binet as a method for predicting which children in Parisian primary grades would succeed in an urban school system and which would be most likely to fail. It has enjoyed success the world over and is used in ways that have gone beyond the original intention of the test (e.g., to determine who will be successful in a particular school system). This traditional view of intelligence is a psychometric one, which has been operationalized in the form of an IQ test. Consequently, IQ is defined in terms of what the IQ test measures. The psychometric view of intelligence is also a static one, meaning that your score on an IQ test should not change significantly no matter what you learn, what experiences you have, or how many times you take it throughout your life. This view of IQ is not a particularly attractive concept for most L2 teachers because most of us like to believe that learning new concepts and developing new skills will result in an increase in intelligence. In addition, most English language teachers work with a diverse set of learners in varied contexts around the world; consequently, most of us believe that it is important to consider how we might influence learning in the classroom, address the needs of the varied and diverse individuals with whom we work, and consider the different ways in which they might be demonstrating different types of intelligent behavior.

Other psychologists, such as Robert Sternberg (1985, 1990) and Howard Gardner (1985, 1997), interpret intelligence, particularly as it relates to learning, in a way that is different from the psychometric view. They believe that smartness or intelligence is a complex set of abilities. For both Gardner and Sternberg, intelligence is dynamic and, therefore, changes as a result of learning and as a result of life experiences.

In his *triarchic theory of intelligence*, Sternberg presents an information processing perspective with three major types of intelligence—*componential intelligence*, which is based on an individual's ability to learn how to do new things and acquire new information; *experiential intelligence*, which is based on a person's ability to solve new problems, to act creatively, and to use insight; and *contextual intelligence*, which is based on a person's ability to use practical knowledge, common sense, one's *tacit knowledge*, in other words, all of the important things in life that you were not formally taught in school. In each case the focus is on learning new concepts or skills or on solving problems.

In Gardner's *theory of multiple intelligences (MI)* (Gardner, 1985a), he introduced seven different kinds of intelligence: (1) linguistic, (2) logical-mathematical, (3) spatial, (4) musical, (5) bodily-kinesthetic, (6) interpersonal (i.e., knowing how to deal with others), and (7) intrapersonal (i.e., knowing about one's self). The original list was not meant to be exhaustive, so he has since added two additional intelligences—the naturalist (i.e., the ability to identify and categorize plants, animals, and other objects in nature) and the existentialist (i.e., a sensitivity, interest, and capacity to tackle deep questions about human existence)—to make nine intelligences in total. Gardner suggests that these intelligences work together in complex ways and are represented differently within each individual. He proposes eight theoretical bases that form the core of his theory and determine the presence of separate intelligences. The idea is that each person possesses all nine intelligences, even though these intelligences are developed to greater and lesser degrees among humans and manifest themselves in different ways.

According to Gardner (1985a), one of the chief problems with the traditional, psychometric view of intelligence is that it only measures the first two intelligences—linguistic and logical-mathematical—and he believes that these are not the only intelligences that can be developed. In addition, Gardner states that intelligence must be made up of a set of skills for problem-solving, enabling the individual to resolve genuine problems or difficulties and create an effective product. This set of skills for problem-solving must also include the potential for finding or creating problems, thereby laying the groundwork for acquisition of new knowledge (Gardner, 1985a). In Gardner's view of intelligence, the learning or acquisition of new knowledge is a manifestation of intelligence in each of these areas. Gardner believes that one's intelligence profile changes throughout one's life as the result of how and what one learns.

Both Sternberg's and Gardner's views of intelligence provide language teachers with attractive alternatives to traditional views of intelligence (Christison, 2005). In each view, intelligence is considered as a dynamic construct. This means that, when students learn new concepts or improve their language skills, they increase their intelligence. In addition, these views of intelligence recognize human diversity in learning and acknowledge that individuals can and do learn differently.

Among English language teaching professionals, there is sometimes confusion between the concepts of multiple intelligences and perceptual learning styles—yet they are different constructs, even though they are frequently confused in the literature. Gardner's MI theory suggests that intelligences are basic to all humans and that brain biology suggests that each intelligence functions separately. Regardless of our preferences, we each have all nine intelligences. No matter what intelligence profile we have today, we have the capacity to change it and to develop or increase all nine intelligences. When we wish to change our profile, we use our preferred ways of learning, such as the difference between developing musical intelligence by listening to a CD (auditory) vs. reading sheet music (visual) in learning a new musical selection.

Task: Expand

Work with a partner or in a small group. Make a list of activities that you can do in a class with L2 learners to promote the development of both language and each of the nine intelligences Gardner proposes in his theory of multiple intelligences.

Cooperative Learning

The most common type of classroom is the competitive classroom, in which students compete with one another for a limited number of resources, such as grades and attention from the teacher. However, in the cooperative classroom learners are committed to helping one another, which is positive interdependence, while at the same time being accountable for their own learning, which is positive accountability (Bassano & Christison, 2010). Because individual learners vary in how they learn best and in how they prefer to learn (Christison, 2003), most English language teachers provide a range of organizational configurations in the classroom. In order to address different learning styles and to provide learners with more complex input and opportunities for interaction (McGroarty, 1992), teachers of English learners have experimented with pair work and small and large group work, as well as provided learners opportunities to work independently. In these different classroom configurations, learners participate in discussion groups, brainstorming sessions, one-centered activities, in which one individual is on focus, and unified group work where success is only possible when the entire group is successful (Christison & Bassano, 1995).

There are many benefits to cooperative learning for English learners. Cooperative learning has been shown to have positive outcomes for learners in general and when compared to intergroup competition, individual competition, and individual student tasks (Johnson, Maruyama, Johnson, Nelson, & Skon, 1981; Walberg, 1999). In terms of language development, English language learners can expect to get more input, more complex language input, and more opportunities to refine communication through natural talk while participating in well-designed cooperative learning activities. In terms of academic and content area skills, English language learners get increased frequency of practice, better differentiation of learning tasks with clearer definitions and presentation of component processes, and an evaluation structure that helps students determine how successful they have been in achieving the goals of the activity (Kagan, 1980, 1988; Long & Porter, 1985; McGroarty, 1992).

In addition to the content and L2 language development benefits for learners, proponents of cooperative learning also suggest that there is a societal benefit as well. Success in most modern societies is based on one's ability to get along with other people; yet we are not born knowing how to cooperate and work together with others. The specific language for use in group work and cooperative learning, as well as cooperative skills, must be taught, and the classroom can be an optimal environment in which to acquire these skills, especially if the teacher understands cooperative learning principles. Cooperative learning is much more complicated than simply putting your students in small groups and giving them an instructional task to complete. Cooperative learning is based on a set of principles, which include specific steps in teaching cooperative skills, such as making certain that learners see the value in group work, that they develop the language skills necessary for functioning in a group, that they are given time to practice the skills, and that they learn how to process their experiences as a group and reflect on them. These principles also include helping to develop a knowledge of the different levels of cooperative learning. These levels include: (1) *forming*, the ability to move into groups quickly and quietly, use quiet voices, stay with the group, encourage participation, use members' names, and avoid put-downs; (2) *functioning*, the ability to complete tasks, maintain good relationships in the group, and use proper speech acts for asking for help, clarifying, explaining, expressing support, and paraphrasing; (3) *formulating*, the ability to help other group members develop a deeper understanding of the material—for example, pointing out ideas that have been missed, synthesizing the material, referring to previously learned concepts; and (4) *fermenting*, the ability of the group members to help one another explore the material more thoroughly—for example, challenge another's ideas, reconceptualize previous thinking, self-evaluate, and evaluate the process. To become skilled in implementing and using cooperative learning strategies with English learners, teachers must first master the basic principles of cooperative learning and develop skills in selecting appropriate tasks for learners and in teaching the skills associated at each level.

Conclusion

This chapter has explored four different concepts related to learning in a classroom—the use of learning strategy instruction, the influence of preferred ways of learning on how and what we learn, the relationship between learning and the development of intelligence, and the extent to which working with others facilitates positive outcomes for learning both language and content. While there are no definitive answers on how to structure learning in a classroom context, experienced English language teachers recognize that each of the concepts introduced in this chapter has contributed to our understanding of classroom learning.

Task: Expand

Visit one of the following websites or select one of your own choosing and find one new concept about classroom learning that has not been covered in this chapter. Share your concepts with a partner, small group, or with your class, and discuss the relevance of the concept you have selected for the context in which you work or plan to work.

www.ku-crl/sim/strategies.shtml

www.pzweb.harvard.edu

www.education.com/activity

www.712educators.about.com

Questions for Discussion

1   There are numerous learning style inventories for perceptual learning styles online and elsewhere. Take one of these inventories and discuss the results with a partner. Did you learn anything about yourself? Do you agree with the results? Disagree?

2   Do you agree or disagree with the authors' statement that cooperative learning is much more complicated than simply putting your students in small groups and giving them an instructional task to complete? Why or why not?

3   What experiences have you had in using or participating in group work in the classroom? What worked? What were some of the problems?

4   The authors mention numerous learning strategies in this chapter. Select one of these strategies and discuss with a partner or small group how you would implement this strategy with your learners in the context in which you work or plan to work. Specifically, what would you do? How might different contexts or different levels of learners (both proficiency and age) mediate how this strategy might be applied?

Notes

1   *Elementary school* is U.S. terminology referring to the first five or six years (excluding kindergarten) of public school.

2   If you are interested, take an official MBTI® (Myers Briggs Type Indicator) from a professional who has met the standards necessary to be qualified to administer the test. An excellent resource for qualified persons is the Association of Psychological

Types. You can identify a qualified administrator in your area through their website (www.aptinternational.org). None of the cognitive-style inventories available on the internet is an official test.

3 For further descriptions of the MBTI®, you may wish to visit www.personalitypath ways.com/type_inventory.html

References

Anderson, N. J. (2005). L2 learning strategies. In E. Hinkel (Ed.), *Handbook on research in second language teaching and learning* (pp. 757–771). Mahwah, NJ: Lawrence Erlbaum.

Bassano, S. K., & Christison, M. A. (2010). *Collaborative language teaching.* Burlingame, CA: Alta Book Center Publishers.

Chamot, A. U., & O'Malley, J. M. (1994). *The CALLA handbook: Implementing the cognitive academic language learning approach.* Reading, MA: Addison-Wesley Publishers.

Christison, M. A. (2003). Learning styles and strategies. In D. Nunan (Ed.), *Practical English language teaching* (pp. 267–288). New York, NY: McGraw Hill International.

Christison, M. A. (2005). *Multiple intelligences and second language learning.* Burlingame, CA: Alta Book Center Publishers.

Christison, M. A., & Bassano, S., K. (1995). *Look who's talking.* Burlingame, CA: Alta Book Center Publishers.

Cohen, A. (1990). *Language learning: Insights for learners, teachers, and researchers.* New York, NY: Newbury House/Harper Row.

Cohen, A. (1998). *Strategies in learning and using a second language.* New York, NY: Longman.

Dörnyei, Z. (2005). *The psychology of the language learner: Individual differences in second language acquisition.* Mahwah, NJ: Lawrence Erlbaum.

Dunn, R., & Dunn, K. (1978). *Teaching students through their individual learning styles: A practical approach.* Reston, VA: Reston Publishing Company.

Dunn, R., & Dunn, K. (1984). *Learning style inventory.* Lawrence, KS: Price Systems.

Dunn, R., & Dunn, K. (1993). *Teaching secondary students through their individual learning styles: Practical approaches for grades 7–12.* Boston, MA: Allyn and Bacon.

Ellis, R. (1994). *The study of second language acquisition.* Oxford, England: Oxford University Press.

Gardner, H. (1985). *Frames of mind: The theory of multiple intelligences.* New York, NY: Basic Books.

Gardner, H. (1997). Reflections on multiple intelligences: Myths and messages. *Phi Delta Kappan, 77*(3), 200–209.

Johnson, D., Maruyama, G., Johnson, R., Nelson, D., & Skon, L. (1981). Effects of cooperative, competitive, and individualistic goal structures on achievement: A meta-analysis. *Psychological Bulletin, 89*, 47–62.

Kagan, S. (1980). Cooperation-competition, culture, and structural bias in classrooms. In S. Sharon, P. Hare, C. Webb, & R. Hertz-Lazarowitz (Eds.), *Cooperation in education* (pp. 197–211). Provo, UT: Brigham Young University Press.

Kagan, S. (1988). *Cooperative learning resources for teachers.* Laguna Nigel, CA: Resources for Teachers.

Kail, R., & Pellegrino, J. W. (1985). *Human intelligence: Perspectives and prospects.* New York, NY: W. H. Freeman and Company.

Kolb, D. (1984). *Experiential learning: Experience as the source of learning and development.* Englewood Cliffs, NJ: Prentice-Hall.

Long, M., & Porter, P. (1985). Group work, interlanguage talk, and second language acquisition. *TESOL Quarterly, 19,* 207–228.

McCarthy, B. (2000). *About teaching: 4 MAT in the classroom.* Wauconda, IL: About Learning, Inc.

McGroarty, M. (1992). Cooperative learning: Benefits for content-area teaching. In P. A. Richard-Amato & M. A. Snow (Eds.), *The multicultural classroom* (pp. 58–69). White Plains, NY: Longman.

Myers, I. B., & McCaulley, M. H. (1985). *Manual: A guide to the development and use of the Myers-Briggs Type Indicator,* 2nd ed. Palo Alto, CA: Consulting Psychologists Press.

Myers, I. B., & Myers, P. B. (1995). *Gifts differing: Understanding personality type.* Mountain View, CA: Davies-Black Publishing.

O'Malley, J. M., & Chamot, A. U. (1990). *Learning strategies in second language acquisition.* Cambridge, England: Cambridge University Press.

Oxford, R. L. (1990). *Language learning strategies: What every teacher should know.* Boston, MA: Heinle and Heinle Publishers.

Oxford, R. L., & Leaver, B. L. (1996). A synthesis of strategy instruction for language learners. In R. L. Oxford (Ed.), *Language learning strategies around the world: Crosscultural perspectives* (pp. 227–246). National Foreign Language Resource Center. Manoa: University of Hawaii Press.

Reid, J. (1997) (Ed.). *Learning styles in the second language classrooms.* Englewood Cliffs, NJ: Regents/Prentice Hall.

Sprenger, M. (2008). *Differentiation through learning styles and memory.* Thousand Oaks, CA: Corwin Press.

Sternberg, R. J. (1985). *Beyond IQ: A triarchic theory of human intelligence.* New York. NY: Cambridge University Press.

Sternberg, R. J. (1990). *Metaphors of mind: Conceptions of the nature of intelligence.* Cambridge, England: Cambridge University Press.

Tarone, E. (1980). Communication strategies, foreigner talk, and repair in interlanguage. *Language Learning 30:* 417–431.

Walberg, H. J. (1999). Productive teaching. In H. C. Waxman & H. J. Walberg (Eds.), *New directions for teaching practice and research* (pp. 75–104). Berkeley, CA: McCutchen Publishing Corporation.

Wenden, A., & Rubin, J. (1987) (Eds.). *Learner strategies in language learning.* Englewood Cliffs, NJ: Prentice Hall.

Part IV

PROFESSIONALISM

In Part IV, we explore what it means to be an ELT professional. While basic knowledge and skills are usually acquired during pre-service teacher education programs, effective teachers commit to continuous improvement. Additionally, what we know about language learning and teaching changes over time. Therefore, teachers engage in a variety of professional development activities to expand their knowledge base, reflect on their practice, and adapt or change their practice, or prepare for new responsibilities.

Crandall (1993) differentiates between professionalism (of educators) and professionalization (of the field). The former refers to teachers acting as professionals, which includes engaging in professional development and inquiry into their own practice in order to improve that practice. Professionalization, on the other hand, refers to the standards required to enter and remain in the profession. Many scholars have written about the lack of professionalization of the field of language education, when contrasted with medicine or the law (see, for example, Nunan, 1999). They generally agree that the criteria for a profession are that

- practice is based on an agreed body of theoretical knowledge and research,
- advanced education in the field exists,
- there are established standards of practice and certification, including disciplinary responsibilities, and
- some members advocate for the profession.

They note that, for ELT, while there are advanced courses and some people do advocate for the profession, disciplinary knowledge appears to be fragmented because it draws on a variety of other disciplines such as linguistics and psychology. However, Freeman and Johnson (1998) and Freeman (2018) have laid out a framework for the knowledge base of second language teaching that focuses on the activity of teaching itself: who is doing it, with whom, and to what end.

Additionally, standards of practice and certification vary widely from country to country, even within one country or institution. Even where there are standards, the profession itself is not responsible for enforcing them, as is the case for medical and legal professional associations. And, if individual teachers are professional in their practice, the question still remains: How does the lack of professionalization of the field affect teachers' practice? Are you likely to lose your job, no matter how professional, qualified, and experienced you are, when the company finds someone they can hire for less money? Does the school commit to the profession's standards, such as hiring only native speakers?

In Part IV we explore how busy teachers can continue their learning and take on additional responsibilities that may require leadership skills and how volunteering, working with volunteers, and advocating for the field can develop their professional practice (Chapter 14). In Chapter 15, we discuss how advancements in digital technologies are changing the context and landscape of English language teaching and language teacher education. We provide an overview of research and offer guidance, suggestions, and resources for teachers' continued learning and skill development.

References

Crandall, J. (1993). Professionalism and professionalization of adult ESL literacy. *TESOL Quarterly*, *27*(3), 497–515.

Freeman, D. (2018). Arguing for a knowledge-base in language teacher education, then (1998) and now (2018). *Language Teaching Research*. Retrieved from https://doi.org/10.1177/1362168818777534

Freeman, D., & Johnson, K. E. (1998). Reconceptualizing the knowledge-base of language teacher education. *TESOL Quarterly*, *32*(3), 397–417.

Nunan, D. (1999). What is a profession, and what is meant by professionalism? [Electronic version]. *TESOL Matters*, *9*. Retrieved from http://davidnunan.com/work/presMess_99Vol9No4.html

14

SUSTAINING PROFESSIONALISM

VIGNETTE

Lai Ping is a PhD candidate in Australia She taught high school English in Hong Kong and in a university English for Academic Purposes (EAP) program in Australia. She is undertaking the PhD so she can teach in a university TESOL program. She recently attended her first international conferences held in the United States—the conventions of the American Association of Applied Linguistics (AAAL) and of Teachers of English to Speakers of Other Languages (TESOL International), giving presentations at each conference. She says of her conference experience: "Apart from gaining more experience in conference presentations, presenting my papers in these two prestigious international conferences enabled me to disseminate my research findings and receive insightful feedback and valuable advice from informed audiences." As well as presenting, she attended paper presentations, colloquia, plenary sessions, and poster and discussion sessions related to her PhD research or that were of interest to her. She says: "Such exposure greatly broadened my horizons as a researcher and helped me to keep abreast of the recent developments in my sub-field." She found particularly helpful the sessions on how to get published because she will need to publish in order to pursue an academic career. She also used the opportunity to meet new people from around the world: "I had opportunities to network with many academics and this may enable collaborations in some future research projects. I also met many other researchers working in my research area." Because her area of research is non-native English speakers in TESOL (NNESTs) in schools in Hong Kong, at the TESOL

(continued)

(continued)

convention she volunteered to staff the Interest Section table for NNESTs and so was able to meet those who both publish in her area and who advocate on behalf of such teachers. She visited a middle school and a high school in the conference region, which "helped me to better understand how English language support was provided for ESL students in these schools." [L .P .F. MA unpublished conference report 2009]

Task: Reflect

1 What follow-up activities might Lai Ping engage in to build on what she learned at the AAAL and TESOL conventions?
2 What other conference activities have you found (or you can think of) that would help you grow professionally?
3 Lai Ping volunteered to work at the TESOL conference. How do you think such volunteering will help her grow professionally?
4 Her research is being conducted in Hong Kong. Why do you think she thought it was useful to learn about schools in the United States?

Introduction

We called the chapter *Sustaining Professionalism* because it begins with the assumption that teachers are professionals, as noted by Crandall (1993) in the introduction to Part IV. One essential aspect of being a professional in any field is to stay current with advances in the knowledge base that underpins the profession. This chapter, therefore, focuses on how busy teachers can engage in both informal and formal professional learning opportunities. To be effective, such professional learning needs to be ongoing, coherent, continuous, context-driven, and collaborative (Myers & Clark, 2002, p. 50; TESOL International Association, 2018). This process has been called *lifelong learning* (European Commission, 2009) and continuing professional development (Edge, 2002a). We will use the term *continuing professional development (CPD)* because for us sustaining professional learning is not, as is so often perceived, a matter of teacher deficit, but rather of teachers being professional and choosing to take the necessary steps to understand their own context and practice.

To become and continue to be a professional in any field requires a commitment to professional competence. To achieve this goal requires lifelong learning and development. Barduhn asks, "Why develop? It's easier not to" (Barduhn, 2002, p. 10). We would respond that, for English language teaching (ELT) educators, the goal of lifelong learning is twofold—to improve instructional practice and to develop new knowledge and skills for new areas of responsibility, such as those related to advances in digital technology (see Chapter 15), as well as taking advantage of leadership opportunities at one's own teaching site or as part of a professional association. We would also argue that it is, in fact, easier to develop professionally than not to do so, because doing the same things and not learning new knowledge and skills leads to burnout, especially as teachers try to juggle a personal life with a professional one. Burnout, which can lead to leaving the profession, is lessened if teachers have peer support: "peers can provide help, comfort, insight, comparison, rewards, humor and escape" (Barduhn, 2002, p. 12). Teachers' job satisfaction is enhanced by feedback from constructive peers and by collegiality (Frase & Sorenson, 1992), all of which can be achieved through a variety of CPD activities. However, many professional development programs are not ongoing, coherent, continuous, context-driven, or collaborative; they are episodic and designed as quick fixes to a problem perceived by administrators or in response to language program change imposed from above, such as the introduction of a new curricular approach. Such an approach to professional learning is an impoverished model (Allwright, 2003; Clarke & Hollingsworth, 2002; Fullan, 1991) because it fails to take into consideration either the context of teachers' lives or the cyclical nature of teacher learning.

In this chapter, we discuss the issues around how to sustain professional development. Then we provide a variety of activities that can help teachers continue their learning and develop professional competence. Many CPD activities include volunteerism—either volunteering to work on the local school fair, agreeing to present a workshop on your teaching, or holding an office in a professional volunteer association. Some of these roles require leadership skills. Understanding the worlds of volunteerism and leadership is an essential aspect of sustaining professionalism; therefore, we include a discussion of the role of volunteers. Another professional role that teachers undertake is as advocates—for their learners and their profession. Such advocacy takes place in a variety of ways, including through volunteer work in professional associations. Because of the importance of advocacy in English language teaching, we include a brief introduction to the concept of advocacy in this chapter. Finally, we end the chapter with a brief introduction to leadership, because it is often an area of CPD that is overlooked until a teacher is holding a leadership position.

Issues in Sustaining Professional Development

There has been general agreement that approaches that focus on the transmission of knowledge are ineffective, leading to little uptake and, therefore, application to the classroom (Bartels, 2005). This lack of uptake is because "knowledge and skill cannot be transmitted" (Burton, 1998, p. 24). Instead, research has shown that "teachers learn by doing, by reflecting and solving problems, and by working together in a supportive environment" (Yates & Brindley, 2000, p. 1). Thus, teacher reflection has been almost universally recognized as essential for most professional growth (Bailey & Nunan, 1996; Borg, 2006). As teachers reflect on their practice, they try to make sense of it and in so doing develop their own principled understandings of instruction. This reflection can take a variety of forms, which we discuss below.

Teaching is often considered a solitary, autonomous practice—you close the door of the classroom and get on with your work! Teaching, and lifelong learning for teachers, however, takes place within the context of their work, work which involves many factors—political, economic, physical, organizational, psychological, cultural, and psychological (Johnson, 1990). Teachers'

> [v]iews held on theories of language teaching and learning and views on the educational process and what happens or should happen in classrooms between the teacher and students are ultimately context specific and derived from the culture of the society in which learning takes place.
>
> (Kennedy, 1987, p. 166)

These factors operate in a context that has formal authority and organizational policies and procedures, as well as informal norms, all of which shape behaviors and beliefs. To understand your own practice requires understanding the context of your work: what shapes your views and what shapes learners' perceptions and those of the institution where you work (see Chapter 5 for a discussion on how to investigate your context). Professional development (PD) needs to be more than the acquisition of skills because, if PD only trains teachers to have students take standardized tests or engage in low-level skills activities, then the hidden goal is to maintain an underclass by ensuring that some students fail in school and in society. When this occurs, teachers become collaborators in this enterprise of maintaining an underclass (Edge, 1996).

Some institutions and governments require a certain number of PD activities each year. There is debate about how to measure the success of any professional learning activity. It is not the number of PD activities, but the process of teacher development and the quality of that process that is essential for changing practice and professional competence. PD should not, therefore, be reduced to quantifiable lists of activities. Some argue that success is indicated by the extent to which the teacher integrates the new knowledge and skills from the PD. Some applied-educational psychologists (Myers & Clark, 2002) argue instead that even integration is an insufficient measure because such integration may eventually lead to the same automatic behavior as practiced prior to the new learning. They argue instead for practitioners to be constantly in learning mode, to be constantly examining, reflecting, and acting on their practice—in other words, to be engaging in continuous professional learning.

A number of activities provide teachers with just this type of reflective experience, but reflection is not sufficient. Professional development needs to be sustained, intensive, and focused on the actual classroom—both on the knowledge of subject and on the teaching methodology. Such activities might include classroom research, peer mentoring, and workshops that provide ongoing follow-up and support. While these CPD activities might be ideal, many teachers are not able to participate in such CPD—perhaps because they are in isolated teaching situations or do not have local support for such activities. In fact, "[f]unding for professional learning is often driven by short-term budget allocations rather than long-term returns on investment" (TESOL International Association, 2018). In this chapter, therefore, we include all types of PD. However, we also argue that teachers should, wherever possible, try to initiate those activities that are known to be most effective, which may require taking a leadership role in one's school. To help you achieve this goal, we offer practical techniques and guidelines that teachers can use in developing your own CPD. We begin with the more traditional approaches to PD, then discuss various reflective approaches. We then explore volunteerism, advocacy, and leadership, all of which provide CPD opportunities.

Traditional Approaches to PD

Traditional approaches are part of the applied science model of teaching; that is, the linking of research with teaching practice by providing research-based training in order to develop teachers' skills (Wallace, 1994). To expand on Wallace's concept, we want to include all the approaches to lifelong learning that view learning as transmission of knowledge. We recognize that people do still learn from these experiences and, with careful planning and opportunities for reflection about the content, teachers can improve their practice. Indeed, one of the premises of the volumes in this series is to promote reflection. We have tried to do this by adding reflective questions, areas for the exploration of your own practice, and collaborative discussion questions within the chapters so that you can learn more about the field and apply new knowledge to your own context.

Conferences

As Lai Ping says in the vignette for this chapter, conferences are an essential part of professional socialization. Not only do we learn about new research findings in the field and hear about other teachers' practice and discoveries, we also interact with colleagues. We have personally found this networking to be an important experience for learning new content and also a means of being emotionally recharged, of re-engaging in the issues and with ideas in our field, and of making new friends. Conferences nourish our spirit as well as our minds. We discover our Communities of Practice (CoPs), ones that go beyond the site where we teach or study. The notion of a CoP was first explored and defined by Lave and Wenger (1991) in their work on apprenticeship. These communities are informal social groupings that come from a commitment to some joint human endeavor. As these groups engage in their practice, they develop shared forms of discourse, values, beliefs, concepts, symbols, and ways of doing things—often opaque to outsiders. Preuss, in the vignette in Chapter 3, was concerned that the field of language teaching had too many disparate CoPs, which inhibited teachers' ability to act in concert to advocate for and support English learners. While we recognize that this is a legitimate concern, we also recognize that, as ELT professionals, we will engage in a number of CoPs.

Task: Reflect

Think about your own experiences so far in the field of English language teaching. What are some of the communities of practice you have engaged in? What forms of discourse, values, beliefs, concepts, symbols, and ways of doing things differentiate the different communities you identified? Share with a colleague.

Formal Learning Opportunities

Teachers can engage in workshops, take further courses, or additional degrees. Schools often require that teachers attend at one or more of these types of activities. As we mentioned above, research shows that, if there is no investment on the part of the teacher and if the program is not ongoing and sustained, the activities are less effective than programs that are ongoing and involve teachers in applying new ideas in their own classrooms and then reflecting on that application. If a transmission model is used, then teachers may add to their knowledge store but may not act. However, you can approach even more traditional PD from a reflection and action perspective. We will provide tools for this in Volume II on facilitating learning.

Readings

One way to keep abreast of new developments in the field or branch out into new areas of expertise, such as English for Specific Purposes (ESP) or English in the workplace, is through professional reading, especially of journals. Again, it is essential to apply such knowledge to your own context. To that end, you can do any of the following:

- Create a reading group at your site to discuss the reading and how it might apply in your situation.
- Use the KWL technique: list what you already know about the topic (e.g., teaching role play) (K); list a series of things you want to know as a result of the reading (W); after reading, list what you have learned that is new (L).
- Take just one idea (no matter how small), reflect on how it might be applicable in your context; apply it in your classroom; evaluate how well it works and why; decide whether you want to incorporate the technique into your future teaching.

Serendipitous PD

A number of activities teachers engage in outside the classroom are in fact opportunities for CPD. In many schools, language examinations are held across several classes so that all students at a particular level take the same examination. In some settings, these examinations are set by a senior teacher without input from other teachers. In other settings, both the writing of the examination and the grading of learners' work are done collegially. Coordination and discussion about the appropriate questions to ask students, and the *benchmark* responses, can lead to a healthy learning opportunity for all involved.

Reflective Approaches to PD

Wallace (1994) suggests a three-part framework for foreign language teacher development: the applied science model, the craft or mentoring model, and the

257

reflective teaching model. We discussed the applied science model in the previous section. The *craft* or *mentoring model* brings together a more experienced, knowledgeable colleague and a less experienced colleague, while the *reflective model* involves teachers in becoming active researchers as they read, observe, critically analyze, reflect, and share. While there is some overlap between these two models, we will discuss each separately to organize the various activities that occur with each model. We also discuss cooperative development, another approach to teacher reflection, as well as teacher research.

Mentoring Models

Some mentoring models are informal, while others are formal. Some experienced teachers take novice teachers under their wing and offer to work with their novice colleagues. This mentoring is also referred to as peer coaching. In some institutions and even some U.S. states, such as in California's Teacher Induction Program (New Teacher Center, 2011), new teachers undergo an induction period during which someone is assigned to them to act as both a sounding board and an experienced other. Mentors often observe mentees' classes and offer advice and encouragement; they may encourage their mentee to read some professional literature, attend conferences, or engage in other professional activities. In some cases, the mentor is also responsible for formal evaluations of their mentee. Unfortunately, this evaluation practice leads to a conflict of interest for the person when acting as mentor. It is far better for an institution that wants to institutionalize mentoring to separate mentoring from evaluation.

Often teachers do not have a human mentor to apprentice them in the craft of teaching. Rather, through the development of specific curricula, content standards, and professional standards, teachers are guided in their practice because the curriculum and standards provide models and samples of best practice (Davison, 2005). The purpose of standards is to change teachers' beliefs, attitudes, practice, and content knowledge (see Volumes II and III for a discussion of curriculum and standards).

Reflective Models

Through a reflective approach, "teachers learn about themselves as teachers and develop a better understanding of teaching . . . [they] recognize and confront their own beliefs, values, and assumptions" (Crandall & Christison, 2016, p. 15) about the entire teaching enterprise. Reflective approaches run the gamut of theoretical foundations, from purely cognitive to sociocultural. For some proponents, reflective teaching is a process of classroom-based thinking that develops "new conceptual knowledge, rather than, say, habits of practice" (Thompson & Zeuli, 1999, p. 356). For others (for example, Zeichner, 1981–2), it is a sociocultural practice because teachers are empowered by reflecting on their own actions, the effect of those actions, and how the classroom, institution, and wider society in which those actions are embedded constrain those actions. Zeichner is concerned that teachers become aware of the ideologies that drive their practice—both their own beliefs and the ideologies of their context. What is common among the reflective approaches is that

> if we want to improve our teaching through reflective inquiry, we must accept that it does not involve some modification of behavior by externally imposed directions or requirements, but that it requires deliberation and analysis of our ideas about teaching as a form of action based on our changed understandings.
>
> (Bartlett, 1990, p. 203)

Task: Reflect

Think of a hobby or sport that you have pursued. How did you first learn the skills of this hobby or sport? How have you developed those skills over the years? Who has mentored you? Who have you used as models? What have you read about the hobby or sport? What methods of learning work best for you?

Cooperative Development

One model that has been shown to be effective and superficially resembles mentoring is Julian Edge's concept of *cooperative development* (1992, 2002b). In cooperative development, two people cooperate in order for one of them to work on self-development to become a better teacher. As can be seen by Edge's definition, cooperative development is different from mentoring, because both parties agree to cooperate and the interaction is on the terms of the one seeking to develop his or her understanding. Although Edge acknowledges that there is certainly a place for frank offering of advice to colleagues or exchange of differing opinions (as in traditional mentoring), his enterprise involves a quite different way of interacting. Edge assigns the roles for the two people as Speaker and Understander. The Understander's role is to help the Speaker discover her own ideas, explore them, and clarify them. To achieve this, he has described in detail, with examples from research, the abilities such interaction requires: attending, reflecting, focusing, thematizing, challenging, disclosing, goal-setting, trialing, and planning. While all of these abilities are vital for such collegial interactions, we will describe just two—reflecting and disclosing—to help you conceptualize the process that Edge is advocating. *Reflecting* refers to a colleague acting as a mirror, telling back the Speaker's ideas so that the Speaker can better understand her ideas, attitudes, and emotions. It is not the Understander's role to interpret in any way what the Speaker articulates. The Understander reflects what the Speaker said and checks whether what the Understander has said is, in fact, what the Speaker intended. *Disclosing* means that it is expected that the Understander will disclose from her own experience but only within the framework of the Speaker. The Understander should offer an illustrative experience of her own only if the purpose is to clarify what the Speaker is trying to say. Disclosing should not be for the purpose of giving the Speaker instruction or explanations.

Practitioner Research

A number of forms of practitioner research fall into the category of reflective professional development, most notably action research, diary studies, and learning logs. These, among other forms of research into classroom practice, will be discussed further in Volume II. For a broad focus on research within TESOL that has a teacher and learning focus, we recommend that teachers explore the *TESOL International Association Research Agenda 2014* (TESOL Research Agenda Task Force, 2014), which provides a map of research in the field of TESOL, discusses assumptions about research, offers an overview of research methodologies, and presents a discussion of research ethics. It also provides information on how stakeholders in TESOL were involved in the creation of the research agenda. In this chapter, we will focus only on the professional development aspect of action research and diary studies.

In broad terms, action research (Kemmis & McTaggart, 1986) involves teachers identifying a question or issue in their practice. For example, an issue might be that some learners do not seem to engage in group work. The teachers then explore the issue and decide on some action that might change the situation. Next, they implement the action, evaluate its impact, and reflect on their observations, which may lead to further action. *Collaborative action research*, an extension of action research, takes place with a group of teachers, who share their observations, their actions, and the effects of those actions (Burns, 1999). "A *diary study* is a first-person account of a language learning or teaching experience, documented through regular, candid entries in a personal journal and then analyzed for recurrent patterns or salient events" (Bailey, 1990, p. 215, our italics). A *learning log* is similar to a diary study, but focuses on what the teacher has learned from a professional development activity or by observing a classroom.

Because these teacher-as-researcher methods include observation of the teaching situation and reflection, teachers' understanding develops. As Burns (1999) notes for collaborative action research:

> [s]uch evidence as exists in the ESL teaching field seems to point to the capacity for collaborative action research to reduce teachers' isolation and to help them generate rich insights about classroom practices and to enhance their own theories about teaching and learning.
>
> (p. 32)

Volunteerism

There are many opportunities for teachers to provide their professional expertise outside the classroom and, in the process, learn new skills and continue to develop their understanding of ELT. Most of these opportunities are volunteer work. In addition, teachers often find themselves managing volunteers, such as in a professional association or aides in a school or classroom. In some situations, teachers' earnings may be so poor that any spare time they have has to be used for additional earnings, rather than on volunteer activities. However, we believe, as a result of our own experiences, that rewarding professional growth occurs through volunteer activities. These activities might include working for a professional association, working for a community organization that supports immigrants or refugees, or providing expert testimony to government departments or local groups. We begin by examining what we already know about voluntarism and how to choose and manage volunteers.

Task: Reflect

What unpaid work have you done in your life? Why did you choose to do it? What skills and knowledge did you gain from these experiences? Did you feel you had sufficient skills to undertake the work? How were you chosen? What criteria were used? Was your work evaluated? How?

There is an extensive research literature on volunteering in general, although very little within the field of ELT. Many people have the mistaken belief that anyone willing should be chosen to do such work and, if their

effort is being provided free, it should not be evaluated. The research literature demonstrates that these are fallacies that lead volunteers and those who
hire them into unfortunate conflict and dissatisfaction. In fact, organizations
that require volunteers find they have to deal with the same issues they do
with paid staff, especially when those volunteers play critical roles and/or
commit a lot of time.

Grossman and Furano's (2002) megastudy of hundreds of studies conducted
in a variety of programs in the United States found that three elements were
vitally important to the success of volunteer programs: screening, training, and
ongoing management and support.

Screening

Often volunteers are not formally recruited, but chosen through word of
mouth. However, as Grossman and Furano (2002) show, the screening process
needs to be sufficiently rigorous to select adults most likely to be successful as
volunteers. The *screening process* looks for individuals who have the appropriate
attitudes, time, and skills needed to succeed. Additionally, the process, as with
hiring of paid staff, should include detailed job descriptions so that both managers and volunteers know exactly what is expected of them and how they will be
held accountable for their work.

To successfully recruit and select volunteers, we need to understand why
people volunteer, so we can meet their needs and expectations, not just the
needs of the organization. A 1987 volunteer survey (Murk & Stephan, 1991)
conducted in the United States found that:

> 97% of people who volunteer do so because they want to help others,
> because they enjoy the work (93%), and because they are personally
> interested in the specific work or cause (89%) for which they volun-
> teer their services. A smaller . . . number of people volunteered as the
> result of a feeling of civic or social responsibility (76%), to fill free time
> (41%), or to make new friends (40%).
>
> (pp. 73–74)

Training

Training includes both initial orientation to the organization and the job description. Additional training should be available if the volunteer does not have all
the skills needed. The orientation and training should be designed to ensure

that volunteers have the specific skills needed to be effective, and that they have realistic expectations of what they can accomplish.

Ongoing Management and Support

Management staff need to ensure that volunteer hours are not wasted and that the volunteers are as effective as possible. Recognition and rewards are essential for successful volunteerism. The rewards do not need to be monetary. As Murk and Stephan (1991) showed, people volunteer for a variety of reasons, including in order to learn new skills, so that they can then obtain paid work. We have found that public recognition and thanks help volunteers feel that their contributions are worthwhile. This appreciation can be as simple as sending thank-you notes or having a ceremony where volunteers are given a paper certificate in acknowledgment of their work.

In our own experience, volunteering has helped us develop new skills, understand the profession in greater depth, and at the same time give back to the field the experiences and learning we have gained. We have both served on the board of TESOL, the professional association, and been its president, an exhilarating, but demanding experience. From these experiences and the research literature, we have come to realize that organizations that rely on volunteers need to use the same professional approach that is used for paid employees. We have also found professional associations to be a platform for advocating for the field, a topic we will now explore.

Advocacy

Advocacy means to plead on behalf of an idea, a proposal, or a person. Although advocacy may seem antithetical to some cultural values in the context in which you teach, in everyday activities, teachers are advocates—for their learners, for the field of English language teaching, for professional practice, for equity, and for justice (as seen in the following task).

Task: Reflect

Each of the following brief scenarios includes advocacy. As you read each one, think about (a) what the teacher had to know to be able to act, and (b) what other action the teacher might have taken.

(continued)

(continued)

- Sam is a refugee from Somalia. His teacher noticed that he is withdrawn in class, but in the playground he is aggressive, often fighting and bullying other children. She spoke to the school counselor about his behavior. The counselor, knowing that some members of his community did not accept psychological counseling, contacted a respected elder from the community.
- At the parent-teacher night, Gabriella's father, a farmer, indicated that he thought teaching English to her was a waste of time. He believed she was never going to work for a multinational company or in the tourist industry. She was going to marry a farmer. The teacher told the father gently that, in today's world, many farmers need English and this will likely increase in the future.
- The language center lets every teacher write their own end-of-course examinations and students then pass into the university based on the teacher assessment. Lisa thinks that there should be some standards so that every student is judged the same way. She talks with some of the other teachers and proposes that they have some common questions on the exam and develop a process for cross-grading so that everyone applies the same standards.

As well as engaging in the everyday activities depicted in the scenarios above, teachers often are advocates for learners, their families, and the profession to policy makers through their professional associations. Teacher professional associations play an important role in disseminating knowledge about the profession to those in a position to make decisions. These associations can amplfy the individual voices of their members. At the same time, each member is empowered through the sharing of knowledge and understandings of professional practice with other members of the profession (see, for example, the Brazilian example in Chapter 15). In an online discussion after the Summit on the Future of the TESOL Profession (TESOL International Association, 2018), Harry Kuchah, an active member of a teacher professional association in Cameroon, reminded us that:

> Practitioners can jolly well influence policy . . . but I would argue that in addition to encouraging policy makers to empower teachers, teachers themselves will need to take the initiative and responsibility of transitioning from mere agents of policy implementation to informed practitioners

capable of articulating the principles which guide their practice and providing evidence that their practices produce quality learning.

(Adoniou, 2017, p. 3)

Learning About Leadership

Many teachers take on leadership roles either within their teaching context or in professional associations. However, most of us receive no training in the various aspects of our new roles. Few courses or workshops exist that help us learn about being managers and leaders.[1] How, then, can we learn about best practice in our new roles? We will first discuss the essential content areas that help inform management and leadership, and then present some tools you can use to learn more about your own practice.

Essential Management and Leadership Skills

In our experience, effective managers and leaders are excellent communicators who understand the context in which they work, understand themselves, can motivate others, and can manage relationships with others in the workplace. Research shows that these are all skills that can be learned. Here we can only touch on some essentials for developing leadership: understanding context, understanding self, and managing relationships. As well as being essential skills for leaders, these are also important skills for all teachers.

Understanding your context. Some recent theories about organizations talk about the effectiveness of learning organizations. They are innovative because they create a culture for all staff to continue learning, value staff contributions, and share knowledge with all staff. These attributes are in contrast to organizations whose culture withholds knowledge because knowledge is considered to be power and is to be held only by those in positions of power. In learning organizations, power resides in the innovations that come from sharing knowledge. There are a number of models of organizational structure that affect how much an organization can become a learning organization (see Chapter 5).

Understanding self. Goleman's (1998) research has shown that understanding oneself is critical for all workers, and especially for an effective leader. He has identified three aspects: self-awareness, self-regulation, and motivation. Each aspect has a number of components. We have listed these in Table 14.1.

Task: Explore

Complete Table 14.1 to rate your own personal competence. What areas do you need to work on as a teacher, and what areas would you need to work on if you held a leadership position? Also use it to rate one leader you admire (i.e., who is effective) and one you feel is not effective.

Managing relationships. Managing our relationships does not mean manipulating others. Rather, it involves a range of skills and activities through which leaders empower staff to reach their full potential and, therefore, contribute to the overall effectiveness of the organization. Goleman (1998) has identified understanding others as the other key component to effectiveness, for both workers and leaders.

Task: Explore

Complete Table 14.2 and rate your own social competence. What areas do you need to work on as a teacher, what areas would you need to work on if you held a leadership position? Also rate a leader you admire (i.e., who is effective) and one you feel is not effective.

Conclusion

From a critical perspective, the political socialization of teachers is viewed as a lifelong dialectical process, because human beings are not only limited and enabled "in what they think and do by existing social relations and ideologies, but they are also active agents who, through their thinking and acting, help to produce and reproduce social structures and ideologies" (Ginsburg & Tidwell, 1990, p. 71). In this chapter, we have explained the importance of continuing professional development (CPD) and provided some tools to help you engage in professional learning. These professional development (PD) activities that we have suggested will help you be an empowered actor in your teaching context, not only a recipient of other people's ideas and mandates.

Table 14.1 Personal competence checklist

	Rate your level of competence			Rate a leader you admire			Rate an ineffective leader		
	Low	Average	High	Low	Average	High	Low	Average	High
Self-awareness									
Emotional awareness									
Accurate self-assessment									
Self-confidence									
Self-regulation									
Self-control									
Trustworthiness									
Adaptability									
Innovation									
Motivation									
Achievement drive									
Commitment									
Initiative									
Optimism									

Table 14.2 Social competence checklist

	Rate your level of competence			Rate a leader you admire			Rate an ineffective leader		
	Low	Average	High	Low	Average	High	Low	Average	High
Empathy									
Understanding others									
Developing others									
Service orientation									
Leveraging diversity									
Political awareness									
Social skills									
Influence									
Communication									
Conflict management									
Leadership									
Change catalyst									
Building bonds									
Collaboration and cooperation									
Team capabilities									

Task: Expand

A number of professional websites provide information on conferences, publications, and also printed research-based materials. These will help you reflect on and grow your practice and knowledge base:

www.ascd.org/Default.aspx is the website for the Association for Supervision and Curriculum Development (ASCD, which focuses on leadership issues in education.

http://iatefl.org is the website for the International Association of Teachers of English as a Foreign Language (IATEFL), which is based in the United Kingdom, but has associates and members worldwide.

www.tesol.org is the website for TESOL International Association, which is based in the United States, but has affiliates and members worldwide.

Casanave, C. P., & Schecter, S. R. (Eds.). (1997). *On becoming a language educator: Personal essays on professional development.* Mahwah, NJ: Lawrence Erlbaum.
This volume uses narrative inquiry to uncover how 16 language educators found themselves as professionals. It provides both thought-provoking stories and models for reflection and scrutiny of practice.

Christison, M. A., & Murray, D. E. (Eds.). (2009). *Leadership in English language education: Theoretical foundations and practical skills for changing times.* New York, NY: Routledge.
This volume covers the broad range of theory and skills that managers and leaders need in order to be effective in language teaching institutions. It includes activities to help readers reflect on their own practice.

Liu, J., & Berger, C. M. (2015). *TESOL: A guide.* London, England: Bloomsbury.
This comprehensive volume explores the profession, the fields of study, and TESOL International Association. It is an excellent resource for anyone involved in the TESOL profession.

Questions for Discussion

1   How do teachers best learn to develop their professional skills?
2   What PD activities are discussed in this chapter? What other PD activities can you think of that teachers can engage in?
3   What are the features of cooperative development?

4   What principles need to be followed when working with volunteers?

5   Why is it important for teachers to understand and practice effective man-
     agement and leadership skills?

Note

1   Exceptions are the extensive programs run by the Association for Supervision and
     Curriculum Development (ASCD) and TESOL International Association.

References

Adoniou, M. (2017). *Professionalism and the profession as change agent.* Retrieved from
    www.tesol.org/docs/default-source/advocacy/misty-adoniou.pdf?sfvrsn=0

Allwright, D. (2003). Exploratory practice: Rethinking practitioner research in language
    teaching. *Language Teaching Research, 7*(2), 113–141.

Bailey, K. M. (1990). The use of diary studies in teacher education programs. In
    J. C. Richards & D. Nunan (Eds.), *Second language teacher education* (pp. 202–214).
    Cambridge, England: Cambridge University Press.

Bailey, K. M., & Nunan, D. (Eds.). (1996). *Voices from the classroom: Qualitative research in
    second language education.* Cambridge, England: Cambridge University Press.

Barduhn, S. (2002). Why develop? It's easier not to. In J. Edge (Ed.), *Continuing professional
    development: Some of our perspectives* (pp. 10–13). Whitstable, England: IATEFL.

Bartels, N. (2005). Applied linguistics and language teacher education: What we know.
    In N. Bartels (Ed.), *Applied linguistics and language teacher education* (pp. 405–424).
    New York, NY: Springer.

Bartlett, L. (1990). Teacher development through reflective teaching. In J. C. Richards
    & D. Nunan (Eds.), *Second language teacher education* (pp. 202–214). Cambridge,
    England: Cambridge University Press.

Borg, S. (2006). *Teacher cognition and language education: Research and practice.* London,
    England: Continuum.

Burns, A. (1999). *Collaborative action research for English language teachers.* Cambridge,
    England: Cambridge University Press.

Burton, J. (1998). Professionalism in language teaching. *Prospect, 13*(3), 24–34.

Casanave, C. P., & Schecter, S. R. (Eds.). (1997). *On becoming a language educator:
    Personal essays on professional development.* Mahwah, NJ: Lawrence Erlbaum.

Christison, M. A., & Murray, D. E. (Eds.). (2009). *Leadership in English language edu-
    cation: Theoretical foundations and practical skills for changing times.* New York, NY:
    Routledge.

Clarke, D., & Hollingsworth, H. (2002). Elaborating a model of teacher professional
    growth. *Teaching and Teacher Education, 18*(8), 947–967.

Crandall, J. (1993). Professionalism and professionalization of adult ESL literacy. *TESOL
    Quarterly, 27*(3), 497–515.

Crandall, J., & Christison M. A. (2016). An overview of research in English language
    teacher education and professional development. In J. Crandall & M. A. Christison

(Eds.), *Teacher education and professional development in TESOL* (pp. 4–34). New York, NY: Routledge.

Davison, C. (2005). The standards solution: The role of standards in developing IT professional competencies and communities of practice in English language teaching. In C. Davison (Ed.), *Information teachnology and innovation in language education* (pp. 255–283). Hong Kong, China: University of Hong Kong Press.

Edge, J. (1992). Co-operative development. *ELT Journal, 46*(1), 62–70.

Edge, J. (1996). Cross-cultural paradoxes in a profession of values. *TESOL Quarterly, 30*(1), 9–30.

Edge, J. (2002a). *Continuing cooperative development: A discourse framework for individuals as colleagues.* Ann Arbor, MI: University of Michigan Press.

Edge, J. (Ed.). (2002b). *Continuing professional development: Some of our perspectives.* Whitstable, England: IATEFL.

European Commission. (2009). *European strategy and co-operation in education and training.* Retrieved from http://ec.europa.eu/education/lifelong-learning-policy/doc28_en.htm

Frase, L., & Sorenson, L. (1992). Teacher motivation and satisfaction: Impact on participatory management. *NASSP Bulletin* (January), 37–43.

Fullan, M. G. (1991). *The new meaning of educational change*, 2nd ed. London, England: Cassell.

Ginsburg, M., & Tidwell, M. (1990). Political socialization of prospective educators in Mexico. *New Education, 12*(2), 70–82.

Goleman, D. (1998). *Working with emotional intelligence.* London, England: Bloomsbury.

Grossman, J. B., & Furano, K. (2002). Making the most of volunteers [Electronic version]. *P/PV Briefs.* Retrieved from www.ppv.org/ppv/publications/assets/152_publication.pdf

Johnson, S. (1990). *Teachers at work: Achieving success in our schools.* New York, NY: Basic Books.

Kemmis, S., & McTaggart, R. (Eds.). (1986). *The action research planner.* Geelong, Australia: Deakin University Press.

Kennedy, C. (1987). Innovating for a change: Teacher development and innovation. *ELT Journal, 41*(3), 163–170.

Lave, J., & Wenger, E. (1991). *Situated learning: Legitimate and peripheral participation.* Cambridge, England: Cambridge University Press.

Liu, J., & Berger, C. M. (2015). *TESOL: A guide.* London, England: Bloomsbury.

Murk, P. J., & Stephan, J. F. (1991). Volunteers: How to get them, train them and keep them. *Economic Development Review, 9*(3), 73–76.

Myers, M., & Clark, S. (2002). CPD, lifelong learning and going meta. In J. Edge (Ed.), *Continuing professional development: Some of our perspectives* (pp. 50–62). Whitstable, England: IATEFL.

New Teacher Center. (2011). *State policy review: Teacher induction.* Retrieved from https://newteachercenter.org/wp-content/uploads/California.pdf

TESOL International Association (2018). *Action agenda for the future of the TESOL profession.* Retrieved from www.tesol.org/summit-2017/action-agenda-for-the-future-of-the-tesol-profession

TESOL Research Agenda Task Force. (2014). *TESOL International Association research agenda 2014*. Alexandria, VA: TESOL International. Retrieved from www.tesol. org/docs/default-source/pdf/2014_tesol-research-agenda.pdf?sfvrsn=2

Thompson, C., & Zeuli, J. (1999). The frame and the tapestry: Standards-based reform and professional development. In L. Darling-Hammond & G. Sykes (Eds.), *Teaching as the learning profession: Handbook of policy and practice* (pp. 341–375). San Francisco, CA: Jossey-Bass.

Wallace, M. (1994). *Training foreign language teachers: A reflective approach*. Cambridge, England: Cambridge University Press.

Yates, L., & Brindley, G. (2000). Editorial. *Prospect, 15*(3), 1–4.

Zeichner, K. M. (1981–2). Reflective teaching and field-based experience in teacher education. *Interchange, 12*, 1–22.

15

TEACHING AND LEARNING LANGUAGE
IN A DIGITAL WORLD

VIGNETTE

Context: Online doctoral class on curriculum. The real-time class is held via a conferencing program that allows for video, audio, display of visuals (e.g., PowerPoint), and chat. This session is about outcomes-based curriculum. The following excerpt is from a chat occurring in parallel with the lecture (names are pseudonyms):

Karen Simpson: (to Everyone)	4:17 PM: Are goals and objectives curriculum-focused, and outcomes student-focused?
Harry Freeman: (to Everyone)	4:18 PM: Could we say that outcomes are objectives that have been met (or not)?
Susanna Morales: (to Everyone)	4:19 PM: I think they're all student-focused.
John Bennett: (to Everyone)	4:19 PM: Tha's my take onit Harry. I always think of outcomes in the past tense
Van Suffolk (to Everyone):	4:19 PM: I think so Harry
Susanna (to Everyone):	4:20 PM: I think of it like if your course is a journey, goals are the destination and objectives are stops along the way necessary to reach that destination.
Harry Freeman: (to Everyone)	4:21 PM: Interesting, Susanna. So how about outcomes?
Rachel Willson: (to Everyone)	4:21 PM: hahaha

(continued)

273

(continued)

Susanna Morales: (to Everyone)	4:21 PM: I think of outcomes as similar to objectives, like the anticipated achievement of the objectives.
Karen Simpson: (to Everyone)	4:23 PM: Every program should know where it is coming from (goals and objectives) and what it is trying to accomplish (outcomes).

Context: Teachers in Brazil use a multimedia platform to interact informally for discussion, presentations, and to share instructional ideas. This excerpt is from the Facebook page, which is publicly available, where one teacher has posed the question "Do you think anyone can learn a language up to C2 [on the Common European Frame of Reference]? What does it take?" (Note: photos have been removed and names are pseudonyms.)

Gabriel Santos *Well, I am C1 in English and PtBr native speaker, but I shall confess my speaking of PORTUGUESE is not that accurate.*

That does bring me down.

Regarding complex conversation and topics, my Portuguese freezes . . . See More

Like

· Reply ·

2

· October 12 at 1:04pm · Edited

Remove

Pedro Oliveira *I'm a C2 and it took me years of study! In fact, I still study the language, not only the 4 skills, but everything else you do with it and I always learn something new!*

Like

· Reply ·

9

· October 12 at 1:14pm

Remove

Luiz Melo *That's the thing people usually don't get: it is a continuous process; it depends on our interest and we're always learning something new.*

Like

· Reply ·

Amanda Rocha *Time*

Like

· Reply · October 12 at 1:37pm

Remove

Felipe Silva *It takes focus, dedication, choice, mind hacks, hard studying, effort, practice, an open mind, passion, devotion, greed, perseverance, resilience, spare time, emotional stability. . . (I could go on forever).*

And, NO, not anybody can do it . . . See More

Like

· Reply · October 12 at 3:06pm

Remove

António Schmitz *In theory? Yes. They need exposure, time and dedication.*

Like

· Reply ·

1

Task: Reflect

1   Why do you think some of the class participants in the curriculum class chose to interact via chat instead of bidding for a speaking turn?
2   How effective do you think the chat was? Why?
3   In the Brazilian example, how would you answer the question?
4   In the Brazilian example, what surprised you about the teachers' points of view?

Introduction

Over the past three decades, Information and Communication Technology (ICT) has expanded its reach around the world. As a result of ICT, we have

developed new ways of communicating among ourselves and sharing information. This digital world impacts English language education at various levels. It
has changed what learners know and are able to do when they enter our classrooms and provided access to new ways of teaching and new avenues for the
development of communities of practice and continuing professional development (CPD). Each of these changes will be discussed in this chapter, while a
detailed discussion on new ways of teaching is provided in Volume II. The issue
of CPD is covered more thoroughly in the previous chapter.

Although we have devoted a chapter to the digital world, in one sense it is not
a standalone chapter but is infused in all the discussions that we have provided thus
far in this volume. We have, however, chosen to devote a chapter to the impact
of digital media and devices on our teaching lives because in the 21st century it has
become salient in our lives outside of the classroom and in teaching. Teachers need
to understand the challenges of digital technologies, as well as their opportunities,
because the digital world provides a context that crosses all the contexts we discussed
in Part I. However, technology for communication has been changing over the centuries, and each new change brings its own challenges and opportunities. To sustain
their professional practice, teachers have always had to understand the changes in the
technologies that impact on teaching and learning. As Hari Krishna Arya, a veteran
educator from India, said: "[t]eachers will not be replaced by technology, but teachers who do not use technology will be replaced by those who do" (dailyedventures,
2015). We begin this chapter by discussing the digital world in general and then
move on to how this digital world is changing the context for teaching and learning.

The Digital World

The digital world appears to be driven by technology, yet, as we have seen with
the introduction of previous communication technologies, the people using the
new technologies have agency. We will, therefore, begin our discussion with a
brief overview of the impact of past technologies before moving to the aspects
of digital world that entered our lives in the early 21st century. While we are all
familiar with these aspects, several issues are especially pertinent for those of us
who are engaged in English language education: unequal access, new literacies,
privacy, and multitasking.

The Historical Impact of Communication Technologies

Writing systems were first introduced in Mesopotamia around BCE 3000 to BCE
2000, providing people with a tool for communicating across time and space.

This Cuneiform system of writing involved using a special tool to cut wedges in intricate designs in clay tablets, but there were limitations on the proliferation of this writing system. Later came the ancient Greek invention of an alphabetic writing system, which was a more simplified form of writing. At the time, scholars such as Socrates and Plato decried this introduction for fear it would disrupt the status quo. They believed only the elite should have access to such writing. Similarly, with the introduction of the printing press to Europe in the 15th century, the Church hierarchy, who controlled the writing of religious scrolls at the time, believed ordinary people should not have access to the Bible, except as interpreted by the Church.

The introduction of computer-based technology in the 20th century, which began as a tool for calculations, became co-opted as a communication tool. However, as in ancient Greece with the alphabetic system and in Europe with the printing press, there have been dire warnings about the perils of email, texting, and Twitter. For example, Walter Ong (1982), a literacy scholar, claimed: "[w]riting is passive, out of it, in an unreal, unnatural world. So are computers" (p. 79), and Sutherland claimed that texting is "bleak, bald, sad shorthand. Drab shrinktalk . . . Linguistically it's all [a] pig's ear … it masks poor spelling and mental laziness. Texting is penmanship for illiterates" (quoted in Crystal, 2008, p. 13).

Despite the dire warnings at the introduction of each new communication technology or tool, researchers have found the people do not adopt new technologies merely because they exist: "Sociocultural precursors to the technological innovation facilitate its acceptance, and the technology amplifies certain sociocultural characteristics (or not)" (Murray, 2013, p. 190). Therefore, we find that Greek culture did not implode as a result of alphabetic writing. Gutenberg filled a commercial need by developing the printing press because already in late Medieval Europe people were interested in texts, memorizing large tracts of material, and literacy was sufficient to support the introduction of printed books. In turn, the Protestant Church encouraged the reading of the Bible and so amplified the need for printed materials. In the late 20th century, people co-opted a technology (i.e., the Internet) which was designed to facilitate business and was an application designed for military research, for personal communication. Email became popular because of global trade and because it was a fast, asynchronous method of communication that facilitated interaction across time zones. Texting became popular because in public spaces, it was far less intrusive than using a mobile phone. Teachers, therefore, need to be aware that the use of technology is first and foremost a sociocultural phenomenon, conditioned by the context(s) in which it is used. Just as they need to consider the contexts of English learners' lives that we discussed in Part I in this volume, they also need to critically examine existing and new technologies and tools as they arise. We now turn to some of the critical issues that English language teachers need to consider—namely, unequal access, new literacies, privacy, and multitasking.

Unequal Access

Much has been written about both the risks and affordances of digital technology (for example, Murray & Christison, 2017a). What has become clear is that the digital world is not monolithic, nor is its full potential available to all equally. One of us (Denise) has been tracking worldwide access to the Internet since 1997, and Table 15.1 shows the incredible worldwide penetration over time.

However, what this table conceals are the following questions (for 2017): Who are the 45.6 percent with no Internet access? What type of access do the 54.4 percent have? Do the 54.4 percent who use the Internet worldwide have the skills to use it effectively? For example, only 35.2 percent of Africans have access. In North America, while 95 percent have access (with two-thirds of Americans being on *Facebook*), the 5 percent who do not have access disproportionately includes the elderly, minorities, and the economically disadvantaged. Impediments to the uptake of information and communications technology (ICT) include low bandwidth, power interruptions, cost, relevance for local needs, digital skills, and cultural barriers. Determining the type of access people have is difficult to judge. However, research has shown that *mobile technology*, especially cell (mobile) phones, has quickly become the device of choice, especially in developing economies. Mobile technology has many advantages over wired formats, especially in terms of rapid and broad diffusion, because the infrastructure is more easily built. In other words, it's easier (and cheaper) to build cell towers than dig underground and run cables to every home, school, and workplace. However, *smartphones* may not have sufficient *bandwidth*, access, or suitable

Table 15.1 Percentage of online users worldwide over two decades

Percentage of online users worldwide					
1997	2002	2007	2010	2014	2017
Network Wizards (reference no longer on the web)	GlobalReach (reference no longer on the web)	Internet World Stats	Internet World Stats	Internet World Stats	Internet World Stats (2018)
6%	9%	18.9%	28.7%	42.3%	54.4%

Note: The Internet World Stats site only has the most recent information.

applications to be effective for school projects. A study in California (Avalos, 2015) found that 21 percent of students had no broadband access and 8 percent had access only via smartphones, which do not facilitate "productivity tasks, or kids doing school work" (p. B6).

Finally, we have to consider how proficient our English learners are in using the digital technology, especially Web 2.0, whose technologies "facilitate user-generated content that can be shared, exchanged, and commented on to create virtual social networks" (Murray & Christison, 2017b, p. 10). While younger generations are *digital natives* (Prensky, 2001), it does not necessarily mean that they will not need any help using the technology effectively for educational purposes. While digital natives may respond well to online class activities because of their familiarity with digital technology, many have limited knowledge of and practical experiences with all computer-based technology (Kim, Rueckert, Kim, & Seo, 2013). Therefore, as teachers navigate the digital world with their learners, they need to know who has what access, how, and what depth of understanding they have to utilize it fully for learning. Furthermore, they need to understand the new literacies that they and their learners need to master to be effective communicators—points that we discuss in the next section.

Task: Explore

Observe your local environments, such as coffee shops, schools, shopping malls, or community centers. Who is using smartphones? Who is using tablets? Who is using laptop computers? Are there generational differences? What percentage of people use one of these devices?

Go to www.internetworldstats.com/stats.htm and check what the Internet usage is for the country where you conducted this observation. Is your local environment typical?

Multimodal Literacy

One aspect of being able to fully utilize the potential of digital technology is one's proficiency with *multimodal literacy*. As noted in Chapter 9, multimodal literacy is when a text combines two or more semiotic systems (Anstey & Bull, 2011). Anstey and Bull give as an example a webpage in which elements such as sound effects, oral language, written language, music, and still or moving images are combined. Although more attention has been paid to multimodal literacy since the advent of digital media, multimodal literacy is not new.

For example, a picture book combines images and linguistic text to create a whole discourse. Even a text with only words may include visuals such as spacing, columns, lists, and so on.

Multimodal literacy, therefore, includes the ability to interact with digital texts that may include linguistic, visual, spatial, and/or audio semiotic systems. To use Web 2.0 effectively for language education requires that learners have the skills to be able to navigate the web and interpret the multimodal texts they encounter. English language teachers need to be able to explicitly teach these skills to ensure that their learners make full use of the language learning opportunities that are provided by instruction using digital technology. However, we must also be aware of some of the hidden dangers (discussed in the next section) that are inherent in the networked world.

Privacy Concerns

While the interconnected world allows us to communicate with anyone in the world at any time, it also means that bad actors or marketers may have access to our communications. With the *Internet of Things* (Watson & Plymale, 2011), privacy concerns have become even more pressing as reports come in of companies (and others) accessing always-on cameras or audio on a variety of devices that are located in the privacy of our homes. These devices are not always transparently computers; they may be home appliances, vehicles, televisions, home thermostats or lights, and smart speakers that connect by voice commands to *intelligent personal assistant* software. *Blogs* and *Twitter* feeds have had endless discussion about whether to be polite to a virtual assistant, with some people contending that we should be polite, because if we are not polite we risk being rude to real people. Others have contended that because it is just a machine, like a toaster or an ATM, it does not make sense to use politeness markers. In fact, it has been shown that many people are beginning to treat personal assistant software as if they are interacting with human beings, using politeness markers such as *please* and *thank you*.

Social media have especially been vulnerable to hacking and also to trolling. *Hacking* refers to someone gaining unauthorized access to a digital device, usually with malicious intent, such as to steal users' identity to sell or to access their bank accounts. *Trolling* refers to deliberately posting an inflammatory comment in order to embarrass or make someone angry. Online communication, such as chat and email, has long had *flaming*, the use of offensive language. In the past this practice was assumed to be prevalent in online communication because of the feeling of anonymity or distance between interlocutors. Social media seem to have amplified this tendency. As language educators, we need to be cognizant of the language used by our learners and alert them to the possibilities of their being trolled, and we need to discuss the potential repercussions of their engaging in such practices. We also need to ensure that we direct them to safe sites, when possible, for our classroom activities. Those learners with limited English skills have been particularly vulnerable to offensive language.

Multitasking

In the vignette at the beginning of this chapter, the students in the curriculum class were engaging in chat at the same time as the professor was eliciting verbal comments from the class through videoconferencing. The professor, therefore, needed to monitor both the audiovisual interaction as well as the text chat. It seems that, more and more, we see people texting while doing other activities, such as driving, crossing the road, having coffee or dinner with someone, or sitting in class. We all think we can *multitask*. However, research has shown that in fact we cannot (Chun, Golomb, & Turk-Browne, 2011; Gorlick, 2009; Junco, 2012), and that multitasking with ICTs in academic contexts can interfere with the learning process. What we actually do is quickly move back and forth between activities. These researchers and others have shown that such constant changing in focus is very inefficient, such that neither task is accomplished well,

---

Task: Reflect

Think about your own uses of digital media. What steps have you taken to ensure the privacy of your data and communications? How did you learn to make these decisions? Share your ideas with a colleague.

Do you try to multitask? The next time you try to multitask, take notes on what you were doing and then reflect on what cognitive processes you were using? Share your thoughts with a colleague.

Changes in the Teaching and Learning Context

Digital media provide new opportunities for learners for interaction and use of English in authentic situations, whether it is through instructional activities or informally through their daily lives. However, using the new technologies may also present a challenge to teachers who did not grow up during the digital age. The technology we are most comfortable with is partly a result of which ones we first used and became comfortable with. For example, in the business world, as *personal computers (PCs)* became available, more executives began using computers. Previously, when all they had was a keyboard and monitor and everything was stored and routed through a mainframe, which was attended by expert technicians, they were reluctant to use them. They adopted PCs not only because the user interface was easier, but because they could use them in the seclusion of their office; no one needed to know when they did something that others might perceive as stupid. Teachers, too, often have their preferred technologies with which they have developed a level of competence, and they may be embarrassed to try using new tools and devices in front of their learners.

Digital Media in Instruction

We will explore the use of digital media in instruction in detail in Volume II. In this volume, our goal is to discuss briefly some of the digital tools that are used for instruction. *Computer-assisted language learning (CALL)*, a term that has been used since the 1970s, has followed the changes in ICT from mainframe computers to microcomputers to networked computers to mobile devices to fully online language courses. The proliferation of mobile devices has led to a subfield of CALL, *mobile-assisted language learning (MALL)*. For a complete history of CALL, see Davies, Otto, and Rüschoff (2013). While the historical trajectory of CALL is fascinating and complex, here we will only discuss activities that are still in general use.

Classroom tools. A variety of 3D *virtual worlds* have been used by many teachers, such as Second Life and *Massively Multiplayer Online Roleplay Games* (MMORPGs) (such as World of Warcraft) because they "can provide opportunities [for learners] to have immediate, visual and affective access to speakers of the language(s) they are learning in a way that is not possible in other online communication formats" (Sadler & Dooly, 2013, p. 159). Such advantages include *task-based learning* through the goal-directed tasks of the games that require collaboration among learners (Dixon & Christison, 2018). *Telecollaboration* is another learning activity that has been embraced by language teachers. In telecollaboration, classes of language learners are brought together online to develop their language skills and intercultural competence through projects and other collaborative tasks. So, for example, a class in Chile learning English may pair with a class in the United States learning Spanish. Traditionally, these interactions have been asynchronous and in text, but with more recent Web 2.0 they may include synchronous audio and video. Discussion lists, chat, email, podcasts, blogs, wikis, and videoconferencing, as well as social media, have also been adapted for language learning purposes.

More recently have been the advances in *Artificial Intelligence (AI)*. Although AI and machine learning have made tremendous advances in speech recognition and speech synthesis, AI is still not general intelligence. It works within limited domains of knowledge and context, such as playing the complex games Chess or Go. It is used especially for decision making, where it is based on data from millions of samples of previous decisions—for example, helping doctors choose the most effective cancer treatment. With the more widespread use of AI systems in many spheres of life, including autonomous vehicles and the military, has come a concern about the ethics of AI. The questions raised include whether machines can ever be sentient or whether they behave ethically. Another concern with AI that has relevance for language instruction is that the decisions made by machines are based on an enormous database of previous examples and, more and more, these machine decisions are becoming accurate in mimicking the human decision-making process. However, the issue is that if the data reflect the biases of a particular society, then the machines will perpetuate that bias.

In ELT, AI has been harnessed for both CALL and assessment. Intelligent CALL (iCALL) has embraced the knowledge from AI, including natural language processing, and has been used for activities across various language learning domains, including grammar, vocabulary, reading, and writing, with a focus on interaction and noticing (Schulze & Heift, 2013).

The assessment of writing provides an example of the potential for bias in AI. For assessment, one particular learner's essay is compared with thousands of other ones written on the same topic. The computer breaks down the essay into different language features. Additionally, AI programs can now assess content; that is, how the learner expresses meaning. While such programs are already in operation, many educators (and AI experts) are concerned that there is insufficient attention paid to essay samples for which the AI program does not know how to score well—that is, it has a bias for the particular linguistic forms that have previously been scored. For example, some responses may be very idiosyncratic, yet still be acceptable responses to the essay prompt. Those who are concerned about this aspect of assessment believe that the AI program should refer any response for which it cannot score with confidence to a live instructor/examiner (Foltz, Hilfer, McClure, & Stavinsky, 2018).

Barriers to using technology in instruction. Not all of the activities mentioned above are accessible in all English language teaching contexts, as we noted at the beginning of this chapter. What technologies are available and able to be used for instruction either in low-tech contexts, when the technology fails, or when the school of a country bans access to certain sites or applications? While each context is unique, there are many examples of teachers using the technological resources available to them in creative ways. We'am Hamdan (2017) teaches in Ramallah in the Occupied Palestinian Territories and tells of one such situation:

> On one occasion, I had to adapt a project-based lesson, where the task for the students was to create a tourism leaflet using an online search. But, you guessed it, there was no internet connection. To replace Google, I used a simple low-tech solution—tourist brochures that an English teacher had brought from the UK. I gave the learners 20 minutes to scan the brochures and choose places and information to include in their leaflets.

This solution in fact had added benefits, because the learners had to work in groups because there were not enough brochures for each person to have one, and so they were able to work together and practice oral English. In addition, they didn't get lost in a Google search or find sites whose language was beyond their linguistic abilities in English. To overcome the lack of access to the Internet, other teachers have used some of the technology from earlier generations of *distance learning*, such as television, radio, CD-ROMs, and mobile phones, even if they are not smartphones. They have used these interactional media in conjunction with activities that learners can accomplish independently on computers.

An additional barrier to integrating ICT into language classrooms is learner attitude. Despite many language learners being digital natives, many teachers have reported that their learners resist the use of computer-based technology in their classrooms, because they consider computer technology to be for entertainment, not for education (e.g., Gonzalez & St. Louis, 2013).

Task: Reflect

Think of all the technology applications you use. Which ones would you want to use for language teaching? Why? Share your ideas with colleagues.

Virtual classrooms. Thus far, we have focused on technology use in the traditional bricks-and-mortar classroom. However, with the advent of Web 2.0 and mobile devices has come the possibility of teaching anyone anywhere at any time in a virtual classroom.

Although many traditional learning institutions have launched online programs, many online companies have been established specifically to take advantage of the flexibility for both teacher and learner. For example, VIPKID in China employs teachers around the world to tutor Chinese children in English. To meet the demand for online teachers, other companies have sprouted up to supply the teachers, often from high-tech hubs such as Medellín, Colombia, and Canggu in Bali, Indonesia. Many young millennials have been attracted by the weather, lifestyle, and ability to earn money on their own terms in these exotic high-tech hubs (Washington Post, 2018). This phenomenon is not restricted to English language teaching but includes many information/knowledge workers in what has been termed geoarbitrage (Ferriss, 2007). *Geoarbitrage* is based on the concept of *arbitrage*, which is an economics term where people take advantage of price differences between two or more markets, such as people who speculate in currency exchange. Therefore, the young millennials only need a laptop and can teach English to anyone in the world, depending on time zones, while living in an attractive and inexpensive environment.

Informal Acquisition

As we mentioned briefly in Chapter 2, Schneider (2016) has identified a variety of English that he calls grassroots Englishes, a variety that occurs as learners interact with others translocally and transnationally through the only common language, English. Vittachi (2010) has called this variety of English *globalese*. Tourism is such an example, but digital media, especially social media, are amplifying this trend and democratizing it, creating Englishes based on affinity groups. *Affinity groups* are where groups with a common interest interact in what Gee and Hayes (2011) call affinity spaces. *Affinity spaces* are characterized by shared interest, distributed (rather than hierarchical) knowledge across gender, races, ethnicity, socioeconomic status, and proficiency in a shared language (which is commonly English). Through this multimodal globalese, learners expand their cultural worlds, develop a new sense of their own identity and their understanding of others and other worlds. Schneider's original hypothesis was based on tourism; however, his argument is that many people are acquiring English through direct interactions. It is in this environment that new Englishes emerge (see Chapter 2 for other Englishes).

Changes in the Professional Development Context

Just as the introduction of digital media has influenced teaching and learning, so too has it affected how teachers engage in CPD. While we focused exclusively on professionalism in Chapter 14, here we'll briefly discuss some of the ways digital media have been used for CPD.

In the vignette, we gave the example of the Brazilian online site for teachers (BrELT). This CPD website has made use of a variety of different tools that are available through the web. As Isabel de Freitas Villas Boas, one of the founders of the Website, says:

> Social media can be a powerful tool to integrate TESOL professionals in a more informal and organic manner. There is an online community in Brazil named Brazilian English Language Teachers (BrELT), created by a group of five educators, with more than 16,000 followers. Here are some of the things they do:
>
> - They have a blog where guests can publish on topics in which they are interested.
> - They organize a chat on Facebook every week.
> - They hold online conferences.
> - They advocate in favor of nonnative-English-speaking teachers' equitable treatment by, for example, publishing posts and videos on the topic and refusing job posts on their page that require native-English-speaking teachers.
> - They defend lesbian, gay, bisexual, and transgender (LGBT) professionals and protest discrimination or unethical practices of English teaching franchises around Brazil.
> - They send roving reporters to conferences who post summaries of what they see.
> - They organized their first face-to-face conference in Rio de Janeiro, which attracted more than 100 participants.
> - They provide a space for teachers who are engaged in research to post their surveys or questionnaires and initiate discussions with researchers and other members on their research topic. This could be an effective way to build a bridge between researchers and teachers and to engage the latter in a meaningful form of inquiry. Guided by an experienced researcher, I am sure the BrELT members would be excited about this type of inquiry.
>
> (TESOL, 2018, p. 10)

While the Brazilian example is of teacher-initiated CPD, the web has also been harnessed by institutions and professional associations. For example, schools and colleges offer online CPD, from self-study through to degree programs. Professional associations offer online courses and resources, sometimes free of charge.

Task: Explore

TESOL International and IATEFL are two international professional associations in the field of English language education. Each has a website where CPD opportunities are listed. Visit each of the webpages and explore the CPD offerings. List those that are totally online and those that require some f2f activities. Then share with a colleague:

www.TESOL.org

https://iatefl.org

Conclusion

In this chapter we have briefly explored the 21st-century digital world. We have introduced you to some of the issues in teaching and learning in this new environment, including the type of access learners have, the multimodal literacy they need to acquire, the risks involved in social media, as well as the opportunities these tools have for language instruction. We have also highlighted how the web has added an additional dimension to CPD for English language teachers.

Task: Expand

Gee, J. P., & Hayes, E. R. (2011). *Language and learning in the digital age*. New York, NY: Routledge.
This volume covers both the advantages and disadvantages of digital media, how digital media are affecting language, and how digital media are being addressed in instruction.

Questions for Discussion

1   Why is differential access to broadband an issue for using the web for instruction?
2   What are some of the societal issues that have arisen with the advent of social media?
3   What types of digital tools are used for language teaching?
4   How can you engage in PD without having to attend an event in person?
5   What skills do learners need to master in order to be able to use digital media effectively?

References

Anstey, M., & Bull, G. (2011). Helping teachers to explore multimodal texts. *Curriculum and Leadership Journal, 8*(16). Retrieved from www.curriculum.edu.au/leader/helping_teachers_to_explore_multimodal_texts,31522.html?issueID=12141

Avalos, G. (2015). Survey: Digital gap persists. *San José Mercury News*, June 16, B5–B6.

Chun, M. M., Golomb, J. D., & Turk-Browne, N. B. (2011). A taxonomy of external and internal attention. *Annual Review of Psychology, 62*, 73–101.

Crystal, D. (2008). *Txtng: The gr8 db8.* Oxford, England: Oxford University Press.

dailyedventures (2015). Teachers will not be replaced by technology, but teachers who do not use technology will be replaced by those who do. Retrieved from http://dailyedventures.com/index.php/2015/03/12/hari-krishna-arya/

Davies, G., Otto, S. E. K., & Rüschoff, B. (2013). Historical perspectives on CALL. In M. Thomas, H. Reinders, & M. Warschauer (Eds.), *Contemporary computer-assisted language learning* (pp. 19–38). London, England: Bloomsbury.

Dixon, D., & Christison, M. A. (2018). The usefulness of massive multi-player online role-playing games (MMORPGs) as tools for promoting second language acquisition. In J. Perren, K. Kelch, J.-S. Byun, S. Cervantes, & S. Safavi (Eds.), *Applications of CALL theory in ESL and EFL environments.* Hershey, PA: IGI Global Publishing.

Ferriss, T. (2007). *The 4-hour work week: Escape the 9–5, live anywhere and join the new rich.* New York, NY: Crown.

Foltz, P., Hilfer, E., McClure, K., & Stavinsky, D. (2018). The agency of Artificial Intelligence. *Language Magazine* (June), 28–32.

Gee, J. P. & Hayes, E. R. (2011). *Language and learning in the digital age.* New York, NY: Routledge.

Gonzalez, D., & St. Louis, R. (2013). CALL I low-tech contexts. In M. Thomas, H. Reinders, & M. Warschauer (Eds.), *Contemporary computer-assisted language learning* (pp. 217–241). London, England: Bloomsbury.

Gorlick, A. (2009). *Media multitaskers pay mental price, Stanford study shows.* Retrieved from https://news.stanford.edu/2009/08/24/multitask-research-study-082409/

Hamdan, W. (2017). *Tips for teaching in a low-tech classroom.* Retrieved from www.britishcouncil.org/voices-magazine/tips-teaching-low-tech-classroom

Internet World Stats. (2018). *Internet users in the world 2017.* Retrieved from www.internetworldstats.com/stats.htm

Junco, R. (2012). In-class multitasking and academic performance. *Computers in Human Behavior, 28*(6), 2236–2243. Retrieved from http://dx.doi.org/10.1016/j.chb.2012.06.031

Kim, D., Rueckert, D., Kim, D.-J., & Seo, S. (2013). Students' perceptions and experiences of mobile learning. *Language Learning & Technology, 17*(3), 52–73.

Murray, D. E. (2013). Technology for literacies. In C. A. Chappelle (Ed.), *The Encyclopedia of Applied Linguistics* (pp. 186–199). Oxford, England: Wiley-Blackwell.

Murray, D. E., & Christison, M. A. (2017a). Going online: Affordances and limitations for teachers and teacher educators. In L. L. C. Wong & K. Hyland (Eds.), *Faces of*

English education: Students, teachers, and pedagogy (pp. 215–230). London, England: Routledge.

Murray, D. E., & Christison, M. A. (2017b). *Online language teacher education: Participants' perceptions and experiences*. Retrieved from www.tirfonline.org/wp-content/uploads/2017/03/TIRF_OLTE_2017_Report_Final.pdf

Ong, W. (1982). *Orality and literacy: The technologizing of the word*. London, England: Methuen.

Prensky, M. (2001). Digital natives, digital immigrants. *On the Horizon, 9*(5), 1–6. Retrieved from http://dx.doi.org/10.1108/10748120110424816

Sadler, R. & Dooly, M. (2013). Language learning in virtual worlds: Research and practice. In M. Thomas, H. Reinders, & M. Warschauer (Eds.), *Contemporary computer-assisted language learning* (pp. 159–182). London, England: Bloomsbury.

Schneider, E. W. (2016). Grassroot Englishes in tourism interactions. *English Today, 32*(3), 2–10.

Schulze, M. & Heift, T. (2013). Intelligent CALL. In M. Thomas, H. Reinders, & M. Warschauer (Eds.), *Contemporary computer-assisted language learning* (pp. 249–265). London, England: Bloomsbury.

TESOL (2018). *Action agenda for the future of the TESOL profession*. Retrieved from www.tesol.org/summit-2017/action-agenda-for-the-future-of-the-tesol-profession

Vittachi, N. (2010). A short course in Globalese. In D. Nunan & J. Choi (Eds.), *Language and culture: Reflective narratives and the emergence of identity* (pp. 215–222). New York, NY: Routledge.

Washington Post. (2018). *For digital nomads, work is where the laptop is*. Retrieved from www.washingtonpost.com/business/economy/for-digital-nomads-work-is-where-the-laptop-is/2018/07/06/3e146a4c-7e34-11e8-bb6b-c1cb691f1402_story.html?noredirect=on&utm_term=.ba58e543bd12

Watson, C. E., & Plymale, W. O. (2011). The pedagogy of things: Ubiquitous learning, student culture, and constructivist pedagogical practice. In T. T. Kidd & I. Chen (Eds.), *Ubiquitous learning: Strategies for pedagogy, course design, and technology* (pp. 3–16). Charlotte, NC: Information Age Publishing, Inc.

INDEX

Golomb, J. D. 281, 288
Gonzalez, D. 284, 288
Good, T. L. 66, 71
Gordon, T. 135
Gorlick, A. 281, 288
Graddol, D. 26, 37
grammar translation 48
Grant, R. 15, 20
Graves, B. B. 121
Graves, M. E. 121
Greenberg, J. H. 208
Grice, H. P. 170–1
Grice's Maxims 170–1
Grossman, J. B. 262, 271
Gumperz, J. J. 13, 18, 24, 37
Gupta, V. 63 72
Guthrie, J. 185, 191
Gutlohn, L. 111

Habermas, J. 171
Habermas's validity conditions 171
Hall, J. W. 121
Halliday, M. A. K. 159
Hamdan, W. 284, 288
Handy, C. B. 76–7, 91
Hanges, P. J. 63, 72
Harley, B. 218
Harlow, H. F. 185
Harmer, J. 181
Harris, R. vii, 27, 38, 46, 57
Hasan Chowdhury, Q. 41, 58
Hatch, E. 205, 222
Havelock, E. 172
Hayes, E. R. 285, 287, 288
Heath, S. B. 172, 175
Heift, T. 283, 289
Henley, N. 10, 20
Hilfer, E. 283, 288
Hinsh, D. 121
Hofstede, G. 61, 63, 71, 72, 75, 91
Holliday, A. 70, 72, 86, 91, 222
Hollingsworth, H. 253, 270
homophones 98
Honig, B. 111
House, R. J. 63, 72
Hyde, M. 70. 72

Ibrahim, A. E. K. 9, 19, 46, 57
identity: and the classroom 14–16, 31, 84;
    conflict 4, 7; cultural 7; exploring 87,
    89; racial 9; shape 6, 33, 45, 83, 89;
    teacher 40

IELTS 47
Ifcher, J. 188
Illeris, K. 181
Ima, K. 43, 58
Imam, S. R. 8, 19
immigrant 41–6; experience 89
inequality 41
information and communication technology
    (ICT) 74, 275, 278, 281, 282, 284; see also
    digital technology
input 220
intelligence 241
intelligences 241–2
interaction 221
interaction analysis 217–19
intercultural 61; communication 65, 70;
    competence 282; exchange 69; interactions
    69; misunderstandings 59; space 69
interlanguage 203
International Association of Teachers of English
    as a Foreign Language (IATEFL) 269, 287
International Phonetic Alphabet, the (IPA) 98, 99
international students 46–7
Internet World Stats 278–9, 288
intertextuality 173
investment: definition 6, 27; in learning
    English 6–8, 12, 15, 27, 44, 46, 74
IPA 98, 99
IQ test 242

Jannen, D. 159
Javidan, M. 63, 72
Jenkins, J. 26, 27, 37
Jensen, E. 69, 72
Jeon, K. 223
Johnson, D. 244
Johnson, K. 74, 91, 249, 250
Johnson, R. 244
Johnson, S. 254, 271
Jordan, S. 83, 90, 92
Judy, J. A. 187
Juel, C. 121
Junco, R. 281, 288
Jussim, L. 66, 72

Kachru, B. B. 25–6, 28, 35, 37, 41, 57
Kachru, Y. 35, 38
Kagan, S. 244
Kail, R. 242
Kalantzi, M. 174
Keenan, E. 208
Kelch, K. 25, 38

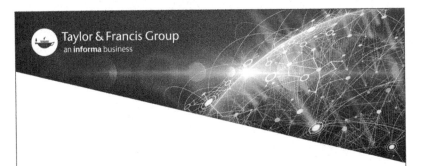

Made in the USA
Coppell, TX
27 July 2022

80469826R00174